JERUSALEM
IN THE BOOK OF EZEKIEL

SOCIETY OF BIBLICAL LITERATURE

DISSERTATION SERIES

David L. Petersen, Old Testament Editor
Pheme Perkins, New Testament Editor

Number 130

JERUSALEM IN THE BOOK OF EZEKIEL
The City as Yahweh's Wife

by
Julie Galambush

Julie Galambush

JERUSALEM
IN THE BOOK OF EZEKIEL
The City as Yahweh's Wife

Scholars Press
Atlanta, Georgia

JERUSALEM IN THE BOOK OF EZEKIEL
The City as Yahweh's Wife

Julie Galambush

Ph.D., 1991
Emory University

Advisors:
John H. Hayes
Carol A. Newsom

Library of Congress Cataloging in Publication Data

Galambush, Julie.
    Jerusalem in the book of Ezekiel : the city as Yahweh's wife /
Julie Galambush.
    p. cm. — (Dissertation series / Society of Biblical
Literature ; no. 130)
    Thesis (doctoral)—Emory University, 1992.
    Includes bibliographical references.
    ISBN 1-55540-755-2.—ISBN 1-55540-756-0 (pbk.)
    1. Bible. O.T. Ezekiel—Criticism, interpretation, etc.
2. Jerusalem in the Bible. 3. Marriage customs and rites, Jewish.
I. Title. II. Series: Dissertation series (Society of Biblical
Literature) ; no. 130.
BS1545.6.J38635 1992
224'.4064—dc20   92-26309
                                        CIP

Printed in the United States of America
on acid-free paper

To my parents,
George and Mary Ellen Galambush

Contents

ABBREVIATIONS

AB	Anchor Bible
ABC	*Assyrian and Babylonian Chronicles* (ed. A. K. Grayson; Locust Valley, NY: Augustin, 1975).
AnBib	Analecta Biblica
ANET	*Ancient Near Eastern Texts Relating to the Old Testament* (ed. J. B. Pritchard; 3rd ed.; Princeton: Princeton University Press, 1969).
AnOr	Analecta orientalia
AOAT	Alter Orient und Altes Testament
AOr	Archiv für Orientforschung
ARAB	*Ancient Records of Assyria and Babylonia* (ed. D. D. Luckenbill; 2 vols.; Chicago: University of Chicago Press, 1924).
ASTI	*Annual of the Swedish Theological Institute*
BA	*Biblical Archaeologist*
BDB	*Hebrew and English Lexicon of the Old Testmaent* (ed. F. Brown, S. R. Driver, C. A. Briggs; Oxford: Clarendon Press, 1952).
BETL	Bibliotheca ephemeridum theologicarum lovaniensium
Bib	*Biblica*
BibOr	Biblica et orientalia
BR	*Biblical Research*
BT	*The Bible Translator*
BTB	*Biblical Theology Bulletin*
BTFT	*Bijdragen: Tijdschrift voor Filosofie en Theologie*
BZAW	Beihefte zur Zeitschrift für die alttestamentliche Wissenschaft
CAD	*The Assyrian Dictionary of the Oriental Institute of the University of Chicago* (ed. I. Gelb; Chicago: The Oriental Institute, 1964-).
CBQ	*Catholic Biblical Quarterly*

EBib	Etudes Bibliques
EI	*Eretz Israel*
ETL	*Ephemerides theologicae lovanienses*
FOTL	Forms of the Old Testament Literature
GKC	*Gesenius' Hebrew Grammar as Edited and Enlarged by the Late E. Kautzsch* (ed. A. E. Cowley; Oxford: Clarendon Press, 1910).
HAR	*Hebrew Annual Review*
HAT	Handbuch zum alten Testament
HSM	Harvard Semitic Monographs
HSS	Harvard Semitic Studies
HTR	*Harvard Theological Review*
HUCA	*Hebrew Union College Annual*
Int	*Interpretation*
JANESCU	*Journal of the Ancient Near Eastern Society of Columbia University*
JAOS	*Journal of the American Oriental Society*
JBL	*Journal of Biblical Literature*
JJS	*Journal of Jewish Studies*
JNES	*Journal of Near Eastern Studies*
JNSL	*Journal of Northwest Semitic Languages*
JPOS	*Journal of the Palestine Oriental Society*
JSOT	*Journal for the Study of the Old Testament*
JSOTS	Journal for the Study of the Old Testament Supplements
JSS	*Journal of Semitic Studies*
KAT	Kommentar zum A. T.
Obo	Orbis biblicus et orientalis
OTL	Old Testament Library
OTS	*Oudtestamentische Stüdien*
PG	*Patrologia Graeca* (ed. J. Migne)
PL	*Patrologia Latina* (ed. J. Migne)
RB	*Revue Biblique*
SBLDS	SBL Dissertation Series
SBLMS	SBL Monograph Series
SJLA	Studies in Judaism in Late Antiquity
TDNT	*Theological Dictionary of the New Testament* (ed. G. Kittel; 10 vols.; Grand Rapids: Eerdmans, 1964-1976)
TDOT	*Theological Dictionary of the Old Testement* (ed. G. J. Botterweck and H. Ringgren; Grand Rapids: Eerdmans, 1974-).
VT	*Vetus Testamentum*
ZTK	*Zeitschrift für Theologie und Kirche*

Acknowledgments

Over the course of my graduate school studies, I have been helped by friends, family, and professors, whose love made the project possible. Among my friends and colleagues, I thank Suzanne Boorer, Ann Byrne, Alice R. Falk, Kathleen A. Forbes, Paul K. Hooker, Gary Stansell, and especially Robert I. Goler. I would also like to acknowledge Jody Greenslade and Jamie Schillinger of St. Olaf College and Patrick Graham of the Candler School of Theology for their generous and careful assistance with this manuscript. Special thanks are due to Luke T. Johnson, without whose encouragement I would not have undertaken graduate studies.

I am grateful for the assistance of my dissertation committee, whose combined patience and enthusiasm have often made the project a pleasure:

Gene M. Tucker, Candler School of Theology, for his guidance throughout my graduate school years, and specifically for his help as a member of the dissertation committee.

Carol A. Newsom, Candler School of Theology, for her generous investment of time and care in the manuscript, and her unfailing, warm encouragement.

John H. Hayes, Candler School of Theology, whose unmatched combination of erudition, common sense, and humor have seen me through.

I

INTRODUCTION

I. GOALS OF THE STUDY

This study will examine the nature and implications of Ezekiel's metaphorical depiction of Jerusalem as Yahweh's wife. The investigation will be performed in two stages.

The study will begin with an analysis of the personification of Jerusalem as Yahweh's wife that makes up the whole of Ezekiel 16 and 23. In these two chapters Jerusalem is depicted metaphorically as a wife who is unfaithful and is therefore punished at the behest of her husband, but at the hands of her lovers. Ezekiel uses the metaphor of the woman's misbehavior to portray two related actions on the part of Jerusalem, both of which he describes as "infidelity" (*tznwt*), and both of which result in "uncleanness" (*ṭmʾ*), the defilement of the city and its temple: idolatry (and possibly other improprieties within the cult) and alliances with foreign nations. The husband's vengeance on the unfaithful wife metaphorically depicts Yahweh's instigation of the destruction of Jerusalem by Nebuchadrezzar.

After the analysis of the personifications of Jerusalem in chaps 16 and 23 will follow an analysis of the language used by Ezekiel to describe

Jerusalem in the rest of the book. Language and imagery used to depict the personified Jerusalem in chaps 16 and 23 will be compared with the language and imagery used to depict Jerusalem in passages in which the city is not explicitly personified. This comparison will help determine the relationship, if any, between Ezekiel's use of metaphoric language depicting Jerusalem as a woman in chaps 16 and 23 and his portrayal of Jerusalem elsewhere in the book.

Analysis of the metaphor of the city as wife in Ezekiel 16 and 23 poses a number of methodological challenges. First, Ezekiel's metaphor is extended into lengthy narratives suggestive of allegory, but which do not conform to usual definitions of "allegory." Thus a working definition of "metaphor" will have to be shaped to the special characteristics of the metaphor of Ezekiel 16 and 23. Second, Ezekiel's repeated allusions in chaps 16 and 23 to events in Israelite and Judean history will require that historical reconstruction be integrated into the literary analysis of the metaphor. Third, Ezekiel's intense concern with ritual purity will require use of the terminology of ritual and symbol analysis. Finally, the peculiar sexual dynamics of Ezekiel's metaphor, with overtones of pornography, voyeurism, and fetishism, will be explicated using terminology drawn from the fields of feminist and semiotic analysis. While the entire study is focused on explication of the nature and function of the metaphor of the city as wife, tools drawn from these various disciplines will be employed at the points where they prove useful to highlight specific aspects of this polyvalent metaphor. The investigation reaches the following conclusions:

Ezekiel's portrayal of Jerusalem, exclusive of the personifications of chaps 16 and 23, may be divided into three parts, corresponding to the generally accepted three-part division of the book:[1] Within Ezekiel 1-24 (the oracles of doom against Judah and Jerusalem) Jerusalem is fully personified as a woman only in chaps 16 and 23. Elsewhere in chaps 1-24 Ezekiel uses key words from the personifications of chaps 16 and 23 to describe the city's wrongdoing. Additional feminine imagery (i.e., depiction of the city as a *nddh*, "menstruant") that is not specifically applied to the woman of chaps 16 and 23 is also used in chaps 1-24 to describe Jerusalem. The combination of Ezekiel's vivid personification of the city in chaps 16 and 23, plus the use of feminine imagery elsewhere in chaps 1-24, combine to give the city an implicitly female persona in this first

---

[1] See, e.g., W. Zimmerli, *Ezekiel 1* (Hermeneia; Philadelphia: Fortress, 1979) 1-2; M. Greenberg, *Ezekiel 1-20: A New Translation with Introduction and Commentary* (AB 22; New York: Doubleday, 1983) 3-4.

section of the book. Chapters 1-24, the oracles of doom against this symbolically female city, culminate with the death of the prophet's wife in chap 24. Consistent with the implicit personification of Jerusalem as female, specifically, as the wife of Yahweh, Yahweh interprets the death of Ezekiel's wife as a sign of the destruction of Yahweh's beloved city, Jerusalem.

In Ezekiel 25-39 (broadly speaking, the promises of restoration to Judah) references to Jerusalem are virtually eliminated, along with the use of feminine imagery for the city. Only in one retrospective summary of Israel's unclean past (36:16-21) does the feminine imagery common in chaps 1-24 recur, when Yahweh compares the *former* ways of the people (violence and bloodshed) with the ways of a *nddh*, a menstruating woman. Neither the city nor its female persona is mentioned; the only trace of Yahweh's former "wife" is the memory of her sexual uncleanness.

In Ezekiel 40-48 the prophet has a vision of the holy city and its temple renewed. Far from being personified as or implied to be Yahweh's wife, however, the new temple is specially constructed so as to exclude those defilements (liaisons with foreign men, the presence of unclean blood) that characterized the old, "female," Jerusalem. Because the metaphoric identification of the city as female intrinsically carries the symbolic potential for defilement (any woman may become unclean through sexual activity, menstruation, or childbirth), the city's female persona must be excluded to ensure the purity of the temple. In the vision of the new temple, feminine verbal imagery, which throughout Ezekiel has meant specifically female infidelity and uncleanness, appears in only a single, retrospective reference to the earlier "whoredom" of the house of Israel (43:7, 9). This suppression of explicitly feminine imagery from the depiction of the new temple, while probably an unconscious rather than a conscious choice, is consistent with Ezekiel's goal of establishing an inviolably pure realm in which Yahweh can safely dwell. Like the thicker walls and more restrictive laws of the new city, the elimination of the city's female persona serves to protect city and temple against the threat of defilement.

Despite the absence of any explicit verbal imagery of the new city/temple as feminine, however, vestiges of the old, female persona persist in Ezekiel's vision of the new city. Though no longer *identified* as Yahweh's "wife," the restored city continues to fill a symbolically feminine role. It is home to and the exclusive possession of Yahweh (foreign men in particular are denied access; 44:9); it is the enclosed space in which the life-bearing power of blood is contained and manipulated (43:18-27); and it is depicted as a source of fertility (47:7-12). The city thus fills the symbolic role of the feminine without the dangers implied by Ezekiel's earlier, metaphorical depiction of Jerusalem as a woman. Ezekiel's ideal city of God is faithful because, being no longer personified, it is no longer capable of infidelity.

II. DEFINING THE METAPHOR OF THE CITY AS WIFE

A. *The Metaphor of the City as Wife: Developing a Working Definition*

In order to analyze Ezekiel's metaphor of the city as wife, it will be necessary at the outset to establish a working definition of "metaphor," and also to describe the ancient Near Eastern tradition of depicting cities as female, since this tradition provides the cultural and literary context for the personification of cities in the Hebrew Bible.

1) *Models of Metaphors*

The nature and definition of metaphor is widely contested in recent research, and no definition of the term can be considered "standard" without further explication. A definition of metaphor will therefore be developed for the purposes of this inquiry, based on some classic definitions, and adapted to fit the situation of Ezekiel 16 and 23.

The terminology developed by I. A. Richards[2] has been employed as a starting point for much of subsequent research and will serve as the basis upon which to build a working definition of "metaphor" for this study. Richards, following the practice of Samuel Johnson,[3] divides metaphor into two constituent parts, naming these the "tenor" and the "vehicle." The tenor is "the underlying idea or principle subject,"[4] and the vehicle the figurative language (sometimes itself called the "metaphor") used to describe the tenor. In the metaphor, "the earth is our mother," the tenor would be "earth" and the vehicle "mother." A

---

2 "The Philosophy of Rhetoric," *Philosophical Perspectives on Metaphor* (ed. M. Johnson; Minneapolis: University of Minnesota, 1981) 48-62, a partial reprint of *The Philosophy of Rhetoric* (Oxford: Oxford University Press, 1936).
3 "Philosophy of Rhetoric," 52.
4 "Philosophy of Rhetoric," 53.

metaphor, according to Richards's definition, is a "double unit" comprised of "two thoughts of different things active together and supported by a single word, or phrase [the vehicle]."[5]

Max Black, focusing on the mutual influence between tenor and vehicle, describes metaphor primarily in terms of the dynamic relationship, the "interaction," between these two parts.[6] According to Black, tenor and vehicle interact so that the vehicle "reorganizes" our perception of the tenor. In the metaphor, "the earth is our mother," the reader's perception of "earth" is "reorganized" by earth's identification with "mother," so that qualities commonly associated with mothers (so-called "associated commonplaces"), such as nurture, fertility, and being an object of gratitude, are highlighted, while qualities *not* commonly associated with mothers (instability, barrenness) are repressed. In addition, not only does the vehicle reorganize our perception of the tenor; the tenor likewise modifies our perception of the vehicle, though to a lesser extent. Thus, while "the earth is our mother" calls attention to the motherlike qualities of the earth (and represses earth's "unmotherlike" qualities), it simultaneously emphasizes the "earthlike" qualities of mothers, such as endurance and impartiality.

Black's theory draws particular attention to the indeterminacy of metaphors, the impossibility of defining with precision what a metaphor "means." Because it is not merely two words or two ideas, but two indeterminate *systems* of culturally associated commonplaces that metaphor brings into contact, the precise interaction between tenor and vehicle is to some extent unpredictable and will differ slightly from reader to reader.[7] This indeterminacy is a prime source of the power of metaphor; a metaphor does not make a single statement (or, to the extent that it does, that statement is always literally false),[8] but provokes the reader to see connections where none had been seen before.

---

5 "Philosophy of Rhetoric," 51.

6 See M. Black (*Models and Metaphors: Studies in Language and Philosophy* [Ithaca, NY: Cornell University, 1962]; "Metaphor," *Proceedings of the Aristotelian Society*, N.S. 55 [1954-55]:273-94, reprinted in Johnson, *Philosophical Perspectives*, 63-82).

7 It is important in this regard to note that commonplaces are culturally determined, and may or may not be *accurate* descriptions of the vehicle. Thus in our example it is irrelevant that not all mothers are stable or nurturing; the system of commonplaces consists of the set of stereotypes commonly applied to the vehicle.

8 The essence of metaphor is that it says a thing *is* something that it *is not*. On the dynamics of this paradox, see T. Brinkley, "On the Truth and Probity of Metaphor," in *Philosophical Perspectives*, 136-53, and D. Davidson "What Metaphors Mean" in *On Metaphor* (ed. S. Sacks; Chicago: University of Chicago, 1978) 29-46.

Taken together, Richards's designation of tenor and vehicle and Black's theory of interaction provide a starting point for the discussion of metaphor. Metaphor is a figure of speech in which a "vehicle" is used to highlight those qualities of the "tenor" commonly associated with the vehicle. At the same time, qualities commonly associated with the tenor but also shared by the vehicle are similarly emphasized. Some useful refinements of this scheme are provided by the work of Janet Soskice,[9] George Lakoff and Mark Johnson,[10] and Paul Ricoeur.[11]

Soskice points out that Black's definition is well-suited "only to metaphor of the form 'A is a B',"[12] whereas metaphor rarely occurs in this two-part form. Soskice cites an example from W. H. Auden:

> The unmentionable odour of death
> Offends the September night

as a case in which the tenor of the metaphor, impending war, is not even mentioned.[13] Soskice proposes a definition of metaphor as "a speaking of one thing in terms which are seen as suggestive of another."[14] Soskice's broadening of the definition of metaphor beyond the "A is B" form will prove useful in looking at the wide variety of metaphorical forms in Ezekiel.

Lakoff and Johnson's work does not change the definition of metaphor per se, but points out additional levels at which metaphors function. Moving the discussion away from isolated, verbal metaphors, Lakoff and Johnson examine "conceptual metaphors," the typically

---

[9] *Metaphors and Religious Language* (Oxford: Clarendon, 1985).

[10] "Conceptual Metaphor in Everyday Language," *Philosophical Perspectives*, 286-329.

[11] See *The Rule of Metaphor* (Toronto: University of Toronto, 1977); "The Metaphorical Process as Cognition, Imagination, and Feeling," *On Metaphor*, 141-58.

[12] Soskice, *Religious Language*, 43.

[13] Soskice, *Religious Language*, 49.

[14] *Religious Language*, 49. Soskice contends that the subject matter of a metaphor is always the tenor (the Auden example is speaking "about" war in terms of odor), a view that seems to contradict Black's claim that a metaphor "says" something new about both tenor *and* vehicle. Soskice's clarification, that the author's subject is, in one sense, always the tenor, does not, however, exclude the possibility that the metaphorical vehicle may also appear in a new light. Auden may well have wished to say something about war and odor *both*. Since the metaphor changes the reader's perception of both tenor and vehicle, there seems no reason to claim, as Soskice does, that the tenor is the exclusive subject matter of metaphor. Nonetheless, her caveat that the interaction between tenor and vehicle is far more subtle than Black's "A is a B" form suggests is valid.

unacknowledged metaphors on which everyday, "literal" language is based. According to Lakoff and Johnson, though "our conceptual system is largely metaphorical,"[15] we are usually unaware of the metaphors that govern our concepts. For example, our language about arguments depends on the unspoken, conceptual metaphor, "argument is war," and it is this generally unrecognized metaphor that accounts for our use of such terms as "defend," "attack," "demolish," "shoot down," and "win" in regard to arguments. At a still more primary level, the conceptual metaphor, "up is good," governs a whole realm of language so common it ceases to seem metaphorical: "feeling up" (or down), "putting someone down," "getting a lift" from something, and so on.[16]

Lakoff and Johnson's observations nuance the discussion of metaphor in a number of useful ways. First, their theory of "conceptual metaphor" accounts for the persistence of metaphors based on dualities such as up-down, in-out, and male-female. Those metaphors most closely tied to primitive, somatic experiences will be most durable. Thus, while "city" is a relatively sophisticated concept, the metaphoric designation of the city as female, and thus as mother, wife, and especially, within a patriarchal culture, as "other," plays on basic male-female, self-other dualities, and so the metaphor may be expected to be deeply rooted and persistent.

Second, the theory of "conceptual metaphor" can be used to describe the mechanism by which a culturally accepted metaphor may keep from becoming "dead" (so widely used as to be no longer perceived as metaphorical) or, if dead, may be "reactivated" so that it is again perceived as metaphor. In the case of any metaphorical concept, only some parts of the metaphor (in Black's language, only some commonplaces) are ordinarily employed. If the Lord is my shepherd (my example), the Lord may feed, carry, chase or chasten me, but he may not kill me and eat me, even though that is one of the things that real shepherds do. If, however, I choose to employ this latent but ordinarily inactive potential,

15 "Conceptual Metaphors," 287.
16 Soskice (*Religious Language*, 81-83) cautions that Lakoff and Johnson's theory could be taken to the extreme of "confusing word derivation with word meaning," and argues for a "synchronic" understanding of word meaning (81). Soskice's criticism, however, misconstrues Lakoff and Johnson's central argument, which is not that meaning is influenced by word *derivation*, but by underlying conceptual models. The culturally shared, but ordinarily unrecognized metaphor, "argument is war," does not reflect the etymology of the word "argument," but exposes the literal phenomenon (tenor) that underlies or provides the basis for figurative language about argument.

then the familiar metaphor of the Lord as shepherd, which had through long use ceased to be provocative or "reorienting," is suddenly new and, in this case, disturbing. This phenomenon of the "active" and "inactive" aspects of a metaphor allows for the possibility of a metaphor's expansion by the activation of facets not previously recognized among the "associated commonplaces" of the vehicle. In the case of the metaphor of the city as wife, Lakoff and Johnson's theory helps account for Ezekiel's transformation of a traditional metaphor which must to some extent have been "dead" (cities in the ancient Near East were understood to "be" female in some important sense) into a provocative, even shocking image.[17]

Finally, Lakoff and Johnson's model takes account of metaphor's moral dimensions. Because most of our fundamental concepts are grounded in metaphor, and because metaphor (as we have seen) highlights some aspects of reality while suppressing others, the metaphors one internalizes will influence one's perceptions of reality. If, for example, one belonged to a culture that included the metaphorical concept, "argument is a dance,"[18] words such as "shoot down" and "win" would not accurately describe one's experience of arguments. Arguments would instead be discussions in which the two partners had different parts that worked together to form a graceful and enjoyable duet. Indeed, in such a culture, the phenomenon denoted by the word "argument" would be a different phenomenon from that denoted by "argument" in a culture with the underlying conceptual metaphor, "argument is war." In this respect metaphors are "like self-fulfilling

---

[17] M. C. Beardsley ("The Metaphorical Twist," *Philosophical Perspectives*, 105-22) likewise describes both the way in which an initially novel metaphor may become "dead," and the possibility of its renovation by the "actualization" of connotations that had hitherto been latent (112-13). Beardsley posits a word's "potential range of connotations," which includes both "staple connotations" (not unlike Black's "associated commonplaces") and other, "lurking" connotations, that may be brought to play, creating a "fresh and novel" metaphor. The primary difference between Beardsley's and Lakoff and Johnson's discussions is in their focus; Beardsley is discussing only "explicit" metaphors, while Lakoff and Johnson raise the possibility that such revitalizing extension of a metaphor may take place even when the metaphor is unstated and unrecognized. That is, not only may unusual connotations of a specific word be brought into a metaphor; the unrealized implications of fundamental, conceptual metaphors may also be effectively exploited. Thus, if argument is war, then the language of death, espionage, and invasion might be used to extend the metaphor beyond its usual range.

[18] "Conceptual Metaphor," 288-89.

INTRODUCTION   9

prophecies";[19] they predispose us to experience reality in certain ways. Metaphors, then, are not value-neutral. Rather, they "sanction actions, justify inferences, and help us set goals."[20] Not surprisingly, the "people in power get to impose their metaphors"[21] and, to that extent, define reality. Because "we define our reality on the basis of metaphor, and then proceed to act on the basis of the metaphor," metaphor has moral, as well as aesthetic and conceptual significance. This recognition of the moral dimension of metaphor will raise the question of how Ezekiel's metaphor of the city as wife colors his perceptions of Jerusalem, and conversely, whether his use of the metaphor only when describing the city as defiled and defiling reinforces "commonplaces" of woman as dangerous and as "other."

Among Paul Ricoeur's contributions to the discussion of the nature of metaphor, especially useful in analyzing Ezekiel's metaphor of Jerusalem as Yahweh's wife is his claim that metaphor involves the "felt participation"[22] of the reader. Ricoeur argues that metaphorical meaning must be seen as occurring on "the borderline between the verbal and the nonverbal";[23] metaphor involves "feeling as well as imagination."[24]

This felt aspect of metaphorical meaning accounts for "the 'illocutionary' force of the metaphor as speech act."[25] Ricoeur's acknowledgment of the role of feeling in metaphor is consistent with Lakoff and Johnson's observations regarding the moral significance of metaphor. Because the apprehension of metaphorical meaning involves, at a certain level, the *assent* of the reader, the effect of metaphor goes beyond the verbal. In the case of Ezekiel, the status of metaphor as speech act helps explain the power of the prophet's use of feminine imagery to describe a city's pollution and degradation, and ultimately, to justify that city's destruction. In addition to accounting for the power of the metaphor, however, the "felt participation" of the reader also implicates the reader as a "participant" in the events depicted. Thus Ezekiel's metaphor not only reinforces the commonplaces of woman as conceptually "other"; it

---

19 "Conceptual Metaphor," 321.
20 "Conceptual Metaphor," 320.
21 "Conceptual Metaphor," 322.
22 "Metaphorical Process," 154.
23 "Metaphorical Process," 149.
24 "Metaphorical Process," 153.
25 "Metaphorical Process," 154.

evokes what Bachelard calls a "reverberation," a partial reenactment by the reader of the experience it depicts.[26]

2) Narrative Metaphor in Ezekiel 16 and 23

Ezekiel uses a variety of figurative language to refer to Jerusalem, ranging from simile ("their conduct was *like* the uncleanness of a *nddh*"; 36:17), in which the comparison of the two terms is explicit, to direct address to the personified city ("Therefore, you whore, hear the word of Yahweh"; 16:35). One hallmark of Ezekiel's style is his use of metaphors that extend over the entire length of a chapter (e.g., the metaphor of the vinewood in chap 15, and of the vine and the eagle in chap 17). The terminology used to describe these chapters varies widely. Although they are most commonly referred to as "allegories" (so, e.g., Greenberg, Zimmerli, Smend), the designation is misleading. Allegory is generally understood as a narrative in which each element represents something or someone else in the real world, so that a point for point correspondence can be drawn between the allegory and its referent.[27] Allegory is thus merely a code in which the allegorical element stands in for the literal, rather than the complex system of interactions that is a metaphor. Northrop Frye distinguishes between "an" allegory, in which "the allegorical reference is continuous throughout the narrative," and a work with "allegorical tendencies," in which allegory is "intermittent, . . . picked up and dropped again at pleasure."[28]

According to Frye's definition, the figures of Ezekiel 16 and 23 have "allegorizing tendencies," but are not allegories per se. Ezekiel's

---

[26] See Ricoeur's discussion of Bachelard in "Metaphorical Process," 148. W. Booth ("Metaphor as Rhetoric: The Problem of Evaluation," *On Metaphor*, 47-70) argues similarly that "to *understand* a metaphor is by its very nature to *decide* whether to join the metaphorist or [to] reject, . . . to decide either to be shaped in the shape [the] metaphor requires or to resist" (63). Furthermore, even the decision to resist is secondary, subsequent to the assenting act of comprehension; thus "the metaphor accomplishes at least part of its work even if the hearer then draws back and says, 'I shouldn't have allowed that!'" (52).

[27] See, e.g., P. Henle, "Metaphor," *Philosophical Perspectives*, 83-104, esp. 91; P. Ricoeur, *The Rule of Metaphor*, 60-61, 84; J. M. Soskice, *Religious Language*, 55-56; E. Honig, *Dark Conceit: The Making of Allegory* (Evanston: Northwestern University, 1959); J. Rosenberg, *King and Kin: Political Allegory in the Hebrew Bible* (Bloomington: Indiana University, 1986); and N. Frye, "Allegory," in *Princeton Encyclopedia of Poetry and Poetics* (ed. A. Preminger; Princeton: Princeton University, 1974) 12-15.

[28] "Allegory," 12. Frye further distinguishes between the naive and moralizing tone generally attributed to "an" allegory, and the richer range of literature that may be interpreted to have allegorical elements.

extended metaphors[29] have the complexity and indeterminacy generally understood to characterize metaphor.[30] Although a few attempts have been made to discuss Ezekiel's extended metaphors using the terminology of allegory in its more nuanced sense,[31] both the inevitable tendency of readers to assume the common definition of allegory, and the close resemblance between nuanced definitions of allegory and definitions of metaphor, argue against the usefulness of describing Ezekiel's figurative language as allegory. For the purposes of this dissertation Ezekiel 16 and 23, in which the metaphor of Jerusalem as a woman is sustained throughout a narrative unit, will be referred to as "extended" or "sustained" metaphor, or as "narrative metaphor."[32]

B. Previous Work on Metaphor in Ezekiel

Before discussing the ancient Near Eastern background of the OT metaphor of divine marriage, previous work on the role and nature of the metaphor of Jerusalem as Yahweh's wife in the book of Ezekiel will be reviewed. It is important to note that interpretation of Ezekiel's metaphor of Jerusalem as wife has hitherto been limited to the interpretation of chaps 16 and 23. No attempt has previously been made to examine the feminine imagery applied to Jerusalem elsewhere in Ezekiel in light of the personifications of chaps 16 and 23. Nor has significant attention been paid to the dynamics of the metaphor in chaps 16 and 23. Instead, interpreters have generally been absorbed either in "decoding" the metaphor or in joining the prophet's harangue against the unfaithful wife.

In nineteenth century German scholarship on Ezekiel 16 and 23, stylistic features of the text tended to be noted only sporadically, rather than treated as a subject for analysis in and of themselves. So, for example, Ferdinand Hitzig[33] makes meticulous observations on the details of Jerusalem's development and dress but never speculates as to the tenor

---

29 Ricoeur's term (*Rule of Metaphor*, 243).

30 On the complexity of Ezekiel's extended metaphors, see e.g., W. Zimmerli, *Ezekiel 1*, 334; M. Greenberg, *Ezekiel 1-20*, 25 and passim in discussion of chaps 16 and 17; R. M. Hals, *Ezekiel* (FOTL 19; Grand Rapids: Eerdmans, 1988) 117.

31 See, e.g., J. Durlesser, "The Rhetoric of Allegory in the Book of Ezekiel" (diss., University of Pittsburgh, 1988).

32 K. Snodgrass (*The Parable of the Wicked Tenants: An Inquiry into Parable Interpretation* [Wissenschaftliche Untersuchungen zum Neuen Testament 27; Tübingen: J. C. B. Mohr (Paul Siebeck), 1983]) defines allegory as "an extended metaphor in narratory form" (19).

33 *Der Prophet Ezechiel erklärt* (Leipzig: Weidmann'sche Buchhandlung, 1847).

of the metaphor, nor does he comment on the use of metaphor as a literary or prophetic device.[34] Hengstenberg[35] provides a close analysis of the historical referents, especially of chap 23, but similarly refrains from systematic discussion or generalization regarding the features of the metaphor itself.[36] Rudolf Smend in his 1880 commentary[37] takes a somewhat different approach. Addressing the question of Ezekiel's allegories in his introduction, Smend expresses an awareness of at least some of their features, and comments on Ezekiel's style as a maker of metaphors (cf. Ezek 20:49): "In seinen Allegorien wirft er fortwährend Sache und Bild durcheinander, unfähig sie klar durchzufuhren wendet er das einmal angenommene Bild nach den verscheidensten Seiten (11, 3. 7), oft bis zur Unklarheit (c. 11. 24), zuweilen bis zum Selbstwiderspruch (c. 15. 17. 19; 16, 31 ff.) [In his allegories he incessantly mixes metaphors, incapable of carrying them through clearly. He turns the image, once adopted, according to its various aspects (11, 3. 7), often to the point of unclarity (c. 11. 24), occasionally to the point of self-contradiction (c. 15. 17. 19; 16, 31 ff.)]."[38] The ambiguity and fluidity so dear to students of metaphor is, for Smend, evidence of the prophet's ineptitude.

The Bible as Literature movement in late nineteenth century England and America provided the occasion for more sustained and sympathetic attention to Ezekiel's use of metaphor. A. B. Davidson, in his 1892 commentary,[39] while not giving detailed analysis of Ezekiel's use of narrative

---

34   So, for example, he notes that "Jerusalem als Weib kann nur mit Männern buhlen; also wird vom Dienste weiblicher Gottheiten, wie z. B. der Astarte, hier abgesehen" ("Jerusalem, as a woman, can have intercourse only with men; the worship of female deities, such as Astarte, was therefore disregarded here"; *Ezechiel erklärt*, 106). This observation is an astute but, sadly, isolated observation on the strictures placed on representation of the tenor by the vehicle of Jerusalem as female (though it might be argued that worship of female deities is not disregarded, but merely masked, indeed, depicted metaphorically).

35   *Die Weissagungen des Prophet Ezechiel* (Berlin: Gustav Schlawitz, 1868).

36   In his discussion of 23:42 Hengstenberg comments regarding the depiction of a "rowdy crowd *in her* [the woman Jerusalem]" that "here the personification is abandoned" (204). This is exactly the type of phenomenon that Moshe Greenberg would later identify as a distinguishing feature of Ezekiel's narrative metaphor, its so-called "permeability." Hengstenberg clearly observed at least some of the traits of Ezekiel's metaphor, but apparently did not think them worth noting, or regarded them as instances of inconsistency.

37   *Der Prophet Ezechiel für die zweite Auflage erklärt* (Leipzig: S. Hirzel, 1880).

38   *Der Prophet Ezechiel*, xxiii. Smend also notes and complains about Ezekiel's "annoying" repetition of his images.

39   *The Book of the Prophet Ezekiel* (The Cambridge Bible for Schools and Colleges; Cambridge: Cambridge University, 1892).

metaphors, advances the literary discussion beyond that in the German scholarship of the period. First, Davidson pays closer attention than had previously been paid to the peculiar texture of the narrative, as for example in his comments on 16:7: "I made you multiply, like the sprouts of the field. And you grew up and matured. And you acquired beautiful adornments. . . ." Davidson observes, "This idea of multiplication in *number* deserts the figure, introducing the notion of the numerical increase of the people. . . . The rest of the verse, however, continues the figure of the child growing up to womanhood."[40] Like Hitzig and Hengstenberg, Davidson notes that the metaphor is interrupted or inconsistent, but rather than stopping at this point Davidson combines a concern for identifying the tenor of the metaphor (the Israelite people) with his concern to describe the *way* that tenor is presented within the metaphor. Like Smend, Davidson passes a somewhat negative judgment on the aesthetic merit of Ezekiel's narrative metaphors, but this too is more considered than Smend's complaint at Ezekiel's "annoying" inconsistencies.[41]

Davidson is also mindful of the relationship of the extended metaphors to the prophetic book as a whole. Noting that the book is characterized by "symbolical figures, symbolical actions, and visions," Davidson concludes, "The three seem all due to the same cast of mind, . . . being all more or less the creation of an imagination or phantasy always grandiose and often beautiful."[42] Davidson posits an interesting connection among aspects of the book not ordinarily seen to be related. Narrative metaphor, one of the most distinctive literary features of the book, is linked to the prophetic sign-act, probably the most striking biographical feature of the book, and both are linked to the governing premise of Ezekiel, that the entire contents of the book is motivated by a series of visions. Though Davidson does not expand on these observations, the passage quoted suggests the profoundly *visual* character of Ezekiel, focusing on visions and sign-acts, and treats the narrative metaphors as akin to visual modes of comunication. Davidson's point, of course, is not to highlight the visual, but the common symbolic nature of Ezekiel's figures, actions, and

---

[40] *Prophet Ezekiel*, 102-03.

[41] In describing the narrative metaphors as a group, Davidson says that Ezekiel tends "to develop his symbols into a multitude of details, which sometimes has the effect of obscuring the brilliancy of the central conception" (*Prophet Ezekiel*, xxvii). In regard to the metaphor of chap 16 specifically, he finds the "allegory of the foundling child . . . powerful," but "marked by a breadth which offends against modern taste" (xxvi).

[42] *Prophet Ezekiel*, xxv.

visions. Davidson also, in this pithy (though, alas, nowhere expanded) statement, moves from observing the common thread among literary features of the book to what in later scholarship would be taken as a statement about its unity, its "single cast of mind." Finally, and most laconically, Davidson points out the peculiar connection between "grandiose phantasy" and "beauty" in Ezekiel. Davidson's treatment, without giving extensive attention to Ezekiel's narrative metaphors, displays a new sensitivity to their shape and their function in the book.

Richard Moulton[43] self-consciously moves toward a definition of the genre of narrative metaphor, and his definition confirms the connection drawn by Davidson between the narrative metaphor and the sign-act. Referring to sign-acts as "emblems" and to the narrative metaphors as "parables," Moulton asserts that "a parable is simply an emblem presented in narrative instead of in visible form";[44] that in "prophecy that is written and not spoken the visible symbol is replaced by the sustained image [the parable]."[45] Moulton thus draws attention to Ezekiel's status as, at least in part, originally *written* prophecy.[46] He also obliquely highlights the element of reader participation implied by metaphor (since in any metaphor it is left to the reader to discern the connection between tenor and vehicle).[47]

The Bible as Literature movement opened up intriguing lines of discussion on Ezekiel's use of metaphor,[48] though no systematic treatment of the subject was produced. In the first half of the twentieth century the focus of the discussion shifted dramatically to problems of the authorship and unity of the book. The widespread conviction that only the "core" of the text derived from the prophet himself eclipsed interest in

---

[43] *Ezekiel* (The Modern Reader's Bible; New York: Macmillan, 1897).

[44] *Ezekiel*, xii.

[45] *Ezekiel*, xxi.

[46] For a further discussion of this aspect of the book, see E. Davis, *Swallowing the Scroll: Textuality and the Dynamics of Discourse in Ezekiel's Prophecy* (JSOTS 78; Sheffield: Sheffield Academic Press, 1989).

[47] Moulton calls attention to Ezekiel's tendency "to seek an external starting-point for discourse," and sees in this tendency a "transitional stage in the development of the modern Text and Sermon" (*Ezekiel*, xxii). This externalization of discourse is also a visualizing tendency, and related to the symbolizing tendency noted by Davidson.

[48] In this category, the pungent metaphor of W. Ballantine (*Ezekiel: A Literary Study of His Prophecy* [New York: Fleming H. Revell, 1892]) on the metaphors of chaps 16 and 23 is noteworthy: "The relentless realism of our author's methods is most startling. . . . down through one step after another we go like men who must explore a sewer and who, as they proceed, sink up to their noses in filth" (20-21). Ballantine nonetheless refers to Ezekiel as "the Dante of the Bible" (8).

the literary style of Ezekiel. This radical turn in Ezekiel criticism was impelled by the work of Gustav Hölscher.[49] Working from romantic assumptions about the "ecstatic" prophet, Hölscher assumed that genuine prophets spoke only in poetry, and that, only in brief outbursts. Prose passages were a sure sign that a later, and clearly less inspired, hand had been at work. After pruning away all the "inauthentic" additions, Hölscher concluded that the pristine product of the prophet himself amounted to slightly more than one tenth of the canonical Ezekiel. In chap 16 he saw little unity, and deplored the repetitions and trivialities that plagued the chapter beginning with v 13.[50] Though appreciative of the poetic rhythm of the passages he judged to be original (chiefly on the basis of that poetic rhythm), Hölscher's dissection of the material, together with his paradigm of the ecstatic prophet who did not compose, but simply ejaculated, his prophecies, prevented him from consideration of metaphor as an intentional, stylistic tool.

Hölscher represents the minimalist position as regards Ezekiel's authorship of the book, but his basic assumptions, that the prophet tended to speak only in poetry, and that prose passages, repetitions, and changes in topic or in genre mark the boundary between the genuine oracle and the inauthentic addition, have dominated Ezekiel scholarship into the second half of this century.[51]

In his two volume commentary, considered a milepost in twentieth-century Ezekiel scholarship, Walther Zimmerli does painstaking work on the text, and reconstructs an original "kernel" that he credits to the prophet Ezekiel. This original kernel was, according to Zimmerli, reinterpreted and updated by successive generations within an Ezekielian school, so that several layers, each commenting on both the kernel and

---

[49] *Hesekiel: Der Dichter und das Buch—Eine Literarkritische Untersuchung* (BZAW 39; Giessen: Töpelmann, 1924).

[50] *Der Dichter*, 92.

[51] See, for example, the works of G. Fohrer and W. Eichrodt. Fohrer (G. Fohrer and K. Galling, *Ezechiel* [HAT 13; Tübingen: J. C. B. Mohr (Paul Siebeck), 1955]) does note (84) that allegory seems more the mark of a writing than a speaking prophet. W. Eichrodt (*Ezekiel: A Commentary* [OTL; Philadelphia: Westminster Press, 1970]) takes a middle course, claiming that the book was in large part compiled by Ezekiel (from his own brief and originally oral speeches; 13, 19). In his introductory comments on chap 16 he notes that "the bright colouring and attractive details make an immediate impression upon the hearer, and make him sensitive to the prophet's concern" (201). That is, Eichrodt is aware of the *rhetorical* power of the narrative metaphor. However, in his analysis of the chapter he divides it into several parts, and so must abandon discussion of the artistry of the whole.

the successive layers, went to make up the canonical book.[52] In the metaphor of Jerusalem as Yahweh's wife in chaps 16 and 23, Zimmerli sees "more than an allegorical image,"[53] but what more, he does not say.[54] He is sensitive to some of the striking traits of the metaphor, such as that "the gap between the metaphor and the fact portrayed can easily disappear,"[55] but in his actual interpretations, he effectively neutralizes this sensitivity by judging most of the metaphor's peculiarities to be the result of later editing.[56]

In recent years a number of scholars have reasserted the substantial literary unity of Ezekiel, and have therefore been free to focus on (among other aspects) Ezekiel's literary style. The Anchor Bible commentary of Moshe Greenberg is the most comprehensive recent work to treat the book as a unity.[57] Reacting against interpretations based on reconstructions of the supposed *ipsissima verba* of the prophet, Greenberg proposes a "holistic" approach,[58] focusing on thematic and stylistic features that are consistent throughout Ezekiel. Greenberg proposes to elicit "the innate conventions and literary formations" of the book "by listening to it patiently and humbly,"[59] that is, by attending to the internal logic connecting the parts to the whole, and to literary patterning such as repetition, inclusio, and reuse of earlier biblical material. Greenberg's literary sensitivity leads him to pay closer attention than have his predecessors to Ezekiel's use of narrative metaphor.[60]

---

52   On this process of *Nachinterpretation*, see Zimmerli (*Ezekiel 1*, 68-73); and also P. D. Scalise, "From Prophet's Word to Prophetic Book: A Study of Walther Zimmerli's Theory of 'Nachinterpretation'" (diss., Yale University, 1982).

53   *Ezekiel 1*, 334-35.

54   Comments such as, "The reality is not simply portrayed artificially, but is present with unusual power in the metaphor" (*Ezekiel 1*, 335), are suggestive, but never elaborated with more systematic attention to Ezekiel's use of metaphor.

55   *Ezekiel 1*, 335.

56   See also the recent form-critical work of R. M. Hals (*Ezekiel*). Hals gives minute attention to a step-by-step analysis of the forms of Ezekiel's speech. In so doing, he is aware of the rhetorical shape of chaps 16 and 23, but pays little attention to metaphor as a stylistic or rhetorical element.

57   As of this writing, only the first of two volumes has appeared.

58   *Ezekiel 1-20*, 17-27.

59   *Ezekiel 1-20*, 21.

60   The commentaries of John Calvin (*Commentaries on the Prophet Ezekiel, I, II* [Edinburgh: The Calvin Translation Society, 1849-50]) should be noted as an earlier example of careful (though not systematic) attention to the dynamics of metaphor in Ezekiel. Calvin is sensitive to changes in the referent (e.g., the mixture of vocabulary from the realms of prostitution and idolatry in 16:16; II, 113) and to nuance and inconsistency in the vehicle (e.g., God's apparently stepping out of character and per-

Greenberg limits thorough discussion of Ezekiel's metaphors to his analysis of chap 17, the "fable" of the vine and the eagle. In Ezekiel 17, the metaphor is initially presented as a riddle (17:2), of which Ezekiel himself gives a two-part explanation. According to Greenberg, over the course of Ezekiel's explanation, "what may vaguely have been thought to be an allegory of apostasy is interpreted as wholly political; but then the political transaction is used as a model from which a theological analogy is drawn. Justice is thus done . . . to the ambiguities of the fable—whose glimmerings of a divine reference are thus affirmed."[61] Greenberg's reading respects the "vagueness" and "glimmerings" that are part of the intentional texture of the extended metaphor. Greenberg also implies an Ezekiel who is fully conscious of the polyvalence of his own metaphor. As exegete of his own ambiguity, Ezekiel leaves some points unexplained, gives others an allegorical (point by point) interpretation, and finally interprets the metaphor as a theological comment on the events depicted. Unfortunately, Greenberg gives no such close attention to other of Ezekiel's extended metaphors, though he makes several valuable, isolated observations. Nor does he attempt to outline the characteristics, either of Ezekiel's figurative language generally, or of the extended metaphors specifically, despite his stated goal of "eliciting the innate conventions and literary formations" of the book of Ezekiel.[62]

Though no other major work has been published that deals specifically with Ezekiel's literary style, the contributions of Carol Newsom,[63] Ellen Davis,[64] and James Durlesser[65] deserve comment. In an article focusing on Ezekiel's oracles against Tyre in chaps 26, 27, and 28, Newsom attempts to show that "the analysis of the rhetoric of metaphor is an essential part of critical exegetical method."[66] Particularly interesting is Newsom's reading of chap 27, in which Tyre is described as a ship that proudly sets out to sea, only to be sunk by an east wind. As Newsom points out, Ezekiel's metaphor depends on the commonplaces associated with Tyre as a wealthy seaport, using those commonplaces to focus the reader's attention on Tyre's pride in its merchant undertakings. Ezekiel then (as Lakoff and Johnson would say) extends the metaphor. If "Tyre is

---

forming "those offices which the nurse discharges for the child" on the post-adolescent woman in 16:9).

[61] *Ezekiel 1-20*, 322.

[62] *Ezekiel 1-20*, 21.

[63] "A Maker of Metaphors: Ezekiel's Oracles Against Tyre" (*Int* 38 [1984] 151-64).

[64] *Swallowing the Scroll.*

[65] "The Rhetoric of Allegory."

[66] "Maker of Metaphors," 164.

a ship," then it can be depicted with a ship's liabilities as well as its abilities; the reader who has tacitly agreed that Tyre is a ship is in no position to object when Ezekiel "shipwrecks" the rival nation.

Newsom provides a helpful reading of Ezekiel's oracles against Tyre within the conventions of literary criticism and demonstrates that Ezekiel's metaphor is more than a mere stylistic ornament. Rather, in chaps 26-28 Ezekiel uses the inherent ambiguity and polyvalence of metaphor to draw out the historical, theological, cultic, and political aspects of God's judgment against Tyre. Newsom elucidates both the mechanics of these four of Ezekiel's narrative metaphors, and the role of metaphor in Ezekiel's rhetoric.

In her 1987 dissertation, Ellen Davis explores the evidence for and implications of Ezekiel's status as a writing prophet. In this context, she also comments on the rhetorical function of metaphor in Ezekiel, using chap 17 as her primary example. Davis sees metaphor as a "collaborative effort" linking the prophet with his audience, a genre whose complexities and even perplexities "serve to deepen [the] relationship" between prophet and audience.[67] Rather than focusing on metaphor's ability to *change* or reorient an audience's view of reality, Davis stresses the communal and traditional aspects of metaphor. Specifically, Ezekiel's reuse of already traditional metaphors establishes a "commonality" with the community from which the metaphors are drawn.[68]

Davis's primary concern in her discussion of Ezekiel 17 is to show the uses of ambiguity in Ezekiel's metaphor. Like Greenberg,[69] Davis maintains that "the text should not be read as a strict allegory, in which each element has a single correct interpretation."[70] Rather, the text simultaneously implies a political, historically bound reading and a universal, theological reading.

In addition to her work on metaphor as a device promoting community between the prophet and audience, and her discussion of the uses of ambiguity in chap 17, Davis notes Ezekiel's reuse of his *own* images, as well as those of the community. Thus, for example, the utter worthlessness of the vinewood, already proven in chap 15, makes the vine's pre-

---

67   *Swallowing the Scroll*, 93.

68   *Swallowing the Scroll*, 94.

69   Davis objects to the notion that the "theological interpretation is finally proved wrong, as Greenberg maintains." The objection is puzzling, given Greenberg's conclusion that "the political transaction is used as a model from which a theological analogy is drawn. Justice is thus done . . . to the ambiguities of the fable—whose glimmerings of a divine reference are thus affirmed" (*Ezekiel 1-20*, 322).

70   *Swallowing the Scroll*, 99.

sumption in chap 19 seem all the more preposterous. Through "the repetition and variation of his own images,"[71] Ezekiel is again, as it were, his own exegete, establishing for the reader the commonplaces on which he will later draw.

Noting that a rhetorical-critical approach "to the allegorical chapters in Ezekiel has not been common in modern biblical studies,"[72] James Durlesser proposes in his 1988 dissertation to study ten "allegorical oracles" in Ezekiel, using the techniques of James Muilenburg to investigate "how an author's utilization of various patterns, devices, and strategies shapes the message of a work."[73]

Though Durlesser calls the passages allegories, he rejects what he considers the widespread "misunderstanding of how allegory works,"[74] namely, allegory as a tale in which a one-to-one correspondence obtains between elements of a fictional story and their real-world referents. Rather, he says, allegory is more like a "sustained metaphor. . . . For this reason, I opt on occasion throughout this dissertation to use the term 'metaphorical narrative' instead of allegory."[75] Why Durlesser chooses to use the term "allegory" at all is unclear, since as he notes, Ezekiel's "metaphorical narratives" do not fit the widespread definition of "allegory." Redefining allegory as "metaphorical narrative," he then neglects to define "metaphor," and is consequently often unclear as to how to describe the phenomena he observes.[76] For each of the ten "stories" analyzed, Durlesser provides a background survey of occurrences of the governing metaphor (vine, lion, prostitute) in the Bible, with occasional references to uses of the metaphor elsewhere in the ancient Near East, a translation of each allegory, and a summary of the argument of each and of the way in which figurative language contributes to the argument.

The broad sweep of Durlesser's survey precludes detailed analysis, and Durlesser sometimes avoids the most problematic sections. In his discussion of chap 23, for example, he skips from v 36 directly to v 45,

---

71 *Swallowing the Scroll*, 94.
72 "Rhetoric of Allegory," 4.
73 "Rhetoric of Allegory," 11.
74 "Rhetoric of Allegory," 21.
75 "Rhetoric of Allegory," 22.
76 For example, in 16:16-17 Durlesser finds the metaphor "so close to the referential track of the story that confusion develops: Is the prophet speaking metaphorically? Or is he allowing the referent to intrude? Such confusion ought not to be criticized, though. Rather, it entices and creates interesting, thought-provoking narrative" ("Rhetoric of Allegory," 156). This generalization is as far as Durlesser goes in explicating the use to which Ezekiel puts metaphorical ambiguity.

dealing with the obscurity of vv 37-44 only by their omission. Of the metaphor of Jerusalem as Yahweh's wife, Durlesser concludes, "Ezekiel utilizes bizarre and graphic images of prostitution as a rhetorical strategy through which he could proclaim the offensiveness of Judah's sins against Yahweh."[77]

To date, research on Ezekiel's use of metaphor is at an early stage. No sustained work has been done on the metaphor of Jerusalem as Yahweh's wife in chaps 16 and 23 or on the use of feminine imagery elsewhere in Ezekiel to describe the city and temple. Consequently, no connection has been drawn between the personifications of chaps 16 and 23, and the metaphor of the city as implicitly female elsewhere in the book of Ezekiel. This study is an attempt to draw those connections.

III. BACKGROUNDS: THE CITY AS A WOMAN IN THE ANCIENT NEAR EAST

The Old Testament metaphor of Jerusalem as Yahweh's wife was developed from the ancient Near Eastern understanding of capital cities as "goddesses who were married to the patron god of the city."[78] This personification of the city as a woman may have functioned somewhat analogously to Lakoff and Johnson's "conceptual metaphor," a metaphor so deeply imbedded in the culture as to be virtually invisible, but nonetheless the source of everyday assumptions and speech about capital cities. Before examining the OT metaphor of Jerusalem as the wife of Yahweh, it will be helpful to examine the metaphor of the capital as consort of the god in the ancient Near East as a whole.

The origin of the personification of cities as goddesses married to male gods is obscure. Julius Lewy argues from West Semitic and Akkadian town names ("The city of Assur is Queen," "The City of Arba'il is Ruler," etc.) and from Assyrian personal names in which "town names appear as feminine theophoric elements"[79] that major cities were

---

[77] "Rhetoric of Allegory," 351.

[78] A. Fitzgerald, "The Mythological Background for the Presentation of Jerusalem as Queen and False Worship as Adultery in the OT," *CBQ* 34 (1972) 403-16. 405; and see his "*btwlt* and *bt* as Titles for Capital Cities," *CBQ* 37 (1975) 167-83. See also the comments of J. Lewy, "The Old West Semitic Sun God Hammu," *HUCA* 18 (1944) 436-43.

[79] "Semitic Sun God," 439.

regarded as female deities, married to the city's patron god.[80] He also cites Hellenistic Phoenician coins depicting women wearing crowns with the turrets of the city on them as evidence of the belief in the city as a goddess.[81] The occurrence of city names that appear to be feminine forms of the name of a male god is taken to support this position. Further, since the deities were presumed to live together in conjugal bliss, "it follows that, on principle, their temples lay within the towns whom [the gods] married. In other words, . . . according to an ancient West Semitic doctrine, the god who chose a town as seat of his sanctuary made that town his divine wife."[82] Thus, according to Lewy, towns were given divine names and considered goddesses *because* "they were the female counterparts of the gods whose sanctuaries they sheltered."[83]

While Lewy makes a strong case that Akkadian and West Semitic cities were considered the female divine consorts of male gods whose sanctuaries were located in the "partner" city, he is less clear as to the *origin* of this perception. At first he argues that the city and god were understood to be married and that it "follows" that the temple of the god should be located within the city. That is, the perception of the city as goddess *precedes* the establishment of the temple. He later claims that the cities were considered goddesses only *because* of the temples they contained. Indeed, he proceeds to postulate that when "towns were founded and named in honor of the gods supposed to own them and dwell therein,"[84] the cities were given the feminine form of the name of the god.

Mary Wakeman, in her article, "Sacred Marriage,"[85] argues for a virtually opposite origin for the image of the city as female. Wakeman

---

[80] On the marriage between gods and goddesses in Mesopotamia, and the ritual participation by kings in renactments of these marriages, see T. Jacobsen, *The Treasures of Darkness: A History of Mesopotamian Religion* (New Haven: Yale University Press, 1976) chap 2.

[81] See also L. Kadman, *The Coins of Aelia Capitolina* (Jerusalem: Israel Numismatic Society, 1956). For an Old Babylonian example of a goddess depicted "wearing" the symbols of her domain, see A. Moortgat, *The Art of Ancient Mesopotamia: The Classical Art of the Near East* (London: Phaidon, 1969). In this case the goddess wears as a headress "an altar or temple facade" (89).

[82] "Semitic Sun God," 441; temples were sometimes referred to as the "bedroom" of the goddess, where the god would pay visits (J.-J. Glassner, "Women, Hospitality and the Honor of the Family," *Women's Earliest Records from Ancient Egypt and Western Asia* [ed. B. Lesko; Brown Judaic Studies 166; Atlanta: Scholars, 1989] 71-90. 87).

[83] "Semitic Sun God," 442.

[84] "Semitic Sun God," 441.

[85] *JSOT* 22 (1982) 21-31.

claims that in the case of Sumer, the goddess Innana is the original patron of the city and is accompanied by a male consort. Only gradually is she transformed into a consort-goddess, a process that is completed with the Assyrian takeover, at which period the mortal king begins to participate as the representative of the god in the divine marriage ceremony, thus sacralizing the hegemony of the male god and his representative over the goddess.[86] In literature depicting the goddess as patron of the city, the temple is considered the goddess's house, and may include her bedroom, but neither city nor temple is personified; rather the goddess herself is depicted as "mother" and protector of the citizens of the town.[87]

Whatever the origin of the concept, it was evidently a given in the West Semitic cultures of the ancient Near East that major cities were considered the female, divine consorts of the male gods whose temples they contained. In his study of the cosmic mountain in the Ugaritic literature,[88] Richard Clifford describes a scene in which Baal has won a victory and decides to build a temple on the "hill of victory." Baal summons the goddess Anat to act as goddess of fertility and help him build "a temple which is to bring about fertility and cosmic harmony."[89] In this example, which would postdate the posited emergence of the male god as dominant, it is the god and goddess together who build the temple, though the god initiates the task and owns the temple, while the goddess seems almost a material principle: she is goddess of fertility and is "needed" for the god to build his temple. This example fits well with the scenario in

---

[86] See also M. Hammond, *The City in the Ancient World* (Cambridge, MA: Harvard University, 1972); M. Falkenstein, "La Cité-Temple sumérienne," *Journal of World History* 1.4 (1954) 784-814; and N. F. Goldsmith and E. Gould, "Sumerian Bats, Lion-headed Eagles, and Iconographic Evidence for the Overthrow of a Female-priest Hegemony," *BA* 53 (1990) 142-56. Fitzgerald ("Mythological Background") claims that "in the WS area cities were regarded from time immemorial as goddesses," but does not speculate as to the origin of this concept. In the Sumerian lamentation over the destruction of Ur (*ANET*, 455-63), the city is personified both as a queen weeping over her palace, and as the mother of the city's inhabitants.

[87] See for example the Nanshe Hymn, in which the goddess is not only the "mother" of her city's people, but also the cause of the women's fertility (in T. Jacobsen, *The Harps That Once . . . : Sumerian Poetry in Translation* [New Haven: Yale University, 1987]) 126-42, esp. 127-28.

[88] *The Cosmic Mountain in Canaan and the Old Testament* (HSM 4; Cambridge, MA: Harvard University, 1972).

[89] Clifford, *Cosmic Mountain*, 74. Cf. the account of Gudea's building a temple which the god and goddess enter together, causing the fertility of fields and filling of the streams (in Jacobsen, *The Harps That Once . . .*, 386-444).

which the female city is inhabited by the male god, and the temple is the particular locus of interaction between god and goddess and the consequent source of fertility. The focus on the goddess's physical association with the temple, and consequently, on the temple as the source of the god's fertility, will be discussed further in conjunction with the marriage metaphor as it appears in Ezekiel.

Ezekiel's use of the marriage metaphor depends for its coherence on the culturally accepted notion that the female capital city is married to a male god. Though, as we shall see, Ezekiel is also dependent on earlier OT authors, none of the OT usage of sexual terminology to describe the relationship between the people and God can be understood apart from the status of the marriage metaphor as part of the worldview of the ancient Near East. Thus the personification of Jerusalem as Yahweh's wife in Ezekiel 16 and 23 forms part of a continuum, a tradition not only within but also preceding the OT, of depicting the capital city as a woman. In these personifications, Ezekiel does not *posit* that Jerusalem is a woman, but can assume a system of commonplaces already associated with the city's feminine persona, and then shape and extend the metaphor to suit his purposes. As will be discussed below, the conceptual metaphor of the city as a woman also influences Ezekiel's depiction of the city in the chapters where the city's feminine persona is not mentioned explicitly. If the city is always implicitly female, then the use of language and imagery drawn from the explicit personifications in chaps 16 and 23 to depict Jerusalem throughout Ezekiel suggests that Ezekiel understands Jerusalem to be, at least implicitly, Yahweh's wife throughout the book. All of Ezekiel's depictions of the city's impurity, infidelity, and abandonment by Yahweh must therefore be reinterpreted in light of the city's female persona.

II

THE MARRIAGE METAPHOR IN THE
OT EXCLUSIVE OF EZEKIEL

I. OT USAGE OF THE NEAR EASTERN METAPHOR:
SOME ESSENTIAL CHANGES

The ancient Near Eastern conception of the capital city as the female, divine consort of its resident god forms the background upon which the OT writers based their depictions of the city as Yahweh's wife. The OT depictions differ in a number of significant ways from their ancient Near Eastern counterparts; three of these differences should be mentioned at the outset of the discussion of OT texts.

First, in the OT the city, though still the consort of the god, is "demoted" from divine to mortal status. Nowhere in the OT is a city, whether Israelite or foreign, referred to as a goddess.[1] Second, the image

---

[1] Depiction of the city as a queen (Isa 47:1f) or as "fit to be queen" (Ezek 16:13) marks the highest rank a city is awarded. Presumably the representation of a divine consort would have been theologically unacceptable to the texts' monotheistic authors. On the relationship between the OT city as queen and the ancient Near Eastern city as goddess, see M. Biddle, "The Figure of Lady Jerusalem: Identification, Deification and Personification of Cities in the ANE," in [The Biblical Canon in Comparative Perspective] (Scripture in Context 4; ed. W. W. Hallo, et al.; Lewiston, NY: Edwin Mellen, 1991) 173-194.

of the personified city is changed in the OT from a positive image to a negative one. Whereas the city-goddesses of the ancient Near East ruled with wisdom and power,[2] in the Hebrew Bible personified cities, almost without exception, are condemned, destroyed, or have their destruction lamented.[3]

Finally, the ancient Near Eastern conceptual metaphor of the city as wife of the god was probably well enough established to have been a "dead" metaphor in biblical times, so ancient and so widely used that its status as metaphor was no longer apparent. In the OT, however, the metaphor is "revived" by its extension to include aspects of marriage that had not previously been active parts of the metaphor. Chief among these previously unrealized aspects of the marriage metaphor is the ability of the city/wife to commit adultery.[4] Not only is the city's infidelity

---

[2] See, e.g., the Babylonian "Hymn to Ishtar" (*ANET*, 383), in which the goddess's supremacy "over the gods" is celebrated, and the depiction of Inanna providing for the citizens of Akkade ("The Cursing of Akkade," in T. Jacobsen, *The Harps That Once . . .*, 361-62).

[3] The single, clear exception is 2 Sam 20:19, in which Abel Beth-maacah is referred to as "a city that is a mother in Israel." Though its precise meaning is unknown, the epithet seems to be a title of respect. Zion in Deutero-Isaiah is loved and comforted, but this apparently positive personification is ambiguous. The promises of comfort to Zion assume the brutal punishment "Daughter Zion" has already, and justly, received for her sins.

[4] Fitzgerald ("*btwlt* and *bt*") argues that the extension of the metaphor to include adultery is the result of the metaphor's transfer to a monotheistic setting. "The city is a goddess married to the patron god of the city. In a polytheist system worship of other gods is permitted, but in the Yahwist system that can only be regarded as adultery" (178). Fitzgerald seems here to equate polytheism with polyandry. If, however, the city and god are depicted metaphorically as wife and husband, then the city's worship of many gods could reasonably be represented as the wife's intercourse with many men—adultery—in any monandrous society, regardless of its worship practice. Acceptance of polytheism (at the level of the tenor) does not imply acceptance of polyandry (at the level of either tenor or vehicle).

A polytheistic (but not polyandrous) culture would simply repress the "adulterous" implications of polytheism within the marriage metaphor. Like the potential for butchery implicit in the OT metaphor of Yahweh as shepherd (who might not only "tend," but also slaughter, the sheep), the potential for adultery implicit in the marriage metaphor would be left inactive. The city might, for example, be understood as married and loyal to its patron god, but the residents of the city understood as her children, who might worship other gods.

In a monotheistic society, or a society in which monotheists are an embattled faction, however, the marriage metaphor's unrealized potential provides an avenue by which to condemn polytheism. The inactive potential of the metaphor is therefore activated and exploited to deride the polytheistic city as an adulteress. The point is not, as Fitzgerald contends, that in a monotheistic system polytheism *must* be re-raised as a possibility in the OT use of the marriage metaphor; condemnation of the city's "adultery" is virtually the only reason the metaphor is employed in depicting the cities of Israel.[5] Israelite cities that are judged, are judged for their (sexual) infidelity; cities that are punished, are punished for infidelity; and cities whose destruction is lamented have been destroyed for the same.

II. THE MARRIAGE METAPHOR IN THE EXTRAPROPHETIC TEXTS

Although OT personification of the city as the wife of Yahweh is limited to the prophetic corpus, the extraprophetic texts do employ the language of sexuality as a metaphor for the relationship between God and the people. Specifically, the root *znh* is applied metaphorically in extraprophetic texts to both the land and the people, to describe their infidelity to Yahweh.

Although the meaning of the root *znh* in its various metaphoric applications is the subject of debate, one literal meaning is generally agreed upon; the participle *zwnh* or phrase *'šh zwnh* is the ordinary OT term for a professional prostitute (as, e.g., in Josh 2:1; Gen 38:15).[6] The verb is most often used, however, in one of two metaphorical senses.[7]

---

garded as adultery, but that only in a monotheistic system would one have reason to exploit rather than repress this aspect of the metaphor.

5   2 Samuel 20:19 is probably the only instance where a fully personified Israelite city is not said to have committed adultery. Foreign cities *may* be depicted as sexually promiscuous (e.g., Tyre in Isa 23:15-17), but may also be punished for vices such as pride (so Babylon in Isaiah 47). Presumably Yahweh was not as concerned with the sexual conduct of other gods' wives as he was with that of his own wife.

6   See S. Erlandsson, "*zānāh*" (*TDOT* IV, 99-104). E. J. Adler (Goodfriend) gives a thorough review of the uses and options for interpreting the root in her dissertation, "The Background for the Metaphor of Covenant as Marriage in the Hebrew Bible" (diss., Berkeley, 1989); see also C. Bucher, "The Origin and Meaning of '*znh*' Terminology in the Book of Hosea" (diss., Claremont, 1988); P. Bird, "To Play the Harlot: An Inquiry into an Old Testament Metaphor," in P. Day, ed., *Gender and Difference in Ancient Israel* (Minneapolis: Fortress, 1989) 75-94; T. D. Setel, "Prophets and Pornography: Female Sexual Imagery in Hosea," in L. Russell, ed., *Feminist Interpretation of the Bible* (Philadelphia: Fortress, 1985) 86-95.

7   If the participle, *zwnh*, derives from the literal sense of the verb ("to be a prostitute"), then this usage of the verb has all but dropped out of use in biblical Hebrew. The Hiph'il occurs in the commandment against making one's daughter a prostitute (*'l thll 't btk lhznwth*; Lev 19:29), but otherwise the verb is used only in figurative senses.

First, the verb *znh* and related abstract nouns[8] can be used to describe illicit sexual activity by a woman.[9] Most women in Israelite society were under the authority of a man (usually a husband or father), who claimed rights of use or disposal over the woman's child-bearing capacity.[10] The woman's sexual intercourse on her own authority violated the rights of the man in authority over her (sexuality), and so was defined as illicit.[11] Thus, extramarital sex by a woman who was betrothed (Deut 22:23-24) or married (Num 5:13), or by a dependent virgin daughter (Deut 22:21) or a levirate widow (Gen 38:24), was forbidden, and was described metaphorically as prostitution, using the verb *znh*.[12] The logic of this usage seems to be that the woman has, like a

---

[8]   *znwt* in Num 14:33 and *znwnym* in Gen 38:24 and 2 Kgs 9:22 are the only extraprophetic uses of the abstract nouns.

[9]   Bucher (" 'znh' Terminology") argues that originally "the root *znh* refers literally to a woman's act of engaging in sexual intercourse with a man to whom she is not formally bound," that "the woman is always unmarried," a prostitute, an unmarried daughter, or a levirate widow, and that the meaning was later "broadened to include the sexual activity of a married woman" (119). Bucher cites no evidence for this two-step process, and the distinction is puzzling. Also, in including prostitutes among those women to whom "the root" applies, Bucher fails to account for the fact that the *verb znh* is never used of a professional prostitute. This is because the sexual activity of the prostitute, while outside formal bonds, is in fact licit. Whatever original, literal meaning the verb may have had, in biblical Hebrew it refers (unlike the participle) to the illicit activity of a woman who is *not* a professional prostitute.

[10]   See Setel, "Prophets," 88-90, and also the excellent study of J. R. Wegner, *Chattel or Person?: The Status of Women in the Mishnah* (New York: Oxford University, 1988). Wegner elucidates in detail the Mishnaic system according to which women are legally persons in most respects, but chattel in respect of their reproductive capacity. This categorization is based on that of the Bible, according to which the woman is the "sexual property" of her father or husband and adultery is "primarily . . . a violation of property" (13). Three classes of legally (sexually) autonomous women were recognized: the "legally emancipated [adult] daughter," the divorcee, and the widow with a male heir (and thus free of levirate status; 14).

[11]   Thus in Israelite law, it is only "the bride, not the husband, who is subject to the laws of adultery"; J. Milgrom, *Cult and Conscience: The Asham and the Priestly Doctrine of Repentence* (SJLA 18; Leiden: Brill, 1976) 134.
     The technical term for adultery per se (illicit sexual activity by a married woman) is *n'p* (so, e.g., in Num 5:11-31). Adultery is a subset of *znwt*, illicit sexual activity by any woman who is not autonomous. In this work the English term "adultery" will be employed in its usual sense, including references to places where the biblical text says that a married party has committed "infidelity" (*znwt*). Thus, for example, cultic apostasy is said to be depicted as "adultery" because an analogy is drawn between cultic and marital infidelity, even though the root *znh* is preferred to *n'p* in the text.

prostitute, allowed more than one man access to her sexuality.[13] The usage of the verb *znh* to refer to a woman's illicit sexual activity (for which she is not paid) will be referred to as the "first level" metaphorical use of *znh*. The woman in question is not a literal prostitute, but she does literally engage in sexual intercourse, and in a manner that implicitly involves more than one man, both the one with authority over her and one without that authority. The subject of this first level metaphor is always female.[14]

The second level at which *znh* is used metaphorically seems to be derived from the first. According to this usage worship of gods other

---

[12] P. Bird,"To Play the Harlot," argues that the original meaning of the verb is, "to have illicit intercourse," where "illicit" means, not extramarital, but transgressing a male's rights of control. Bird considers all extramarital intercourse by a woman to have been "illicit"; she does not consider the possibility of the legally autonomous woman. Bird argues that the literal meaning of the root is derived from the verb, and that "to be sexually unfaithful" is the literal usage. Perplexingly, she also claims that "normally, *zana* does not carry the notion of infidelity" (81). If the verb *znh* does not carry the notion of infidelity, it is difficult to imagine what notion it *does* carry, particularly if its meaning is, as Bird claims, "to be sexually unfaithful." A root meaning of infidelity would, however, make it difficult to explain the root's application to the professional prostitute, who seems to fall into the category of the sexually independent woman. Bird claims that "in Hebrew conception the prostitute is essentially a professional or habitual fornicator, a promiscuous or unchaste woman" (78), but in fact the prostitute is the one woman whose extramarital sex is *not* condemned as fornication or unchastity in the legal sense, presumably because it violates the rights of no man. Though their social status seems to have been a low one, prostitutes are never condemned in the Hebrew Bible for their sexual activity (see Bucher, "'znh' Terminology," 96; Setel, "Prophets and Pornography," 89; Adler, "Covenant as Marriage," 349-52).

[13] Note, however, that in order to have "prostituted" herself, the woman need not have had intercourse with more than one man. In the case of a (formerly) virgin daughter who is found to have "prostituted" herself (Deut 22:13-21), for example, it is her *father's* rights over her reproductive capacity that have been usurped and given to another man. Thus "prostitution" in its figurative sense refers to a situation in which more than one man (the one in authority and one unauthorized) is allowed power over a woman's sexual activity, rather than a situation in which more than one man actually has intercourse with the woman.

[14] The subject is female because only women are legally circumscribed in regard to *their own* sexual activity. Men are under no sexual obligation to spouse or parents (except for possible expectations of endogamy); their activities can only be illicit in respect to the rights of other *men*. Thus, if a married man seduces a dependent virgin, the wrong is understood to have been committed against the father of the (former) virgin (Exod 22:15-16; Deut 22:28-29; and see Wegner, *Chattel or Person*, 13). The man's offense is more like theft than like prostitution, and the verb *znh* does not apply.

than Yahweh is referred to by the verb *znh*.[15] The male Israelite's worship of other gods is understood as parallel to a woman's illicit sexual activity, because in each case the offender has transferred the exclusive rights of the one in authority (at the second level, Yahweh, rather than husband or father) to a second, competing party (the other god). Unlike the first level metaphor, the second level metaphor is applied to cultic activity and does not ordinarily entail any literal sexual activity.[16] The subject of the

---

[15] The nominal forms are not used outside the prophetic corpus at this second metaphorical level (idolatry).

[16] There is no evidence that the apostate Israelites engaged in sexual intercourse as part of their "whoring around on Yahweh." A thorough review of the extrabiblical texts commonly assumed to contain evidence of cultic sex in the ancient Near East can be found in Bucher ("'znh' Terminology," 29-31). Bucher concludes that even in the sacred marriage rituals of Sumeria and Babylonia, literal sexual intercourse may not have taken place. The only known mortal participant is the king; the participation of women has simply been assumed. The *nadītu*, often taken to have a sexual function in the cult, was actually forbidden intercourse (see also E. J. Adler, "Marriage as Covenant," 317-49; R. Westbrook, *Old Babylonian Marriage Law* [AOr 23; Horn, Austria: Ferdinand Berger & Sohne, 1988, 64]; B. F. Batto, *Studies on Women at Mari* [Baltimore: Johns Hopkins, 1974] 93-113; and R. Harris, "The naditu-Woman," *Studies Presented to A. Leo Oppenheim* [Chicago: The Oriental Institute, 1964] 106-35). Likewise, no sexual activity is recorded on the part of the *qadistu* (on the nonexistence of sacred prostitution in Israel and the ancient Near East generally, see E. J. Fisher, "Cultic Prostitution in the Ancient Near East: A Reassessment," *BTB* 6 [1976] 225-36; R. A. Oden, "Religious Identity and the Sacred Prostitution Accusation," in his *The Bible without Theology* [1987] 131-53; K. Van der Toorn, "Female Prostitution in Payment of Vows in Ancient Israel," *JBL* 108 [1989] 193-205; J. G. Westenholz, "Tamar, Qedesa, Qadistu, and Sacred Prostitution in Mesopotamia," *HTR* 82 [1989] 245-65; A. van Selms, *Marriage and Family Life in Ugaritic Literature* [Pretoria Oriental Series 1; London: Luzac, 1954] 80).

In only two instances in the OT (Exod 34:15-16; Num 25:1) is the verb *znh* used to link literal sexual activity with cultic infidelity. In Exod 34:13-16 the people are warned against accepting an invitation to eat with the inhabitants of the land, lest the Israelites be moved to participate when the Canaanites "prostitute themselves to their gods." Likewise, the Israelites' sons are not to marry the Canaanites' daughters, lest the wives entice the husbands to "prostitute themselves to their gods" along with them. In short, the Israelites are urged not to mingle with the Canaanites, lest they participate in Canaanite worship, a worship metaphorically referred to as "prostitution" (the Canaanites' worship of their *own* gods is pejoratively termed "prostitution/infidelity"). Though this passage does discuss both sexual relationships and idolatry, it is social, not sexual, intercourse that is considered dangerous.

In Num 25:1 the Israelite sons do indeed "prostitute themselves with" (ʾl, not ʾḥry, the usual form referring to idolatry) the daughters of Moab. The phrase *znh* ʾl here has two possible meanings: 1) the Israelites prostitute themselves *along with* the Moabites; that is, they engage in the latter's idolatrous practices, or 2) the Israelites

verb *znh* as a second level metaphor is always male or of mixed gender, since it is the Israelite male whose cultic activity (like the female's sexual activity) is legally circumscribed. The male Israelite was the legal "person" to whom the commandments were addressed.[17] Ordinarily, the verb *znh* is followed by the preposition *ʾḥry*,[18] plus the object of the offending worship. In Lev 20:5 the apostate "prostitutes himself to Molech" (*znh ʾḥry hmmlk*) and in Deut 31:16 the people "prostitute themselves to the strange gods" of the land (*znh ʾḥry ʾlhy nkr-hʾrṣ*). The meaning of *znh* at the second metaphoric level is "to violate the obligation of exclusive fidelity to Yahweh." Twice removed from its literal meaning as prostitution, the second level metaphor (a metaphor based on the metaphor of illicit sexual activity as "prostitution") thus depends on a comparison between idolatry and adultery, not one between idolatry and prostitution.[19]

---

marry the Moabites despite having been forbidden (in Exodus 34) to do so, and their sexual relationship is therefore illicit (and would constitute the unique case of men as the subject of *znh* as a first level metaphor). As predicted in Exodus 34, the Moabite wives invite the Israelites over to feast and to sacrifice, which they do (v 2). Note that although sexual intercourse between the Israelites and Moabites is clearly implied (cf. v 8), intercourse has no connection with worship per se.

[17] Thus in Exod 20:15 the "people" are told, "Be ready on the third day; do not go near a woman," and in Exod 20:14 the commandment against coveting the neighbor's *wife* is not matched by a commandment against coveting the neighbor's husband; the community to whom the law is addressed is the community of Israelite males.

[18] Outside the prophetic books the verb occurs in six locations (out of a total of forty-four extraprophetic occurrences) without *ʾḥry*. In 2 Chron 21:11, 13 and Lev 19:29 the Hiph'il form designates someone's causing someone else's (in Leviticus, the land's) "prostitution"; in Ps 106:39 the people's idolatry is summarized, "They performed acts of prostitution"; Ps 73:27 condemns "all who prostitute themselves 'away from'" Yahweh (*mʾḥry*; implying that they do so "after" someone else); and in Num 25:1 the people prostitute themselves "together with" (*ʾl*) the daughters of Moab, by marriage or by sacrificing to their gods.

[19] There appears to have been relatively little stigma attached to prostitution as a profession (in this regard, see Bucher, "'*znh*' Terminology," 96; Adler, "Marriage as Covenant," 349-52). Rahab, for example, is depicted as a person of integrity (Josh 2:1-21; 6:25), and in rabbinic tradition is even said to have married Joshua (L. Ginzberg, *The Legends of the Jews*, 7 vols. [Philadelphia: Jewish Publication Society, 1968] 4. 5). While priests are forbidden to marry prostitutes (Lev 21:7), there is no prohibition against such marriages for lay Israelites. The lack of overt condemnation of prostitutes may reflect a relative lack of concern as to the sexual conduct of the (rare) woman who was not under male authority. When, however, the root *znh* is used of anyone to whom it does not apply literally (sexually disobedient females or idolatrous males), it describes a violation of authority, and is a term of strong opprobrium. Thus, males are forbidden (Lev 19:29) from making their own daughters prostitutes,

The biblical metaphor of apostasy as sexual infidelity cannot be understood apart from Israel's theological stance of being bound in an exclusive relationship with Yahweh. Israel described its relationship to Yahweh in terms of a political treaty—a covenant (Hos 8:1; Exod 24:7-8; Deut 29:1; Josh 24:19-28; etc.).[20] The vassal treaties on which the biblical covenant is modeled establish a relationship between a superior (suzerain) and an inferior (vassal) party, in which the suzerain swears to protect the vassal, and the vassal swears exclusive loyalty and obedience (including the payment of tribute) to the suzerain. The treaty, while mutual, establishes roles that are neither identical nor equal. The suzerain king who imposes the treaty remains the superior party and, though obliged to protect the vassal, is under no obligation of exclusive allegiance. The vassal, however, must swear loyalty to the suzerain alone. The Israelites' covenant with Yahweh parallels this arrangement.[21] Yahweh is the sovereign lord who, in exchange for his provision and protection, imposes a pledge of obedience and exclusive fidelity on the people.[22] The worship of gods other than Yahweh is thus considered a violation of Israel's covenantal obligation of exclusivity, and therefore

---

and the sons of Jacob consider Shechem's act of treating their sister "like a prostitute" (Gen 34:31) sufficient justification for murderous revenge.

[20] On Israel's covenant with Yahweh, and its relation to political treaties, see C. T. Begg, "Berit in Ezekiel," Proceedings of the Ninth World Congress of Jewish Studies (Jerusalem: World Union of Jewish Studies, 1986) 77-83; P. Kalluveetil, Declaration and Covenant (AnBib 88; Rome: Biblical Institute, 1982); D. J. McCarthy, Old Testament Covenant: A Survey of Current Opinions (Oxford/Richmond: Basil Blackwell/John Knox, 1972); E. Nicholson, God and His People: Covenant and Theology in the Old Testament (Oxford: Clarendon, 1986); G. M. Tucker, "Covenant Forms and Contract Forms," VT 15 (1965) 487-503; M. Weinfeld, "bĕrîth," TDOT I, 253-79; and G. Widengren, "King and Covenant," JSS 2 (1957) 1-32.

[21] The use of the treaty/covenant form to describe the relationship between Yahweh and Israel would fit well with the Israelite designation of Yahweh as "king" (see Weinfeld, "King and Covenant," 278). On the use of the term mlk in connection with Yahweh see G. C. Heider, The Cult of Molek: A Reassessment (JSOTS 43; Sheffield: Journal for the Study of the Old Testament, 1986); S. Olyan, Asherah and the Cult of Yahweh in Israel (SBLMS 34; Atlanta: Scholars, 1988) 11-13.

[22] The treaty is depicted as ritually enacted with the king serving as intermediary between the people and Yahweh (as, e.g., in 2 Kgs 11:4, 17). Although the age of this practice is unknown, as early as Hosea Yahweh claims that the people have broken his covenant (8:1). Weinfeld notes that such "a covenant between a deity and a people is unknown to us from other religions" (278).

just cause for Yahweh to revoke his promise of provision and protection.[23]

The dynamics of covenant loyalty and disloyalty form the basis for the depiction of apostasy as adultery.[24] Israelite marriage was, like vassaldom, a relationship of mutual obligation between two parties, one (the husband) superior and the other (the wife) inferior in terms of their legal status. As in a treaty agreement, the husband was required to protect the wife (in this case, provide food and clothing)[25] and the wife was to obey the husband and to refrain from sexual relationships with other men. The husband, like the suzerain, was free of any such obligation of exclusivity.[26] The Israelite covenant with Yahweh shares this basic shape with both international and marriage agreements. Yahweh is Israel's (suzerain) king and Israel is his vassal. As suzerain Yahweh's role in

---

[23] See, e.g., the "treaty-curses" in Deut 28:15-68 and cf. D. R. Hillers, *Treaty-Curses and the Old Testament Prophets* (BibOr 16; Rome: Pontifical Biblical Institute, 1964).

[24] P. A. Kruger comments ("Israel, the Harlot [Hos. 2:4-9]," *JNSL* 11 [1984] 107-16) that the image of the god and followers as married is not an ancient Near Eastern commonplace, but is "peculiar to the OT" (107).

[25] For ancient Near Eastern antecedents, see M. Malul, *Studies in Mesopotamian Legal Symbolism* (AOAT 221; Neukirchen-Vluyn: Butzen & Bercker Kevelaer, 1988, 174-75), who cites the husband's duty to provide food, oil, and clothing, "the three basic staples of life"; cf. Kruger, "Israel, the Harlot."

[26] The exact nature of the marriage agreement continues to be a matter of debate. The ancient Near Eastern evidence seems to indicate that marriage was a two-stage process in which a contract (not covenant) was established between the groom and the parents or guardian of the bride, and then the marriage proper entered into by the groom's (and possibly the bride's) verbal declaration (see S. Greengus, "The Old Babylonian Marriage Contracts," *JAOS* 89 [1969] 505-32; Westbrook, *Marriage Law*). Westbrook suggests (58) that the procedure for marriage conformed to that of adoption, in that the only mutual agreement was between the man and the parents, and that this agreement plus the declaration by the man created a legal status between him and the new son/wife, the terms of which were a matter of statute, rather than of individual decision.

There is, however, evidence to suggest that Israelite custom differed from Mesopotamian in at least some details, and that in at least some cases, the declaration of marriage included (like a covenant) an oath in the name of Yahweh (cf., e.g., Ruth 3:13; Mal 2:14; Ezek 16:8; Prov 2:17; and see Weinfeld, "berîth," 278). Given that Israelite religious ritual departed from ancient Near Eastern custom generally by including a covenant between God and the people, there is no reason marriage rituals might not also have differed in their inclusion of covenant vows. Whether or not Israelite marriage included covenant vows in some or all cases, however, does not affect the fact that the dynamics of obligation between husband and wife match closely those between the two parties of Israel's international covenants and the covenant depicted between Israel and Yahweh.

relation to Israel parallels that of the husband in relation to the wife; he is the superior party who gives protection in exchange for obedience and exclusive loyalty. Cultic apostasy, the worship of gods other than Yahweh, can thus be seen as a parallel to marital infidelity, a violation of Yahweh's right to exclusive control over the inferior covenant party.[27]

Another dynamic of the international covenant relationship affects the OT use of the adultery metaphor. Treaties in the ancient Near East were sworn before the deity. The name of the god (or gods) was invoked as guarantor of the fidelity of (at least) the inferior party.[28] In Israel, Yahweh's role as guarantor of covenants between Israel and other nations meant that the breaking of a covenant was an offense against his name, impugning both his power (as avenger) and his honor. In his covenant with Israel, then, Yahweh would have played a double role, as both participant in and guarantor of the covenant, and the king's or people's breach of covenant would therefore have constituted a double offence against Yahweh. Not only would Yahweh suffer dishonor as a king whose vassals had disobeyed, but also as a god whose name had been defiled.[29] This aspect of Israelite apostasy—the defilement of the divine name—may have contributed more than any other to the use of the adultery metaphor to describe apostasy. Although adultery did not defile the name of the husband, the shame created by Yahweh's failure to keep his subjects "at home" would have found powerful expression in the image of the god as a cuckolded and therefore shamed husband.[30]

---

[27] The language of human (sexual) relationships was an element of ancient treaty-making; the language of love of God (in Deut 6:5, and so on) should probably be understood in this context (see W. Moran, "The Ancient Near Eastern Background of the Love of God in Deuteronomy," *CBQ* 25 [1963] 77-87; J. A. Thompson, "Israel's Lovers," *VT* 27 [1977] 475-81). Treaty-loyalty was termed "love," and disloyalty "hate" of the sovereign. The same terminology was used in regard to the *legal* (and not emotional) aspects of marriage and divorce. So, a man who rejected his wife was said to "hate" her (*zerum*). Though ordinarily used to describe the reason for divorce (personal preference rather than cause), in some circumstances the mere statement, "I hate my wife," constituted a declaration of divorce. According to Westbrook, this is the meaning of "hate" (*śnʾ*) in Deut 24:3 (Westbrook, *Marriage Law*, 22-23; Westbrook, "The Prohibition on Restoration of Marriage in Deuteronomy 24:1-4," *Studies in Bible* [ed. S. Japhet; Scripta Hierosolymitana 31; Jerusalem: The Magnes Press, 1986] 387-405).

[28] See M. Cogan, *Imperialism and Religion: Assyria, Judah, and Israel in the Eighth and Seventh Centuries B.C.E.* (SBLMS 19; Missoula, MT: Scholars, 1974) 44-49.

[29] On treaty violation as violating the name of Yahweh, see Milgrom, *Cult and Conscience*, 13-22.

[30] The shame of adultery is often understood to adhere to the *man* rather than to the offending woman (see esp. the survey of this evidence by U. Wiken, "Shame and

The intense emotional and cultural sanction surrounding female adultery would have provided an appropriate vehicle for venting the powerful rage and shame of the humiliated god.[31]

III. THE MARRIAGE METAPHOR
IN THE PROPHETS

A. *Distinctive Characteristics of the Marriage Metaphor in the Prophetic Books*

In addition to employing the metaphor of apostasy as adultery (using the root *znh*), the prophets also exploited the ancient Near Eastern tradition of personifying capital cities as women married to the god. The image of the city as a benevolent goddess was changed by the prophets, however, into an image of the city as a weak and degraded mortal woman, and above all, an adulteress.

The prophetic use of the marriage metaphor differs not only from that in the ancient Near East generally, but also from the use of the metaphor of apostasy as adultery elsewhere in the Hebrew Bible. The

---

Honour: A Contestable Pair," *Man* 19 [1984] 635-47; and see also M. Bal, *Murder and Difference: Gender, Genre, and Scholarship on Sisera's Death* [Bloomington: Indiana University, 1988] 115-20; S. Brandes, "Like Wounded Stags: Male Sexual Ideology in an Andalusian Town," in S. B. Ortner and H. Whitehead, eds., *Sexual Meanings: The Cultural Construction of Gender and Sexuality* [Cambridge: Cambridge University, 1981] 216-39; J. G. Peristiany, *Honour and Shame* [London: Weidenfeld and Nicholson, 1965]; and J. Pitt-Rivers, "Honor," in D. L. Sills, ed., *Encyclopedia of the Social Sciences* [New York: Crowell Collier and Macmillan, 1968] 6. 503-11, and *The Fate of Shechem and the Politics of Sex* [Cambridge: Cambridge University, 1976] 78-83, 161). In the OT the public shaming (or capital punishment) of the woman transfers the shame onto her, and serves to vindicate the honor of her husband or clan.

[31] Interestingly, the image of apostasy as adultery requires that the Israelite audience (and authors) accept the change in gender implicit in the metaphor. The male Israelites, who constituted the legal community of Israel, were cast in the role of the unfaithful wife. In the context of adultery this role-reversal is shaming (and see, e.g., Nah 3:13), though the assignment of the female gender role to a man may not have been shaming in itself. Malul (*Studies*, 171-72) mentions that in healing/exorcism texts, "demons and sicknesses possessing a person always play the male role, while the sick person is perceived as the female [sexual] partner, even if he is a male." Like the role reversal in the exorcism texts, the gender-reversal implicit in the adultery metaphor was a "dead" metaphor, and was probably not even consciously perceived by its users. A comparable phenomenon would be the mental distortion unconsciously performed by speakers of modern English who use "he" and "man" to refer to women.

marriage metaphor, the depiction of the relationship between Yahweh and the people in terms of sexual obligation, occurs in both prophetic and extraprophetic texts, but the metaphor is used differently in the two bodies of material. Most striking is the contrast between the total absence of personification of the capital city in the extraprophetic texts, and its prominence in the prophetic corpus.[32] A second distinctive feature of the prophetic texts is the use of *bt* followed by the name of the city (e.g., "daughter Zion" in Isa 1:8).[33] This minimal personification is common in the prophets but almost entirely absent from the rest of the OT.[34] Third, the phrase *znh ʾḥry* followed by an object, the usual extraprophetic expression designating cultic infidelity (e.g., Exod 34:15-16),[35] occurs only twice in the prophets, both times in Ezekiel (Ezek 6:9; 20:30; but cf. Hos 1:2). Fourth, whereas outside the prophets the second level use of *znh* refers exclusively to cultic infidelity, in the prophets the verb may have either a cultic or a *political* referent.

Finally, in the prophetic personification of cities, the city may be punished by Yahweh. In addition to exploiting the metaphor's ability to

---

[32] Strong personifications of cities occur in Hosea, Isaiah, Nahum, Jeremiah, Lamentations, Ezekiel, and Deutero-Isaiah (Zeph 3:1-2, 14 and Zech 9:9 also contain brief addresses to personified Jerusalem). The epithet, "daughter" or "virgin" is applied to a city in Amos, Isaiah, Micah, Jeremiah, Zephaniah, Zechariah, Lamentations, and Ezekiel.

[33] D. Bourguet (*Des Métaphores de Jérémie* [EBib 9; Paris: Gabalda, 1987]) notes that the usage "daughter X" is not applied to cities in the ancient Near East generally. The expression "virgin X" is also not used of cities, though it may be used of the patron goddesses themselves, especially Anat (482-84).

[34] Outside the prophets, the expression is used only three times, all in the Psalms: 9:15 (Eng 9:14); 45:13 (Eng 45:12); 137:8. A parallel expression, *btwlt* plus the name of a nation, is a related metaphor, again designating the capital city; *btwlt yśrʾl* (Jer 31:4), "virgin of Israel," refers to Jerusalem (as does the compound form, *btwlt bt sywn*, "virgin daughter, Zion," Isa 37:22). Use of *btwlt* to designate a city is entirely lacking outside the prophets. Fitzgerald argues ("*btwlt* and *bt*," 178-79) that *btwlt yśrʾl* in, e.g., Amos 5:2 should be translated "virgin Israel," assuming that the "house of Israel" in 5:1 and the "virgin Israel" in 5:2 "clearly refer to the same institution," namely, the kingdom. Amos's lamentation, however, calls on the "house" to lament the fall of the "virgin." The "house," the ruling family or inhabitants of the North, are summoned to lament over Samaria, the capital, the "virgin of Israel."

The expression "daughter X" in reference to a capital is frequently used without further personification, and by prophets (e.g., Amos) who use no other forms of personification of cities, and so was probably a "dead" metaphor, part of the ancient Near Eastern metaphoric conception of cities as female.

[35] For a thorough review of the range of use and meaning of the phrase *znh ʾḥry*, see Adler ("Marriage as Covenant," 317-49).

express Yahweh's outrage, the prophets also exploited the Israelite custom of publicly shaming the unfaithful woman. This shaming of the personified city would have provided a metaphorical means of transferring the shame of cuckoldry from the husband/god onto the woman/people. Thus the prophetic extension of the marriage metaphor to depict the city as an adulteress simultaneously expressed the horror of the god's loss of honor and provided the means by which that honor could symbolically be restored.

Because the depiction of apostasy as adultery differs in such consistent and significant respects in the prophetic and the extraprophetic texts, the marriage metaphor of the prophetic and the extraprophetic writings may best be understood as two different metaphors. In the extraprophetic texts the metaphor always applies to the (male) people as a whole, or their ruler as a representative, and is for all intents and purposes "dead"; the verb *znh* is employed as a second level metaphor, with no further elaboration of either tenor or vehicle, and "whoring after other gods" is the metaphor's full extent. The comparison between the people's obligation to Yahweh and a wife's obligation to her husband, and hence the comparison between apostasy and adultery, are implicit in the phrase, "prostitute [oneself] after strange gods" (Deut 31:16), but the metaphor is never extended by more detailed personification of the nation or any group within it as an adulteress.[36]

The usual pattern within the prophetic corpus is, on the contrary, to employ the adultery metaphor *only* in the context of personification, particularly the personification of capital cities. In fact, within the prophetic corpus, the personification of capital cities is a "dead" metaphor, as shown by the use of stock expressions, "daughter X" and "virgin of X" to denote capital cities, even by prophets (e.g., Amos 5:2) who employ no further personification of cities and make no use of the marriage/adultery metaphor. The nearly exclusive domains of the *bt/btwlt* metaphor and other forms of personification of cities in the prophets, and of the expression *znh ʾḥry* in the extraprophetic texts, plus the prophetic use of the metaphor to describe both cultic and political infidelity, indicate that the figurative use of *znh* to denote apostasy (used throughout the OT, but most common in extraprophetic texts) and the figurative lan-

---

[36] The personification is so minimal that the verb *znh*, when used to describe the behavior of the people, is used with masculine verb forms.

guage of the prophets, personifying cities as women (especially, as adulteresses) are distinct, though related, metaphors.[37]

B. Personification of Foreign Cities as Women

The prophetic reuse of the ancient Near Eastern personification of capital cities was not limited to excoriation of the prophets' own capital cities. Foreign capitals were subjected to the humiliation of being demoted from goddess, to woman, and finally, to whore. The prophetic condemnations of personified foreign capitals serve, like oracles against foreign nations generally, to affirm Israel at the expense of its enemies.[38] Personification of the foreign capital as a woman provided an especially graphic mode for displaying the vices and the downfall of the enemy.

Not being "married" to Yahweh, the foreign cities could not, however, be accused of adultery against him, nor did the prophets dwell on the misdemeanors committed within legal and religious systems different from their own. Rather, the personification of foreign capitals served as a rhetorical tool by which the prophets could malign and belittle enemy strongholds. The virtues traditionally attributed to the personified cities—wisdom, strength, and care of their "children"—were denied by the prophets, who instead focused on the vices that might be implied by the cities' personification. In place of the positive commonplaces associated with womanhood, the prophets exploited negative commonplaces such as deceit, weakness, sexual infidelity, and finally, vulnerability to rape, to belittle and threaten these neighboring powers.

1) Isaiah

In Isaiah 23, Sidon, Tarshish, and Tyre, three famous seaports, are personified as women. The simplest of these personifications is that of Tarshish, who in v 10 is addressed as "daughter Tarshish." Sidon (vv 4 and 12) gets a somewhat fuller treatment. In v 4 she is addressed as "oppressed virgin daughter Sidon" and in v 12 is told that she will cease to exult and will find no rest. The imagery of v 4 is more difficult to follow; Sidon is told to be ashamed, because the sea/stronghold of the sea is mourning the loss of its young men and women. Sidon might appropri-

---

[37] It is not clear which is the earlier usage, especially since the prophetic personification seems to play on the general ancient Near Eastern practice, while the extraprophetic usage is more closely related to the Israelite metaphoric labeling of adultery as "prostitution."

[38] See J. H. Hayes, "The Usage of Oracles Against Foreign Nations in Ancient Israel," *JBL* 87 (1968) 81-92.

ately be depicted as the "stronghold of the sea," in which case v 4 would be a picture of mother Sidon mourning the death of her children, the inhabitants of Sidon. This, however, ignores the parallelism between "the sea" and "the stronghold of the sea," which seems at least loosely to identify the sea with its stronghold. It is the sea (and its stronghold) that has spoken and that is bereaved of its children.[39]

In the depiction of Tyre in vv 15-18 Isaiah makes a more rhetorically interesting use of the city's traditional female persona.[40] Having already lamented (vv 1, 13, 14) Tyre's (hoped for) destruction, Isaiah sets out in v 15 to describe what will transpire afterwards. Tyre will be forgotten for seventy years, after which its situation will be "just like that in the song about the prostitute" (v 15). Tyre is not fully personified here, though the preceding personifications of Tarshish and Sidon predispose the reader to picture Tyre as a woman. At this stage the comparison between "forgotten" Tyre's situation and the prostitute's is merely suggestive. In the song (v 16) a "forgotten" prostitute is instructed to pick up a harp and walk around the city singing so that she will be "remembered." She is evidently being encouraged to come out of retirement and drum up a little business. Thus far, Tyre's situation is only *compared* with that of the prostitute, but the comparison is apt, playing both on Tyre's traditional personification as a woman and on its famous commercial success, hiring out its ships to any customer.[41] In v 17 the forgotten harlot's song ends and the narrative about Tyre resumes, "after [her] seventy years" (v 15) of being forgotten. At that time Yahweh will visit (*pqd;* "remember"?) forgotten Tyre and "she will go back to wage-earning, and prostitute herself to every kingdom on the whole face of the entire world." Over the course of three verses Isaiah moves from predicting that the commercial capital will be "forgotten," to a comparison between Tyre's situation and that of a "forgotten" but newly enterprising whore, and finally to a prediction that after seventy years Tyre (likewise) will return, not to her commerce—but to world-wide prostitution! Isaiah uses the song about

---

[39] If, with LXX, we omit *l'mr*, the verse could be translated, "The sea has spoken, O stronghold of the sea: 'I have not labored, nor given birth . . .'," in which case Sidon is addressed as the stronghold of the sea, who is bereaved by the death of the sea's children, who in turn can logically be only the people of Sidon.

[40] Lewy ("Semitic Sun God," 439) cites evidence for Tyre's and Sidon's self-representation on hellenistic coins as women, "wearing turreted crowns," though we have no proof of this self-identification in the eighth century.

[41] F. Hauck and S. Schulz (*"porne,"* TDNT VI, 579-95), among others, have suggested that trade was generally thought of as a less than "honest calling" in ancient Israel (587).

the whore as a kind of hinge connecting his depiction of Tyre as city with his depiction of Tyre as whore. Playing on the already available comparison between city and woman, Isaiah exposes Tyre's much vaunted commercial success as a type of commerce particularly associated with women: prostitution. Indeed, says Isaiah, even Tyre's prostitution will be allowed to prosper only because it is Yahweh who will receive the proceeds of her work.

2) Nahum

The fall of Nineveh is predicted in Nahúm 3, a graphic account of the city's future suffering. In the prophet's opening call, "Woe, bloody city" (cf. Ezek 22:2-3; 24:6; 36:17), the city's personification is already implied by the use of direct address. Nahum then depicts an invading army, tumbling in their haste over the dead bodies of the Ninevites, "because of the many prostitutions of the whore—good looking, entrancing, who sells out nations by her prostitutions and peoples by her entrancement" (v 4). Nineveh is identified not only as a woman, but as a deceitful prostitute whose "entrancing" charms mask her genuine treachery. Note that in this depiction Nahum never *posits* that Nineveh is female; apparently the culturally assumed persona allows him to move directly to attacking her for "prostitution." "Prostitution" is defined in this case as "selling out" (*mkrt*) nations and peoples through prostitution (*mrb znwny zwnh*, v 4)—presumably, through treaty violations. Though "unfaithful," Nineveh is not pictured as married to any "man" (or male god), perhaps because of the awkwardness of depicting Yahweh as defending another god's honor or even acknowledging the other god's existence. Instead, Nineveh is presented as a stereotypically seductive but deceitful foreign woman (cf. Prov 2:16-19; 7). Her punishment for treachery, then, depicts simultaneously the humiliation of a powerful political enemy and the humiliation of the foreign woman whose attraction threatens the community.

Yahweh will take responsibility for Nineveh's punishment (at the hands of the Babylonians), even though he makes no claim to have been personally injured by Nineveh's infidelities. Yahweh tells Nineveh, "I will raise your skirts over your face, and make nations look at your nakedness and kingdoms at your 'shame.' I will pour refuse on you, and mock you, and have you stared at" (vv 5-6). That is, he will subject

Nineveh to public punishment as an adulteress.[42] Nineveh, dazed, will "be drunk" (v 11)[43] and try, staggering, to hide from the enemy. At the level of both metaphorical vehicle and tenor, Yahweh acts as the defender of the right, sexually humiliating the alien woman (including pouring excrement onto her), and also destroying the political oppressor on behalf of "nations and peoples."

In vv 8-10 Nineveh is compared to Thebes, a "woman" who suffered a similar fate, "carried away" while her little ones were smashed in the street and her strong men bound in chains. Nahum's depiction of Thebes illustrates well the dynamics typical in personifications of the city as a woman. First, though in v 10a Thebes is pictured as a woman being "taken away," in the next hemistich Nahum refers to her children as being in her "streets." The two pictures are logically incompatible: either Thebes is a woman carried away, or she, though symbolically "mother," is a city with buildings and streets that are not portable. The reader, however, automatically follows Nahum's alternation between vehicle (a woman carried away) and tenor (a city with streets), and so Thebes is depicted as simultaneously the female city and the wife and mother of its male and juvenile citizens. In v 10 Nahum tells the fate of the men and children of the city but ignores the fate of the Theban women. The literal women of Thebes (unlike the literal men and children) have no place in the anticipated destruction.[44] Because Thebes itself is depicted as the ravished bride of "her strong men" and the mother of "her" murdered children, the actual Theban women become superfluous. The personified city has taken over the role of the women of Thebes. Thebes is thus depicted as simultaneously a location, a woman, and as the representative of the city's female inhabitants.

Nahum's description of Nineveh and Thebes reveals the assumptions, the "associated commonplaces," underlying the prophetic personification of the capital city. First, the vehicle of the woman, specifically of female sexuality, is used to highlight Nineveh's treachery and infidelity (selling out nations by her prostitiution). Second, in describing the city's

---

[42] The form of punishment parallels that cited by S. Greengus in "A Textbook Case of Adultery in Ancient Mesopotamia" (*HUCA* 40 [1969] 33-43), in which the offending wife has her pudendum shaved and her nose bored, and is then led around the city (39-43).

[43] Cf. Jer 13:13; 25:15-29; 48:26; 49:12; 51:7, 39; Obad 16; Hab 2:15-16; Zech 12:2; Lam 4:21; Ezek 23:31-34.

[44] Cf. the Sumerian lamentation over Ur (*ANET*, 455-63), in which the goddess says, "My daughters and sons verily . . . have been carried off—'alas for my men' I will say" (460).

punishment, the depiction of Nineveh as female focuses attention on the city's helplessness[45] (she will be carried away, her skirts lifted up) and shame (through her public exposure). Nahum exploits the attributes of infidelity, helplessness, and shame, commonplaces culturally associated with "woman," to reorganize the reader's perception of Nineveh from that of a threatening power to that of a deceitful but ultimately helpless female victim who has earned her punishment at the hands of the male god.[46]

3) Deutero-Isaiah

The only other substantial personification of a foreign city as a woman in the OT is that of virgin Daughter Babylon in Isaiah 47.[47] Isaiah's personification of Daughter Babylon plays on Babylon's identification as a queen. Rather than referring directly to the city's regal status (and thus acknowledging it), however, the prophet systematically strips her of the signs of office: "Come down and sit in the dust . . . sit on the ground without a throne" (v 1). Babylon's robe will be taken off, and she will no longer be called "the mistress of kingdoms" (vv 2, 5). Instead, her

---

[45] Note that in 2:12-14, depicting Nineveh's strength, "she" is pictured as a *male* lion.

[46] Nahum's comment in v 13 regarding the men of Nineveh reinforces the link between femaleness and helpless victimization and shaming. "Behold," says Nahum, "your people are women in your midst." The metaphor focuses the reader's attention on the commonplaces already evoked in 3:1-11, of women as helpless, panicking, and vulnerable (note the sexual implications of the succeeding phrase, "they have been opened wide to your enemies"). Moreover, the true tenor of the metaphor is not the "people" of Nineveh, but precisely her *men*. Though Nahum says, "Your *people* are women," it is only men who can be referred to metaphorically as women (like the "wife and mother" Thebes, Nineveh may, for the purposes of the metaphor, have no women inhabitants). This brief insult intensifies both the sense of Nineveh's powerlessness (even her men are women!) and the association of femininity with powerlessness and shame.

[47] One other abbreviated reference is Jer 49:4, in which Yahweh addresses Rabbah as "faithless daughter," asking her why she has bragged about her "flowing valley" (reading ʿmqk hzb with W. Holladay, *Jeremiah 1, 2* [Hermeneia; Philadelphia: Fortress, 1986, 1989] 2. 369). In the context of the tradition (and Jeremiah's practice) of impugning the sexual mores of personified cities, the reference to Rabbah's "flowing valley," which is otherwise difficult to interpret, may be a sexual euphemism. D. Bourguet (*Métaphores*, 495) supports this interpretation, which he connects (484-85) with the possible sexual connotations of Rabbah's question in 49:4, "Who will come to me?"

"nakedness will be uncovered" and her "shame exposed" (v 3), and she will be widowed and bereft of her children (v 9; cf. Nah 3:10).[48]

Though the punishments meted out to Queen Babylon are exactly those imposed on Nineveh in Nahum 3 (public exposure, widowhood, and the loss of children), the reason for Babylon's punishment is not "adultery." Pride is the chief sin of which she is accused (vv 7-8, 10, 12), though "evil" (v 10) and "enchantments and entrancements" (v 12; cf. Nah 3:4) are also named. Babylonian wisdom is apparently the central issue here. Remarkably, Queen Babylon's sexual integrity is never impugned; instead Babylon is told that though she expects to be saved by sorcery and entrancement, her "knowledge" and "wisdom" (v 10) and the counsel of her stargazers (v 13) have led her astray. Yahweh will both rescue his people and prove his superior power by destroying the haughty Babylon.

C. Personification of the Capital City as Yahweh's Wife in the Prophets

The prophetic depictions of foreign capitals as women focus on negative traits associated with women (promiscuity, treachery, weakness), while the strengths commonly attributed to the cities as women are either ignored or (as in the cases of Queen Babylon and "forgotten" Tyre) deliberately undermined. Neither the cities' status within their own cultures as goddesses, nor their marriages to their various gods is mentioned by the Israelite prophets. Instead, the cities are depicted as married to their powerless male inhabitants, whose death leaves them

---

[48] C. Cohen ("The 'Widowed' City," *JANESCU* 5 [1973] 75-81) demonstrates that the ordinary biblical meaning of "widow" (*ʾlmnh*) is "a once married woman who has no means of financial support and who is thus in need of special protection" (77). That is, the term refers only to women who have no male relative to take over the financial responsibilities of their deceased husbands (cf. the Akkadian *almattu*, "woman without support, widow," *CAD* 1.1. 362-64). Cohen argues that the term, when applied (four times in the OT) to cities, refers to "a once independent city which has become a vassal of another state" (79). Though Cohen never connects this usage with the practice of personifying cities as women, the two are clearly related. The vassal city is "widowed" only because she once was "married," that is, under the protection of the male god. Her vassaldom is the consequence, not of her god's death, but of his having removed his patronage and consequently his protection.

Babylon, according to v 47, has believed herself immune to "widowhood," but Isaiah says she will experience both widowhood and the loss of children. The city's "widowhood," then, is simultaneously the death of its male inhabitants/protectors, and its consequent vassal status.

"widowed."[49] The prophetic personifications transform the "ruling women" of the ancient Near East into immoral, vain, and ultimately defeated and humiliated women.

In their treatment of their own capitals, the prophets take much the same approach, with a few key modifications. First, Israelite capitals, when personified, are always depicted as married to Yahweh, even though there is no known tradition of a sacred marriage between Yahweh and the capital.[50] Second, the occasion for the personification of Jerusalem and Samaria as women, apart from the use of the epithet "daughter" is always "adultery" on the part of the city. The prophets are charged by Yahweh with making his accusation of infidelity against his wife, either specifying the terms of her return (e.g., Jer 3:12-13) or announcing the form of her punishment (e.g., Hos 2:11-12; Eng 9-10).

1) *The Marriage Metaphor in Hosea*

The book of Hosea presents special problems for a survey of the metaphor of the city as Yahweh's wife. Hosea is often cited as the source of the OT marriage metaphor,[51] but Hosea's use of the metaphor is notoriously subtle and difficult to explicate.[52] Though Hosea, especially in chaps 1-3, makes extensive use of the metaphoric vehicle of "marriage," the metaphor's tenor is virtually impossible to follow. The metaphoric

---

[49] The cities are metaphorically "widowed" because the death of the male inhabitants both leaves the personified city without "her men," and makes her vulnerable to becoming a vassal (see note on "the widowed city" above).

[50] If Yahweh was understood within Israelite tradition as having an actual (and not merely a metaphorical) consort, such a relationship is not acknowledged within the Hebrew Bible. The strongest evidence for Israelite belief in a consort for Yahweh suggests that the consort was not a personified city, but Asherah (see S. Olyan, *Asherah*, 4-9; 70-74).

[51] Bird, "Play the Harlot"; Setel, "Prophets and Pornography"; H. W. Wolff, *Hosea* (Hermeneia; Philadelphia: Fortress, 1974) xxvi, 44.

[52] According to F. I. Andersen and D. N. Freedman (*Hosea* [AB 24; Garden City: Doubleday, 1980]), "while the basic narrative is straightforward and superficial, the underlying, or second, level is fragmentary and discontinuous" (120). For a review of the literature on Hosea's metaphors, see L. J. Braaten, "Parent-Child Imagery in Hosea" (diss., Boston University, 1987) 12-16; and see also F. C. Fensham, "The Marriage Metaphor in Hosea for the Covenant Relationship between the Lord and his People (Hos. 1:2-9)," *JNSL* 12 (1984) 71-78; M. A. Friedman, "Israel's Response in Hosea 2:17b: 'You Are My Husband'," *JBL* 99 (1980) 199-204; Kruger, "Israel, the Harlot."

Hosea lacks much of the stock imagery used by the other prophets, including his contemporaries. The *bt/btwlt* language for capital cities, already present in Amos (5:2) and Isaiah of Jerusalem (16:1), is entirely absent from Hosea.

vehicle (adultery) is consistent, but the tenor is extraordinarily fluid, consistent only as a general accusation of infidelity, and apparently mutable in its referent.

The sign-act of the prophet's own marriage as the basis for the metaphor is unique to Hosea and may help account for Hosea's equally unique combination of a clear and forcible vehicle with an elusive tenor. Rather than basing the metaphor of Yahweh's marriage on a personification of the capital city, Hosea takes an action, marriage to a "woman of infidelities," as the starting point for his prophecy and his metaphor. The vividness of this initial symbolic action guarantees the clarity of the metaphoric vehicle and establishes the general sense of the tenor as infidelity; an infidelity equivalent to that of an adulterous wife has been committed. Hosea's use of the sign-act actually allows the infidelity of the nation to be doubly signified: Hosea depicts Israel's relationship to Yahweh using both his symbolic action and his symbolic language (metaphor), rather than depending on the use of metaphor alone.[53] This combination of symbolic action with metaphoric speech strengthens the impact of Hosea's prophecy while increasing its flexibility. The sign-act, unlike simple, verbal personification, in which the figure of "the faithful (or unfaithful) city" clearly links tenor and vehicle, may be applied to a wide range of tenors. This flexibility of Hosea's marriage metaphor accordingly makes it virtually impossible to "decode" in terms of a single tenor represented by a single vehicle.

The initial command of Yahweh to the prophet establishes that Hosea's wife, Gomer, represents the land of Israel. Hosea is told to marry an ʾšt znwnym, a woman of "prostitutions" (1:2),[54] as a sign that "the land is utterly unfaithful to Yahweh" (ky znh tznh hʾrṣ mʾḥry yhwh). Metaphorically, the vehicle is the "prostituting" woman and the tenor

---

53 Cf. the comments of Davidson on Ezekiel's sign-acts, in *Prophet Ezekiel*, 102-3.

54 The questions raised even by this brief command are legion, ranging from whether Hosea's marriage ever actually took place, to the problem of whether Gomer was in fact a whore, and whether she was already promiscuous before the marriage or only became so afterward. On the question of her literal prostitution, there seems no reason to assume this as her profession, since the text never refers to her by the word "prostitute," zwnh or ʾšh zwnh. On these questions see Bird, "Play the Harlot"; Setel, "Prophets and Pornography"; H. W. Wolff, *Hosea*; Bucher, "ʿznhʾ Terminology"; J. L. Mays, *Hosea: A Commentary* (OTL; Philadelphia: Westminster Press, 1969); F. I. Andersen and D. N. Freedman, *Hosea*; H. L. Ginsberg, "Studies in Hosea 1-3," in M. Haran, ed., *Yehezkel Kaufmann Jubilee Volume* (Jerusalem: Magnes Press, 1960) 50-69.

the "prostituting" land.[55] But what does it mean for "land" to "act as a prostitute"? The land is personified as a woman who acts as a (first level) metaphoric prostitute—she is sexually unfaithful. Her metaphoric prostitution is in turn metonymous for the metaphoric prostitution of the land's inhabitants. The people commit infidelity that is metaphorically represented in sexual terms.[56]

The nature of the inhabitants' "prostitution" is not specified, but cultic infidelity seems to be implied. First, the phrase *znh m'hry* is clearly a variant of "*znh 'hry*," a phrase that is used exclusively to denote idolatry (cf., e.g., Exod 34:15-16; Deut 31:16; Ezek 6:9) in both prophetic[57] and extraprophetic texts. Second, and more problematic, is the possibility that Hosea here is referring obliquely but specifically to the worship of Baal. In Ugaritic mythology the land is a "mother" married to the sky-god, Baal. Baal fertilizes the earth with rain and enables her to bring forth food to support humans, who are understood to be her children.[58] The personification of the land as Yahweh's wife in Hosea 1 may be intended to evoke the Canaanite personification of the land as consort to the god, but Hosea 1 claims that the land is *Yahweh's* wife (rather than Baal's) and that her (inhabitants') involvement with Baal constitutes infidelity.

The tenor of Hosea's sign-act and metaphor of the unfaithful wife in 1:2 may be understood as the land, and the tenor of the metaphoric depiction of the land's infidelity may be understood as Baal worship. Such an interpretation, while perhaps valid for Hosea 1, is only partially

---

[55] It is unusual to speak of an actual person as a metaphoric "vehicle." Gomer, however, is presented in the text, not as a strictly *fictional* character, but as one whose only significance is her role as a symbol. Her function in the text may therefore be considered metaphoric; she is a type of the unfaithful woman, evoking commonplaces regarding unfaithful women in order to refocus the reader's perception of the unfaithful land.

[56] Two additional biblical references to the land are instructive here. In Deut 24:4 the people are commanded not to "cause the land to sin" by *their* infraction of marriage laws. In Lev 19:29 fathers are told not to defile their daughters by causing them to prostitute themselves, and not to cause the land to prostitute itself (both Hiph'il forms of *znh*), or fill it with perversion. The implication is that the daughters' actions are tantamount to the land's. In both Deut 24:4 and Lev 19:29 the land is personified and has been made to prostitute itself as a result of the sin of its inhabitants. The land that "commits great whoredom" in Hos 1:2, then, like the land that "sins" in Deut 24:4 and Lev 19:29, does so as a metonymous representation of its inhabitants' infidelities. In Lev 18:24-30, however, the land is depicted as "vomiting out" its sinful inhabitants, rejecting rather than reflecting their sins.

[57] In prophetic literature the phrase occurs only in Ezek 6:9 and 20:30.

[58] See Wolff, *Hosea*, 15-16.

supported by Hosea 2. In 2:7 (Eng 2:5) the woman claims that her "lovers" have provided for her. The list of the woman's provisions plays on commonplaces of both the marital and the cultic domains. Within the vehicle of marriage, the provisions represent the necessities of life which the husband was obligated to provide.[59] The provisions listed here, however, go beyond the food, clothing, and oil required of the husband. Rather, the woman is given food, water, wool, flax, oil, and drink—the produce of the land. The (personified) land has failed to understand that Yahweh was the source of this abundance and believes that Yahweh's competitors have made her fertile. Moreover, in 2:10 (Eng 2:8) Hosea depicts Yahweh's rival as "the baal" and claims that the woman has used both her agricultural produce and silver and gold "for the baal." In response to this infidelity Yahweh will take back his gifts to the woman (2:11; Eng 2:9) and expose her publicly,[60] his rights as the divorcing husband (2:4; Eng 2:2) of an unfaithful wife.[61] In 2:13-14 (Eng 2:11-12) Yahweh promises to end the woman's festival observances, as well as revoking the land's fertility. Hosea uses the language of marriage and fertility (2:7; Eng 2:5) and of divorce and sterility (2:11; Eng 2:9) to elaborate on the image of the land as Yahweh's wife. As in the initial description of the provisions given the woman, so here also vocabulary emphasizing the gifts as the fruit of the earth suggests the tenor of Yahweh as the true custodian of the land's fertility,[62] which he will withhold because of the land's (its people's) disobedience. Note that while the sin of the land is figurative, metonymous for the sin of the people, the punishment of the land by the removal of crops is literal.

Much of the language of Hosea 1-2 supports the metaphoric identification of Gomer with the land, which, particularly because of its femi-

---

[59] Malul, *Studies*, 175; Wolff, *Hosea*, 35.

[60] The woman's exposure takes place "before her lovers' eyes." The male lovers could constitute the condemning populace (cf. Ezek 16:27 and perhaps Lam 1:8), but this is awkward at both the level of the vehicle and of the tenor. The claim of Andersen and Freedman (*Hosea*, 249) that a husband would invite over his wife's lovers to gloat over her punishment (rather than being punished themselves) seems unlikely, as does the idea that Yahweh should favor competing gods with the status of scornful witnesses to the land's desertification. Rather, the force of the punishment "before the eyes of the lovers" must be the lovers' impotence. The woman/land had trusted their power, but is now denuded before their very eyes.

[61] See S. Greengus, "A Textbook Case"; R. Westbrook, "Restoration of Marriage."

[62] Hosea's phrase, "my grain in its time, and my wine in its season," parallels Yahweh's covenant obligation that if the people "love" him (Deut 11:13) he will give "rain for your land in its season . . . that you may harvest your grain and your wine and your oil" (Deut 11:14; cf. 28:12; Lev 26:4).

nine role in the Baal cult, has been made "unfaithful" by the cultic apostasy of its inhabitants. This identification between woman and land is not, however, consistent throughout chaps 1-2. Already in chap 1 contradictions surface. Gomer has children who are identified by their symbolic names ("Not My People") with the inhabitants of the land. This identification is consistent with the identification of Gomer with the land; the people are the land's children. To the extent that the land itself represents the people, however, Hosea's children are redundant, since the people are represented by both Gomer and her children. In 2:4 (Eng 2:2) the problem becomes compounded when the children (the people) are told to plead with their mother (the land, which represents the people). How are the people to "convince" the land to change its ways, if its "sin" is only a metaphoric representation of their own?[63]

Additional inconsistencies make it impossible to sustain a simple reading of the woman as representing the land in Hosea 1-3. In 2:5 (2:3 Eng), for example, Yahweh threatens to strip the woman and expose her, making her "like a wilderness . . . , like a desert land." The imagery *compares* the woman to the land, but does not identify woman and land, as does the metaphor in 1:2. If the woman "is" the land, why threaten to make her "like" a wilderness rather than turning her "into" a wilderness? Why the change from metaphor to simile? A similar problem arises in vv 16-17 (Eng 14-15), where Yahweh promises to bring his wife "into the wilderness," where she will respond as she did "when she came out of the land of Egypt." As before, the woman is associated with wilderness imagery, but (since the land will not be "brought" into the wilderness) can only with difficulty "represent" the land.[64]

---

[63] Andersen and Freedman (*Hosea*, 219) recognize this problem, but consider it "a dialogue going on within the covenant community." Such an interpretation (particularly since the mother does not respond) stretches the metaphor, besides assuming that the listening or reading audience would have picked up on the double level at which the metaphor of "land" is employed. Friedman ("Israel's Response") offers the simpler explanation that this is a mixed metaphor, noting "Israel's double metaphorical role—God's children and His bride" (201).

[64] Meir Malul's observations on Ezek 16:1-7 ("Adoption of Foundlings in the Bible and Mesopotamian Documents: A Study of Some Legal Metaphors in Ezekiel 16.1-7," *JSOT* 46 [1990] 97-126) may illuminate the function of the wilderness in this passage. Malul discusses the function of the wilderness as an "ownerless area outside the domain of society" (103). Yahweh's plan to take his wife to "the wilderness," then, promises not merely a return to the exodus period but to Israel's unmarried status, whence Yahweh will betroth her anew (cf. S. Talmon, "The 'Desert Motif' in the Bible and in Qumran Literature," *Biblical Motifs* [ed. A. Altman; Cambridge, MA: Harvard University, 1966] 31-63).

The most consistent role of the woman in Hosea 2 is as a personification, not of the land, but of the capital city, Samaria.[65] As has been noted, Hosea 2 begins with a request by Yahweh that is inconsistent with the metaphoric tenor of the woman as the land; the "children" are to plead with their "mother" that she end her adultery (2:4; Eng 2:2). The image of the city as a mother to her inhabitants is familiar from both earlier ancient Near Eastern[66] and later Israelite usage.[67] Moreover, the image of a city "becoming a desert" (2:5; Eng 2:3) has ancient Near Eastern precedent,[68] as well as occurring in later Israelite literature.[69] The imagery of 2:8 (Eng 2:6) continues to depict the woman as a city, now under siege: "I will block in her wall, so that she cannot find her paths." This identification of the woman with Samaria would be consistent with Yahweh's warning to the priest in Hos 4:5 (cf. v 10) that his "mother" (the cult center) will be destroyed.[70]

Hosea's specific references to Baal may also be interpreted in light of the possibility that in chap 2 it is Samaria, and not the land, that is depicted as a woman. In chaps 1-2 Hosea never uses "baal" as a name, but always as a title: "the baal" (2:10; Eng 2:8) or "the baalim" (2:15, 19; Eng 2:13, 15).[71] Hosea may be condemning Samaria's dependence, not on a Canaanite god, but on human "baalim," the foreign powers with which she had liaisons.[72] In 8:9-10 Hosea depicts Ephraim as having "lovers," who are clearly other nation-states and may be the same "lovers" as the

---

65 J. Schmitt argues that the woman is Samaria throughout Hosea 2 ("The Wife of God in Hosea 2," *BR* 34 [1989] 5-18).

66 See, e.g., *ANET*, 460.

67 See the discussion of Nahum, above.

68 See H. W. F. Saggs, "The Nimrud Letters, 1952—Part VI" (*Iraq* 25 [1963] 70-80), in which towns are apparently referred to as having become "deserts" (*mu-da-bi-ri*; 79-80.)

69 Cf. Yahweh's threat to Jerusalem in Jer 6:8 ("Lest I make you a wasteland, a land without inhabitants") and mention of the *mdbr* of Zion in Isa 51:3.

70 Hosea's recollection of bringing the woman "out of Egypt" (2:17; Eng 2:15) and his reference to the "day of [her] birth" (2:5; Eng 2:3), while apparently inappropriate to describe either land or a city, are both images used later by Ezekiel to describe the city, Jerusalem (16:4-5; 23:3).

71 There is no evidence that Israel worshiped several "Baals" (e.g., Baal Melqart, Baal Zaphon) simultaneously. S. Olyan (*Asherah*, 62) takes the Bible's plural usage (*b‘lym*) as designating "foreign gods generally understood" (62). Olyan also argues, however, for the presence of both a Baal sanctuary and a Yahweh sanctuary in Samaria. If a specific, known "Baal" were being worshiped in Samaria, it would seem odd that Hosea would refer to "baalim," foreign gods generally, rather than to the particular "Baal" at issue.

72 Cf. the use of the term "baalim" in Gen 14:13 and Isa 16:8.

"baalim" of chap 2. Foreign alliances are often considered but a prelude to idolatry in the Hebrew Bible (cf. Exod 34:15; 1 Kgs 16:31; 2 Kgs 16:10-12; Ezek 23:7) and the prophet may be intentionally connecting reliance on foreign "lords" for protection with the supplication of their gods for sustenance. Thus the condemnation of Samaria's various "baalim" may play on the name of Baal, but only in the context of condemning the capital's devotion to foreign political powers.[73]

In addition to this apparent personification of both the land and the city of Samaria as Yahweh's unfaithful wife, Hosea uses the verb *znh* as a second level metaphor[74] to describe the "unfaithful" behavior of the nation as a whole and its leadership (see 4:10, 11, 12, 15, 18; 5:3; 6:10; 9:1; and the charge that Ephraim has taken [male] "lovers" in 8:9).

Hosea also includes one instance of the "first level" metaphorical use of *znh* and one of the noun, *znwt*. In 4:13 Yahweh describes the "*znwt*" of the male Israelites "sacrificing on the mountains." He then tells his audience that because of this infidelity "your daughters prostitute themselves (*tznynh*) and your daughters-in-law commit adultery (*tn'pnh*)." Yahweh will not punish the women for their *literal* fornication (but only figurative prostitution; v 14), because the men have likewise (figuratively) prostituted themselves. The charge against the men, that they "split off with prostitutes and sacrifice with 'holy women'," is usually interpreted as describing literal sexual activity.[75] There is no reason, however, to depart at this point from reading the accusation of prostitution as metaphorical, as elsewhere in the book.[76]

---

[73] The use of the verb *'šm* in 4:15 to denote Judah's potential (and Israel's actual) offense suggests that a trespass violating the sanctity of Yahweh's name had been committed (see Milgrom, *Cult and Conscience*, 13-22). Israel's breaking of its treaty-vow with Assyria (an action it was urging on Judah) would constitute such a trespass.

[74] J. Schmitt argues ("The Wife of God," 7; and cf. "The Gender of Ancient Israel," *JSOT* 26 [1983] 115-25) that the use of the verb *znh* does not constitute personification of Israel as a woman (note the use of masculine verbal forms).

In 4:15 Hosea pleads with Israel (2ms) not to pass on its "prostitution" to Judah. Israel is not fully personified as a woman, but merely made the subject of the verb *znh*. The comparison between Israel and Judah, however, with the implication that Judah might learn "the tricks of the trade" from Israel's example, may be the source of Jeremiah's later personification of Israel and Judah as two sister prostitutes (3:6-11), an image taken up by Ezekiel in 16:44-63 and 23:1-35.

[75] So Andersen and Freedman, *Hosea*, 370; Bird, "Play the Harlot," 85-88; and Wolff, *Hosea*, 87-88.

[76] If Hosea's polemic is in part political, then the followers of Pekah, who had "split off" from Samaria and were now loyal to Damascus, would fit this description

Beginning with the sign-act of his own marriage to Gomer, Hosea uses the figure of the unfaithful woman as a unifying symbol embodying the full range of people and institutions he considers complicit in "infidelity" against Yahweh: the people, the land (both as metonymous for its inhabitants and possibly as a mythological participant in Baal worship), the capital city, its priest, the "nation" Israel, and its government. Commonplaces associated with female sexual infidelity provide the common link among Hosea's various accusations. The strength of Hosea's sign-act and his subsequent metaphorical imagery overcomes a multitude of unmarked changes in the tenor; the unfaithful woman goes from receiving produce from her lovers (as the personified land) to having her walls attacked (as the personified city) with no disruption in the story of the unfaithful wife.

Rather than focusing on a single set of people or events and depicting them *through* the metaphoric vehicle of the woman, Hosea focuses on the unfaithful woman and uses this image as the means of addressing the various objects of Yahweh's anger. In places where the land or the city is personified, existing traditions personifying both land and cities as women apparently help the reader follow Hosea's transfer from the infidelity of the land to the infidelity of the city. In the cases where the nation (which is traditionally personified as male),[77] the priest, or the people are depicted, Hosea conforms to the extraprophetic practice of using the verb *znh* with masculine subjects, thus avoiding identifying male subjects directly with the woman.

Two additional aspects of Hosea's use of the marriage metaphor deserve mention. First, and connected with the ambiguity of the tenor, is the lack of a strong persona for the land, the capital city, or the people of Israel. As compelling as Hosea's use of the sexual metaphor is, no identifiable figure, such as Isaiah's forgotten prostitute Tyre or Deutero-Isaiah's Daughter Babylon, emerges. The reason for this lack of strong personification may lie, like the constant change in the tenor, in Hosea's use of symbolic action as the basis for his metaphor. Rather than depicting accused Israel (or its representative) as an adulteress, Hosea depicts

---

nicely. The verb *prd* ("split off") never has sexual connotations, and though this is the only occurrence of the Pi'el, the root frequently refers to familial or political divisions (Gen 10:5; 25:23; Prov 18:1; 19:2; 2 Sam 1:23). Syrian loyalty might well have included support for the worship of Baal. Thus the reference to "splitting off with prostitutes" would be a pointed metaphorical slam against Pekah's rebellion, while the reference to "sacrificing with 'holy women'" would be a literal reference to the worship practices of the pro-Damascus faction.

77 See Schmitt, "Gender of Ancient Israel."

an *actual* adulteress and proceeds to reflect on her as the prototype of Israel's infidelity. The role of the woman as a figure of infidelity in Hosea is filled by Gomer; a strongly personified "Daughter Samaria," for example, would be redundant.

A second striking aspect of Hosea's use of the marriage metaphor, an element that may fairly be assumed to have originated with him, is the personification of Yahweh as husband. The extraprophetic denotation of cultic infidelity as *znwt* is a "dead" metaphor, entailing neither strong personification of the male Israelites as a wife nor of Yahweh as a husband—the metaphor is not elaborated beyond its labeling of idolatry as equivalent to marital infidelity. In the prophetic personifications of foreign cities as women, Yahweh is only somewhat more strongly personified; he interacts with the foreign "woman," but acts only as, so to speak, himself, the omnipotent avenger. Hosea's personification, however, implicates Yahweh at a deeper level. Though he retains his status as omnipotent in revenge, Yahweh is impotent in respect of his wife's fidelity. In order to accuse his wife of "adultery," Yahweh must accept the role of the rejected and injured husband. The metaphor demands Yahweh's vulnerability. This potential for the compromise of Yahweh's honor, implicit in the marriage metaphor, creates a problem ultimately resolved only in the book of Ezekiel, in which Yahweh's honor is finally safeguarded by the destruction of his unfaithful wife.

2) *The City as Yahweh's Wife in Isaiah*

Isaiah 1-39 contains only a brief personification of Jerusalem as Yahweh's wife. In 1:21 Isaiah laments over Jerusalem, "How has 'the faithful city' become whorelike" (*hyth lzwnh*). This scant personification depends for its effect on the reader's previous familiarity with the personification of Jerusalem as Yahweh's wife. Earlier in the same chapter, Israel has been depicted as Yahweh's sons (v 2) and as a diseased body (vv 5-6), both of which metaphoric vehicles are explicitly introduced in the text ("I raised sons . . ."; "From the sole of the foot up to the head . . ."). The depiction of the city as wife, however, apparently requires no such introduction. The mere epithet "faithful city" suffices to tell the reader which city this is, to whom she owes fidelity, and in what capacity: her fidelity is not that of a son or slave, but of a wife.[78] The reader must recognize the epithet "faithful city" as a reference to Jerusalem the

---

[78] Zech 8:3 also predicts a time when "Zion" will be called "the faithful city." The epithet may have been a traditional title of Jerusalem.

faithful wife in order to appreciate Yahweh's accusation of infidelity. With remarkable economy, Isaiah extends the conventional metaphor. Simply by replacing "faithful" with "whorelike," he achieves the turn from the commonplace to the shocking.

The verses following Isaiah's accusation of infidelity (vv 22-26a) abandon the sexual metaphor and instead employ the metaphor of pure versus alloyed metals to depict the corruption of the city's rulers and judges.[79] Yahweh briefly describes Jerusalem's "corruption," swears to burn out the city's "dross," and then promises rehabilitation. "I will restore your judges . . . ," says Yahweh, and "afterward, you will be called 'the city of righteousness, the faithful city.'" Jerusalem's reputation, both as a just town and as a respectable woman, will be restored. The question of Jerusalem's fidelity or infidelity (in 1:21 and 26), expressed through the use of the epithet, "faithful city," thus forms a tidy inclusio.

3) The City as Yahweh's Wife in Jeremiah

Jeremiah uses the image of Jerusalem as Yahweh's wife often, but not in a sustained way. Like Hosea, Jeremiah often changes tenors in the middle of an oracle (e.g., from city to nation), but Jeremiah is prone to change vehicles as well. An address may begin by depicting the city as a woman and conclude depicting her as a camel (2:23-24). The one point of consistency in Jeremiah's metaphors is that the city of Jerusalem is always feminine[80] and is therefore usually addressed as Yahweh's wife.

The first oracle Jeremiah is directed to deliver is to Jerusalem (2:2), and from the outset the city's persona as Yahweh's wife is implicit: "I remember the devotion of your youth, your love as a bride."[81] Jeremiah expands on Hosea's suggestion (2:16-17; Eng 2:14-15) that, contrary to the account in Exodus and Numbers, Israel[82] was faithful in the wilderness

---

[79] Although the metaphors of sexuality and metallurgy are taken from different realms of experience, both describe the city using the categories of purity and impurity.

[80] Schmitt ("Gender of Israel") argues that while Jerusalem is feminine, Israel is always masculine. Both Israel and Judah, however, are depicted as either masculine or feminine in Jeremiah. In fact, Israel may be referred to as masculine (4:1) or feminine (3:6), singular (4:1) or plural (3:12). Judah, feminine in 13:19 and masculine in, for example, 11:13, is always referred to in the singular.

[81] W. L. Holladay (Jeremiah 1, 83) argues that both terms of youthful Israel's "affection," ḥsd and ᵓhbh, are terms of covenant loyalty, suggesting a "political nuance."

[82] Whereas in Hos 2:16-17 the intended tenor is unclear, here the addressee is unquestionably Jerusalem, which is said to have spent time "in the wilderness." The

period. Jeremiah depicts Yahweh's bride following faithfully through the desert.[83]

In v 3, while apparently maintaining the image of the idyllic past ("Israel was holy to Yahweh"),[84] Jeremiah abruptly switches to third person masculine singular discourse (v 3a)[85] and then to third person masculine plural ("All who ate it sinned"; *yᵓšmw*). After a concluding formula (*nᵓm yhwh*) Jeremiah addresses the "families of the house of Israel" and continues in vv 4-13 in second person masculine plural address. Verses 14-15 depict Israel with verbs in third person masculine singular form, and in v 16 second person feminine singular address is resumed, continuing through v 25. Though Jerusalem seems to stand for city, state, and members of the state simultaneously, each of these entities is addressed or discussed separately, as if Jeremiah were turning to them one by one as he speaks.[86]

The feminine "you" of 2:16-25 is never identified but can be assumed to be Jerusalem. The woman is said to have "abandoned Yahweh [her]

---

capital city thus metonyously represents the entire nation, apparently including the life of that nation before it had Jerusalem as its capital.

[83] M. V. Fox argues that it is not Jerusalem, but *Yahweh* who was devoted in the desert and loving in Jerusalem's "bridal days" ("Jeremiah 2:2 and the 'Desert Ideal'," *CBQ* 35 [1973] 441-50). While Fox may be right that the emphasis is on Yahweh's provision rather than Jerusalem's loyalty, the image of the woman "following" during a time happily remembered still points toward a Jerusalem originally faithful to Yahweh.

[84] J. Neusner (*A History of the Mishnaic Law of Women* [SJLA 33/1; Leiden: Brill, 1980] ix) argues that the Israelite wife was "holy" to the man in authority over her; cf. Milgrom's observations in *Cult and Conscience*, 134, that the adulteress committed *mᶜl* against her husband; and J.-J. Glassner's assertion that in ancient Mesopotamia the wife was "holy" to the husband ("Honor of the Family," 75). Jeremiah's designation of Israel as "holy to Yahweh" may be intended here to call further attention to the parallel between the loyalty owed to a husband and that owed to Yahweh, especially since the phrase follows Jeremiah's description of the woman Jerusalem's devotion to him. Only in 2:3b does it become clear that Israel is "holy to Yahweh" because "he" is identified with the first fruits of the land (Deut 26:2).

[85] MT reads, "Israel was holy to Yahweh, the first-fruit of *her* produce." This would be consistent with the usual usage of *tbwᵓh*, which is frequently connected by the possessive suffix with the source of the produce (Exod 23:10; Lev 25:7, where the produce of the land is *tbwᵓth*; Lev 19:25, *tbwᵓtw* for the produce of a tree, and so on). Israel, then, would be the first-fruits of the *land*'s (her) produce. The MT is corrected in the massora to read *tbwᵓtw* (as do the Qumran manuscripts), "Yahweh's produce," but this may reflect the gender confusion built into the metaphor rather than a better text. Holladay (*Jeremiah 1*), in his comments on this verse, notes the change to 3ms, but continues to refer to *Israel* as "her" (1. 84-85).

[86] See Schmitt ("Gender of Israel") for a detailed analysis of gender in this passage.

God when he led [her] on the road" (v 17), evidently a reference back to Jerusalem's honeymoon days described in 2:2.[87] In v 20 the woman is depicted as "bending over" as a prostitute,[88] but the metaphor is further compounded; the already metaphorical "woman" is called in turn a wild vine (v 21) and a camel in heat (vv 23-24). In v 25 Yahweh urges the woman to "keep [her] feet from going bare, and [her] throat from thirst." Apparently, having confronted his wife with her infidelity, Yahweh is giving her a final chance to avoid divorce and the consequent withdrawal of her food and clothing (cf. Hos 2:11; Eng 2:9).[89] Jerusalem, however, has made her choice, and, abdicating her right to Yahweh's protection, answers, "I have loved strangers and will follow them." Jerusalem's "loving" and "following" strangers reverses her "youthful devotion," when she "loved" and "followed" only Yahweh (2:2). Verse 25 forms an inclusio with v 2, focusing the intervening material on the question of Jerusalem's loyalty: whom will she love and whom follow?

Jeremiah continues with masculine terminology for the people until vv 32-36. In v 32 Yahweh compares "my people" to a bride and himself, not to the groom, but metonymously, to her ornaments.[90] In v 33 he resumes direct discourse to the woman, addressing her as a "teacher" of women already wicked themselves (cf. Ezek 16:44-63), guilty of the blood of the innocent poor, but claiming her innocence. Yahweh asserts that the woman will be "shamed" (v 36) by both Egypt and Assyria,[91] who are implied to be her lovers. Whatever choices are left to Jerusalem, return to

---

[87] The references to "drinking the waters" of Egypt and Assyria reflect Jerusalem's hope that one of these nations will offer protection.

[88] The charge against the woman apparently changes here from one of political wrongdoing to the charge of idolatry, as evidenced by the activities' location on "every high hill and under every lush tree" (see W. L. Holladay, "On Every High Hill and Under Every Green Tree," VT 11 [1961] 170-76).

[89] R. P. Carroll (Jeremiah: A Commentary [OTL; Philadelphia: Westminster, 1986]) reads this as "a reference to frantic journeys (in the desert) which wear out shoes and cause thirst" (133). The basis for such a reading is unclear, since the only restless desert journeys mentioned in the text are those of the estrous camel.

[90] "Could a young woman forget her ornaments . . . ? Yet my people have forgotten me" (2:32).

[91] It is unclear whether the woman's "shaming" represents her punishment at the hands of the lovers (cf. Ezek 16:27) or the inability of her lovers to protect her (cf. Hos 2:12; Eng 2:10). J. Bright (Jeremiah [AB 21; Garden City: Doubleday, 1965] 17-18) reads the shaming as subjection to vassaldom under Assyria and "humiliation at the hands of the Egyptians in 609," but this ignores the depiction of Jerusalem's seeking these partners in 2:18, as well as contradicting his own translation of 2:36: "Egypt too will disappoint you, Just as Assyria did." The image of Jerusalem led away as a captive in v 37 strongly suggests the failure of Egypt and Assyria to protect her.

Yahweh is no longer among them (3:1).[92] Yahweh apparently cites the law against a divorced and remarried woman's return to her husband (Deut 24:4), claiming that after her prostitution his return to her or hers to him would pollute (*ḥnp*) the land.[93] Indeed, her prostitution has *already* affected the land, causing the withholding of rain threatened in Deut 28:23-24.[94]

Verses 6-11, a prose section dated to "the days of King Josiah," paint a vignette that is related to but distinct from the foregoing personifications of Jerusalem. Here it is not the city, but Israel and Judah who are personified as Yahweh's faithless wives who prostitute themselves "on every high hill" (3:6). Yahweh divorces Israel for her infidelity, but Judah refuses to be warned and instead follows suit. Yahweh concludes that "even perverse Israel is more righteous than deceitful Judah" (v 11). The passage, unique to Jeremiah in its explicit personification of the nations rather than the city as wife, and in its inclusion of the North in the marriage metaphor (cf. Ezekiel 23), echoes Hosea's plea to Israel in 4:15 not to corrupt Judah as well. Apparently, Yahweh's concern about Judah,

---

[92] Perhaps Jerusalem's refusal of Yahweh's offer of 2:25 and her stated preference for lovers constitute Yahweh's grounds for divorce.

[93] See Westbrook ("Restoration of Marriage"), who argues that the basis of the prohibition is financial rather than due to concern over ritual purity. The first husband, divorcing his wife for "unchastity," would have kept her bridal money. The second husband, divorcing without "cause," would have had to pay the woman "divorce money" in addition to returning her bridal money. If the first husband were to remarry the woman, he would then have the benefit of two payments of bridal money. The prohibition is against estoppel on the part of the first husband.

Although Westbrook's argument is strong, it does not explain why such an action should bring sin (*ḥṭʾ*) upon the *land*. Only three kinds of sins are said to pollute the land itself: murder, idolatry, and sexual abominations (T. Frymer-Kensky, "Pollution, Purification, and Purgation in Biblical Israel," in *The Word of the Lord Shall Go Forth* [Winona Lake, IN: Eisenbrauns, 1982] 399-414; 408), and the remarried woman's return seems to belong to the third category. The case in Jeremiah 3 is even more vexed, since the question is the wife's infidelity, not divorce and remarriage, nor did Jerusalem's lovers send her away. Westbrook thinks, perhaps rightly, that Jer 3:1 is not connected with Deut 24:1-4 (405). This would leave the pollution of the land in Jer 3:1 still unexplained.

[94] The woman calls Yahweh, "My father, the companion of my youth" (v 4), apparently in an attempt to get him to restore her as his wife. The phrase, "companion of [one's] youth," as an epithet for "husband" is attested in Prov 2:17, but reference to the husband as father occurs only here. The superior party of a treaty is called "father" by the loyal "son" (S. M. Paul, "Adoption Formulae: A Study of Cuneiform and Biblical Legal Clauses," *MAARAV* 2 [1980] 173-85), and such usage would be consistent with the use of the epithet in 3:19 (where it has a 2mpl subject).

voiced by the earlier prophet, was well-founded, but his plea went unheeded.

In 3:20 Jeremiah states explicitly the rationale for the use of the marriage metaphor: "Just as a deceitful woman betrays her companion, so have you betrayed me, O house of Israel." This simple explication of the metaphor marks a break in Jeremiah's rhetoric. Having "decoded" the metaphor—Israel's deceit is like that of an unfaithful woman—Jeremiah then largely abandons it. In the following section (vv 21-25) it is the sons who are called back from their "infidelity" on the hills and pictured returning to Yahweh; the metaphorical woman of the previous three chapters is effectively replaced with her literal referent. After the explication of the metaphor in 3:20, Jerusalem is personified as a woman only briefly, in three sections depicting the woman attacked (4:30-31), exposed (13:22, 26), and bereaved (15:5, 9).[95]

In its opening chapters, the book of Jeremiah makes effective use of the already traditional metaphor of Jerusalem as Yahweh's wife, interweaving it with direct accusations against the people. The constant and usually unmarked oscillation between discourse to the woman and discourse to the people establishes the identity of woman and people as much by juxtaposition as by the content of the metaphor. The city as woman is not a central image in the book as a whole, however, but primarily a rhetorical tool of the first three chapters, emphasizing the severity of the people's infidelity and the urgency of the call to repentance. As in Hosea, personification of the city also results in a strong personification of Yahweh, here depicted as a lover desperately attempting to win back his unfaithful wife and ultimately punishing her instead.[96]

---

95 In 31:3b-5 Yahweh addresses a promise of restoration to the "virgin of Israel," Samaria.

96 Carroll (*Jeremiah*, 142) comments on Jeremiah's "cuckold god," "pathetic and ranting . . . , [who] can only retaliate by smashing up the place and destroying everything." This blunt assessment of Yahweh's situation and his response is certainly an accurate enough description of the dynamics of Yahweh's role within the marriage metaphor. By and large, however, it is not as "husband" that Yahweh "smashes things up" in Jeremiah. The marriage metaphor has been all but dropped by the time Jeremiah's God gets violent. It is only with Ezekiel that the full emotional implications of the cuckolding of God will be played out within the terms of the metaphor.

4) *The City as Yahweh's Wife in Lamentations and Deutero-Isaiah*

Although neither Lamentations nor Deutero-Isaiah predates Ezekiel,[97] both make substantial use of the metaphor of Jerusalem as Yahweh's wife. While their imagery cannot have contributed directly to Ezekiel's, they provide a further look at the range of the metaphor in the context of Israelite religion in the sixth century BCE. The use of the marriage metaphor in each of these books will therefore be given brief consideration.

Lamentations 1-2 focuses on the woman Jerusalem after she has been punished, and as such, represents the culmination of the generations of prophecies predicting her demise. The city is depicted as a "widow,"[98] abandoned by her lovers, betrayed by her friends (1:1-2), and deprived of children taken (1:5). The city's situation as described in Lamentations is remarkably like that *predicted* in Ezekiel. Those who "pass by" (2:15; Ezek 16:6, 8) are astonished that this city had once been called "perfect in beauty" (2:15; Ezek 16:14); she "remembers" her former complacency (1:7, 9; Ezek 16:61, 63) after she has been punished for admitting foreigners to the sanctuary (1:10; Ezek 44:7; and see comments below on 23:44); she is compared unfavorably with Sodom (2:4; Ezek 16:48), and likened to a *nddh* (1:17;[99] Ezek 36:17); and she has been made drunk and strips herself (4:2; Ezek 23:31-34).[100] If neither Ezekiel nor Lamentations was a written source for the other, this correspondence between the punishment called for (by Ezekiel) and that received (according to the author of Lamentations) suggests that the metaphor of Jerusalem the unfaithful wife must have been widespread by the early sixth century, and included a fair amount of fixed vocabulary with which to accuse the city. Deutero-Isaiah depicts the next stage of the fate predicted by earlier prophets for

---

[97] Although Lamentations postdates the earliest parts of Ezekiel, its vivid description of the conditions in post-siege Jerusalem would suggest a date soon after the fall of the city (see D. R. Hillers, *Lamentations* [AB 7a; Garden City: Doubleday, 1972] xviii). It may therefore actually predate the earliest version of Ezekiel as a whole. This, of course, would make it theoretically possible that Lamentations was a source for Ezekiel (or even vice versa), though Ezekiel's Babylonian provenance, if accepted, would make such a connection unlikely.

[98] Or vassal; see the discussion of Cohen ("The 'Widowed' City"), above (and cf. Isa 47:9). The parallelism of the lines, "How she has become like a widow, who was great among the nations/ Princess of the provinces, become a vassal," confirms the identification of the "widowed" city as a vassal city.

[99] On the question of whether she is also called *nddh* in 1:8, see Hillers, *Lamentations*, 23-24.

[100] In Lamentations, the "pride of the eyes" (*mḥmdy-ʿyn*) of Jerusalem is slain in her "tent"; in Ezekiel 24, the pride of Jerusalem's eyes is the temple.

the woman Jerusalem. Beginning in chap 51, the author announces her restoration by Yahweh. "Daughter Zion" has been punished with bereavement of her children (51:18), forced drunkenness (51:17, 21-22), shameful "widowhood" (54:4),[101] and God's anger. Now her tent will again be pitched in safety (54:2); she is now promised children, "lasting love," and a "lasting covenant" (51:8, 10) from Yahweh.[102]

D. Conclusions

The Israelite prophets, surrounded by cultures in which the capital city was revered as a beneficent goddess, created a second, distinctive strand in the tradition of personification. This new tradition is not one of veneration but of condemnation. Now a mortal woman, the city has become both corrupt and vulnerable. The city's cultic and political proceedings are defined as violations of an exclusive loyalty to her husband/god, who punishes her as an adulteress. No longer a metaphor for the city as mother or queen of her inhabitants, the personification is cast in the prophetic corpus strictly in terms of the city's obedience or disobedience to her husband/god. In prophetic rhetoric, personification of the city serves to expose and decry the distance the "faithful city" has fallen in becoming a "whore."

---

[101] The fact that the woman's "widowhood" is listed as part of her "shame" supports Cohen's thesis ("The 'Widowed' City") that a widowed woman is not one whose husband has died, but one who has lost a male provider. Thus a woman whose husband was living, but who had been divorced with cause (and thus without support) might also be a "widow." Yahweh's promise in the succeeding verses that though he has abandoned the woman, he will now take her back, confirms this reading of "widowhood." As in Isaiah 47, the metaphorical "widowhood" of the city is its vassaldom.

[102] The feminine imagery for the restored Jerusalem is continued in Trito-Isaiah, where the city is also promised a new name, "My Delight Is in Her" (62:2-4), an interesting possible variant on Ezekiel's name for Jerusalem, "My Tent Is in Her" (23:4), and his reference to the city as the "delight" of the people's eyes (24:20).

III

EZEKIEL'S DISTINCTIVE USE
OF THE MARRIAGE METAPHOR

Ezekiel's use of the marriage metaphor, comprising the whole of chaps 16 and 23, depends for both its general outline and for various details on earlier prophetic treatments, particularly those of Hosea and Jeremiah. Ezekiel's use of the metaphor is, however, distinctive in style, content, and function. A brief summary of Ezekiel 16 and 23 will precede an annotated translation, after which will follow a discussion of the distinctive traits of Ezekiel's marriage metaphor as compared to those of earlier prophets.

I. EZEKIEL 16 AND 23: FOUR
METAPHORICAL NARRATIVES

Chapters 16 and 23 follow a structure typical in Ezekiel: each consists of two sections, the first and longer of which tells the narrative, and the second and shorter of which elaborates some element of the narrative taken from the first section.[1] Each chapter concludes with a brief "coda,"

---

[1] Both of these chapters have frequently been interpreted as composites consisting of Ezekiel's original oracles plus the work of later editors (see, e.g. Eichrodt, *Ezekiel*, 202, 330, 333-34; Zimmerli, *Ezekiel 1*, 333-34). In light of the overall stylistic and struc-

which combines the language and themes of the two preceding sections.[2] Ezekiel's use of this two-part pattern in chaps 16 and 23 means that the oracle against the woman is in effect delivered four times, twice in each chapter. Because the details of accusation and punishment differ slightly from section to section, each section will be summarized briefly.

A. *Ezek 16:1-43*

Ezekiel 16:1-43 traces the life and times of the woman Jerusalem, providing, as Greenberg says, "the adulterous wife of Hosea and Jeremiah with a biography."[3] Ezekiel is commanded by Yahweh to inform Jerusalem of her abominations (v 2), after which Yahweh proceeds to recount the story of Jerusalem's life. Born of Canaanite and Hittite ancestry (v 3), Jerusalem is not recognized by her parents but is instead exposed to die in her birthblood (vv 4-5). Yahweh, however, passes by, claims, and rescues the infant.[4] After the girl reaches puberty, Yahweh passes by a second time (v 8) and now marries her. He then (vv 9-14) proceeds to cleanse her and to dress her in elegant attire, until her beauty is "perfect."

In vv 15-34 the woman undoes step by step the good Yahweh has done for her. Prostituting herself with "every passerby" (v 15), she uses Yahweh's gifts to build shrines, to populate them with idols, and to provide the idols with offerings, including Yahweh's own children. Next, the woman builds public platforms for her prostitution with "every passerby" (v 25), now the Egyptians, Assyrians, and Chaldeans, none of whom can satisfy her lust (vv 23-29).

In vv 35-43 Yahweh announces Jerusalem's punishment: Yahweh will gather her lovers and expose her to them, after which they will

---

tural unity of the book, and because chaps 16 and 23 conform to Ezekiel's usual pattern of oracles consisting of two related sections plus a conclusion, there is no compelling reason not to regard these chapters as the work of a single author, or of an editor who is responsible for the canonical shape of the book. In the present work the book's author will be referred to as "Ezekiel."

[2]   Greenberg (*Ezekiel 1-20*, 25-26) observes this pattern and its use in chap 16. In the introduction to his commentary he does not list chap 23 among the chapters following this two-part division, though his explication of chap 23 is not published at this time.

[3]   *Ezekiel 1-20*, 299.

[4]   M. Malul ("Adoption of Foundlings") argues persuasively that the girl's exposure while still in her birth blood signifies the parents' renunciation of any legal claims (106), and that Yahweh's commanding her in her blood to live constitutes his formal adoption of the girl as if from her birth (111).

remove Yahweh's gifts and then stone her, slice her open, and burn her houses.

B. *Ezek 16:44-58*

The second section of chap 16 begins with a reiteration of Jerusalem's dishonorable parentage (v 45), adding that Samaria is her elder and Sodom her younger sister. Jerusalem has not only learned abomination from her siblings (v 47), but has outdone them in corruption. In vv 53-58 Yahweh promises to "restore" all three sisters, but only so that Jerusalem may be ashamed at her unworthiness.

C. *Ezek 16:59-63*

Verses 59-63 form the coda to chap 16. Yahweh here accuses Jerusalem of breaking "the covenant," but then promises to establish a new covenant with her (cf. v 8). After her "purification" (*kpr*; v 63) Jerusalem will recognize the authority of Yahweh[5] and be horrified, shamed, and silenced.

D. *Ezek 23:1-35*

The opening section of chap 23 takes up the idea of 16:44-58 that Jerusalem and Samaria are sisters and claims they spent their youth in prostitution in Egypt before being married to Yahweh. Their names symbolize their worship practice: Samaria is "Oholah" ("She Has a Tent," i.e., her own sanctuary) and Jerusalem is "Oholibah" ("My Tent [Yahweh's sanctuary] is in Her").[6] Yahweh tells the story of Samaria's prostitution with the Assyrians and their idols and of his consequent handing her over to her Assyrian lovers for punishment (vv 5-10). Jerusalem's story is patterned after Samaria's, but despite seeing Samaria's punishment, she becomes still worse. Jerusalem is unfaithful even to her illicit lovers, abandoning Assyria for Chaldea, and the Babylonians for the Egyptians (vv 12-21).

---

[5] Yahweh's goal throughout the book of Ezekiel is that both Israel and the nations should "know that [he is] Yahweh" (the phrase, with variations, occurs over seventy times in the book). In the context of the metaphor of the unfaithful wife, "knowing Yahweh" signifies Jerusalem's acknowlegment of Yahweh's authority which she has flouted. For an analysis of Ezekiel's use of the phrase, "You will know that I am Yahweh," see P. Joyce, *Divine Initiative and Human Response in Ezekiel* (JSOTS 51; Sheffield: Journal for the Study of the Old Testament, 1989) 89-95; and also Zimmerli, *Ezekiel 1*, 37-40.

[6] See Zimmerli, *Ezekiel 1*, 483-84 for a discussion of the significance of the names, and also see Chapter Four.

Yahweh therefore announces his punishment of Jerusalem (vv 22-34). Parodying his earlier description of the lovers' grandeur, Yahweh describes in detail the regalia with which the nations will arrive to destroy Jerusalem (vv 23-24). The former lovers will cut off Jerusalem's nose and ears, capture her children, and strip her, as Yahweh's retaliation for her "prostitution with the nations" and her pollution with their idols (v 30).

E. *Ezek 23:36-45*

In the second section of chap 23 Yahweh charges the sisters with "adultery" and "bloodshed," metaphors for idolatry and child sacrifice, respectively (v 37). In addition, Yahweh describes Jerusalem's preparations to greet "men summoned from afar," to whom she offers Yahweh's incense and oil (vv 40-41). Omitting a detailed description of their punishment, Yahweh predicts only that "righteous" men will punish the women (v 45).

F. *Ezek 23:46-49*

In the conclusion to chap 23, Yahweh no longer merely predicts Jerusalem's punishment, but actually sets it in motion, issuing the call for the mob to assemble. The avenging host is to stone and cut her, kill her children, and burn her houses. Yahweh's call for the avengers completes the story of his unfaithful wife. At last she is to suffer her long-threatened punishment; having suffered, she will come to recognize the authority of Yahweh (v 49).

II. TRANSLATION AND NOTES:
EZEKIEL 16 AND 23

Two considerations guided the following translation. First, the translation is intended to reproduce the graphically sexual tone of the Hebrew, avoiding euphemism except where euphemism characterizes the Hebrew text. Thus, in 16:25, *wtpśqy ʾt rglyk lkl ʿ wbr* is translated, "you spread your legs for every passerby." This straightforward rendering keeps intact the euphemism of the Hebrew *rglym*, replacing it with the comparable English euphemism (presumably the woman opened more than her legs). The translation does not, however, obscure the sexual force of the Hebrew, as does, for example, RSV's "offering yourself to any passerby."

Second, because of the complicated word-plays and repetitions in Ezekiel 16 and 23, words derived from a single Hebrew root are when possible translated with words derived from a single English root. Thus, *znh*, *tznwt*, and *znwnym* are translated, "to be a prostitute; to prostitute oneself," "prostitution," and "prostitutions," respectively. While *znwnym* may be a plural of amplification (GKC §124e) and so best translated "promiscuity," faithful representation of the root *znh* was considered a more important criterion than the most idiomatic word choice in English.

A. *Ezekiel 16*

[1]The word of Yahweh came to me saying, [2]Mortal, make known to Jerusalem her abominations, [3]and say, "Thus says Lord Yahweh to Jerusalem: 'Your origin and your birth were of the land of the Canaanite; your father was an Amorite and your mother a Hittite.[a] [4]As for your birth—on the day you were born your umbilical cord was not cut, and you were not rinsed with water to cleanse you.[b] You were not rubbed with salt,[c] nor swaddled in cloth. [5]No one took pity on you to do any one of these things for you out of compassion for you; you were thrown onto the open field, your life abhored on the day you were born.

[6]Then I passed by you and saw you wallowing in your blood,[d] and I said to you in your blood, "Live."[e] [7]I made you a multitude, like the sprouts[f] of the field. And you grew and matured.[g] And you attained beautiful adornments; your breasts had developed and your hair sprouted, but you were stark naked.[h]

[8]When I passed by you and saw you, you were at the age for love-making, so I spread my skirt over you and covered your nakedness. Then I made a vow to you and entered a covenant with you, declares Lord Yahweh, and you became mine.

[9]Then I rinsed you with water and washed your blood off you, and anointed you with oil. [10]And I dressed you in multicolored fabric, shod you with fine leather,[i] wrapped you in fine linen, and covered you with silky cloth.[j] [11]I adorned you with ornaments and put bracelets on your hands and a necklace around your neck. [12]I put a ring in your nose and earrings in your ears, and a treasured crown[k] on your head.

[13]So you were adorned with gold and silver, and your clothing was fine linen, silky cloth, and multicolored fabric. You ate fine flour and honey and oil; you grew extremely beautiful—you became regal. [14]Your fame spread among the nations because of your beauty, for it was perfect through my splendor which I placed upon you, declares Lord Yahweh.

[15]But you trusted your beauty and prostituted yourself on the basis of your fame, and showered forth your prostitutions on anyone who passed by—it was his.[l]

[16]Then you took some of your garments and made yourself brightly colored shrines, and prostituted yourself on them,[m] coming to him—and it was his.[n] [17]And you took your treasures,[o] made from my gold and my silver that I had given you, and made for yourself phallic images; then you prostituted yourself on them. [18]And you took your multicolored garments and covered them, and my oil and my incense you set before them. [19]My food that I had given you, fine flour and oil and honey I had fed you, you set before them as a sweetly scented offering—thus it was,[p] declares Lord Yahweh.

[20]Then you took your sons and your daughters whom you had borne to me, and sacrificed them to them for food. Was your prostitution not enough?[q] [21]Yet you slaughtered my children and gave them up, passing them over[r] to them.[22] In all your abominations and your prostitutions you did not remember the days of your youth when you were stark naked, wallowing in your blood.

[23]And then, after all your evil—woe, woe to you, declares Lord Yahweh—[24]you built yourself a platform[s] and made yourself a stand in every square. [25]At the end of every street you built your stand, made your beauty an abomination, and spread your legs for anyone who passed by. Then you multiplied your prostitutions. [26]You prostituted yourself to the Egyptians, your big-membered neighbors; you multiplied your prostitutions so as to anger me. [27]Therefore, see how I stretched out my hand against you and cut back your territory, and handed you over to the rapacity of those who hate you, the daughters of the Philistines, who were ashamed at your perverted behavior.[t]

[28]Then you prostituted yourself to the Assyrians, since you were unsatisfied. You prostituted yourself with them,[u] but still you were not satisfied. [29]So you multiplied your prostitution, with the commercial land[v] of Chaldea,[w] but even this left you unsatisfied. [30]How hot is your lust,[x] declares Lord Yahweh, in doing all this, acting like a headstrong prostitute, [31]building[y] your platform at the end of every street and setting up your stand in every square.

But you behaved unlike a prostitute in disdaining payment—[32]the adulterous woman who in place of her husband receives strangers!—[33]Gifts are given[z] to every prostitute, but you . . . you gave your gifts to all your lovers. You bribed them to come to you from every direction, in your prostitution. [34]Thus it was that you were different from other women in your prostitution: no one solicited prostitution from you.aa By giving payment while no payment was given you, in that way you were different.

³⁵Therefore, prostitute, hear the word of Yahweh. ³⁶Thus says Lord Yahweh: Because your dischargebb was showered forth and your nakedness exposed in your prostitution with your lovers and with all your abominable idols, and for the bloodcc of your children whom you gave them,

³⁷therefore, look—I am gathering all your lovers whom you pleased, all you loved together with all you hated; I will gather them against you from every direction, and I will expose your nakedness to them, so that they may see all your nakedness. ³⁸And I will judge you with the punishment against adulterous women, and against women who shed blood, and will put the blood of rage and jealousy upon you.dd ³⁹Then I will hand you over to them, and they will tear down your platform and pull down your stands, strip you of your garments, take your treasures, and leave you stark naked. ⁴⁰Then they will bring up a hoard against you and stone you with stones, split you openee with their swords, ⁴¹burn your houses with fire, and bring judgments upon you before many women. I will put an end to your prostitution; truly, you will give payment no longer.

⁴²Thus I will calm my rage against you and my jealousy will subside from you; I will be quiet and will no longer be angry. ⁴³Because you failed to remember the days of your youth and enragedff me with all this, I will indeedgg lay the consequences of your actions upon you, declares Lord Yahweh. Have you not engaged in perversion together with all your abominations?hh

⁴³See here—everyone who makes proverbs will say this proverb about you: like mother, like daughter. ⁴⁵You are the daughter of your mother, who loathes her husband and children, and a sister of your sisters,ii who loathe their husbands and children. You women's mother was a Hittite and your father an Amorite. ⁴⁶Your big sister is Samaria, she and her daughters who live north of you. And your little sister who lives south of you is Sodom, with her daughters.

⁴⁷But you did not follow in their paths or perform their abominations, for they were too minor;jj you were more degenerate than they in all your behavior. ⁴⁸As I live, declares Lord Yahweh, neither your sister Sodom nor her daughters behaved the way you and your daughters have. ⁴⁹Look—this was the wrong of your sister Sodom: she had the pride of abundant foodkk and the tranquility of security for herself and

her daughters, but she would not support the poor and the needy. [50]They were exalted, but they committed abomination before me. So I removed them, for I saw it.[ll] [51]Samaria has not committed even half your sins; you made your abominations greater than theirs, justifying your sisters through all the abominations you committed.

[52]As for you, bear your disgrace, by which you intercede for your sisters; committing abominations worse than theirs, you have made them more just than you. So be ashamed, you, and bear your disgrace at having justified your sisters.

[53]For I will restore their fortunes, the fortunes of Sodom and her daughters and the fortunes of your captives in their midst, [54]so that you may bear your disgrace and be ashamed of all you did to console them. [55]As for your sisters, Sodom and her daughters will be restored to their former state and Samaria and her daughters will be restored to their former state, and you and your daughters will be restored to your former state.

[56]Was not your sister Sodom the object of your gossip[mm] in the days of your pride, [57]before your own evil was exposed, now a taunt of the daughters of Aram and all those around her, and the daughters of Philistia, who despise you from every direction? [58]The consequences of your perversion and your abominations, you bear, declares Lord Yahweh.

[59]For thus says Lord Yahweh: I will do to you just as you did when you disregarded the oath by breaking covenant. [60]Then I will remember my covenant with you from the days of your youth, and will establish for you an everlasting covenant. [61]Then you will remember your behavior and be ashamed when you receive your sisters, the older ones along with the younger; I will give them to you as daughters, but not because of[nn] your covenant. [62]I myself will establish my covenant with you, and you will know that I am Yahweh, [63]wherefore you will remember and be disgraced, and will no longer be able to open your mouth in the face of your shame, when I purge you of all you have done, declares Lord Yahweh.'"

Notes

a   MT: "the Amorite"; emending to agree with LXX and with Ezek 16:45.
b   mš'y is a hapax legomenon and is not attested in either LXX or Syriac. The translation, "to cleanse," is based on T and is the logical consequence of rḥṣ.
c   Lit: "the salt you were not salted."
d   bdmyk. Although the plural form is frequently used to denote violently shed blood (so BDB, 196), the usage is by no means consistent. Bloodshed is denoted

by the singular, *dm*, in Gen 9:6 and Lev 17:4, while the plural is used of a woman's bleeding after childbirth in Lev 12:4, 5, 7. In the case of an unwashed newborn, the plural would denote afterbirth.

e   Deleting with some Greek texts and the Syriac the repeated line, "and I said to you in your blood, 'Live.'"

f   The image reflects the tenor of Jerusalem as a growing multitude rather than the vehicle of a growing girl. The more usual translation, "grow like a weed of the field" (cf. RSV, Zimmerli), requires emendation of *rbbh* to *wrby* (so Zimmerli, *Ezekiel 1*, 324) and obscures the imagery of flourishing vegetation (see Greenberg, *Ezekiel 1-20*, 276).

g   Or "you became great." Whereas the preceding *rbbh* applies to the city's population, here the verb *wtrby* applies to the girl's growth.

h   Lit: "and you naked and nakedness." "You with your nakedness exposed" would capture the sense of the phrase, but the idiom "stark naked" is used here to avoid confusion with the phrase *glh ʿrwh*, which is used (vv 36, 37) to describe part of the punishment for adultery.

i   *tḥš*. The word is used only here and for the covering of the tabernacle in Exod 26:14, etc. For a review of the discussion as to the type of leather, see Zimmerli, *Ezekiel 1*, 340-41.

j   *mšy* is a hapax whose etymology is unknown. For a review of the literature, see Zimmerli (*Ezekiel 1*, 324) and Greenberg (*Ezekiel 1-20*, 278-79).

k   Lit: "a crown of splendor." Rather than translating, "a splendid crown" (so NJPS), the English root "treasure" is used here to highlight the repetition of *tpʾrt* in vv 17 and 39 (and cf. 23:26).

l   The 3ms form is unexpected here. Zimmerli (*Ezekiel 1*, 325) emends to *lwyty*, "you clung [to every passerby]." The entire phrase is unattested in some Greek mss and in Syriac, raising the possibility of a later (but garbled) addition. Context suggests emending to 2fs, "you were his," to contrast with the phrase, "you were mine," in v 8. G. R. Driver ("Ezekiel: Linguistic and Textual Problems," *Bib* 35 [1954] 145-59, 299-312) translates "that it [namely, her beauty] might become his" (151). Driver's use of the subjunctive is superfluous, since the indicative mood maintains the parallel with v 8, highlighting the transfer of sexual rights from Yahweh to an unnamed other.

m   Or "because of them." The 3mpl suffix does not agree with *bmwt*, nor is Zimmerli's suggestion (*Ezekiel 1*, 326) of *bgdym* as the antecedent convincing. The suffix probably refers to *bmwt*, incorrectly substituting the 3mpl for 3fpl suffix (cf. GKC §135o; M. F. Rooker, *Biblical Hebrew in Transition: The Language of the Book of Ezekiel* [JSOTS 90; Sheffield: Almond Press, 1990] 78-79; and cf. Ezek 23:45).

n   *lʾ bʾwt wlʾ yhyh*. The phrase is usually translated, "the like has never been, nor ever shall be" (RSV). Such renderings assign the same referent to both the fpl *bʾwt* and the ms *yhyh*. Greenberg (*Ezekiel 1-20*, 280) translates "such things will never be," reading *lʾ bʾwt* as "not coming things."

Driver ("Ezekiel," 151) emends with Cornill to *lw bʾt wlw yhyh*, "thou didst go in to him, so that it [again, her beauty] became his," a reading closer to that of LXX "you will not go in." This emendation, which assumes an error of the ear, confusing *lw* for *lʾ*, allows the verse to follow the pattern of vv 8 and 15: what should be Yahweh's has become "his."

o   Lit: "the vessels of your splendor." This is commonly translated "jewelry," i.e., "beautiful objects," but such a rendering ignores the ambiguity of the Hebrew. *kly* most commonly denotes containers (even baggage); "objects" is a translation of last resort. *tpʾrt* is used in MT most frequently to describe priestly or royal garments (e.g., Exod 28:2; Isa 10:12). Thus the phrase, "vessels of your splendor" suggests temple paraphernalia (the tenor) as strongly as it does personal adornment (the vehicle). The translation "your treasures" could similarly refer to either personal or cultic objects.

p   The placement of the verb *hyh* at the end of the verse conforms to its use as an ending for vv 8, 15, and 16, though here it does not announce who has had sexual access to the woman, but rather emphasizes the events just recounted.

q   Lit: "Was it less than your prostitutions?"

r   I.e., as an offering by fire (cf. 2 Kgs 16:3).

s   *gb*. Lit: "back; rim." But see Ezek 43:13 in which it designates the base or stand of the altar. The Greek, *oikēma pornikon*, apparently derives from the context only.

t   Lit: "your way of perversion." The noun, *zmmh*, occasionally denotes "plan" or "device," as in Job 17:11. Most often, however, it has a negative, and sexual, connotation, as in Lev 18:17, "You must not uncover the nakedness of a woman and her daughter . . . it is *zmmh*."

u   The verb *znh* is used twice in the verse, first with the preposition *ʾl*, and then with the d. o. suffix. The Greek text attests no object in the latter case. Keil (*Biblical Commentary on the Prophecies of Ezekiel* [2 vols.; Grand Rapids: Eerdmans, 1950] 1. 210) interprets the sequence to mean, first, "immoral pursuit," and then its fulfilment, "adulterous intercourse." The verb also occurs with the preposition *ʾl* in v 16 and with *b* in v 17; the nuances of these differences are unknown, although it is possible that the use of a direct object refers, as Keil concludes, to the act of sexual intercourse per se (cf. Isa 23:17; Jer 3:1, "you have screwed many lovers").

v   Or, "the land of Canaan," which is awkward in context.

w   The form, *kśdymh*, is anomalous, and seems to be meant to clarify the relationship of apposition between *ʾrṣ knʿn* and *kśdym*. That is, *knʿn* is not to be read as "the land of Canaan" (in which case the *h* directive would be attached to *ʾrṣ*; cf. Zimmerli, *Ezekiel 1*, 328), but as "the commercial land, Chaldea." Jerusalem's sexual "trade" is seen to extend to Chaldea, *kśdymh*.

x   *mh ʾmlh lbbtk*. If *lbbtk* is taken as a variant of *lbb* and *ʾmlh* as 3fs perfect of *ʾml*, the phrase can be translated, "how weak is your will" (so BDB, 51b). This, however, is inconsistent with the end of the verse, "acting like a headstrong prostitute." It seems unlikely that the woman should be accused of being both weak-willed and strong-willed in a single verse. The best reading is that of F. Stummer ("*ʾmulla* [Ez xvi 30a]," *VT* 4 [1954] 34-40), basing *ʾml* on the Arabic *mll*, "to be hot."

y   MT's *bbnwtyk*, "with your daughters," is an interesting possibility, but does not fit in context. A more likely explanation is that the infinitive is here treated as a plural (cf. GKC §91l, and versions from the Cairo Geniza).

z   The subject is indefinite: "they give gifts."

aa   Pu'al. Lit: "after you it was not prostituted."

bb   Lit: "brass; bronze." Greenberg (*Ezekiel 1-20*, 285-86) cites the Akkadian *nḫš*, "be abundant, overflowing," and sees reference here to "female genital 'distillation' produced by sexual arousal." The versions read "copper," presumably referring to the reverse-prostitute's payment to her clients (Judah's payments of tribute).

cc   *kdmy*. Reading *k* as "in accordance with" (cf. R. Williams, *Hebrew Syntax: An Outline* [2nd ed.; Toronto: University of Toronto, 1976] §259), or, given the context, "in recompense for."

dd   Lit: "put you blood of rage and jealousy." LXX translates, "put you in blood," and Greenberg (*Ezekiel 1-20*, 286), "make you into a bloody object." G. R. Driver ("Linguistic and Textual Problems: Ezekiel," *Bib* 19 [1938] 60-69, 175-87) reads the text as parallel to 23:25, *wntty bk hmḥ wqnʾh*, reading *dmy* as "an example" of rage and jealousy (65). Ezek 14:19, "I will pour out my rage on it with blood," attests to the combination of "rage" and "blood" as elements of judgment in Ezekiel.

ee   *btq* is a hapax legomenon. F. Greenspahn (*Hapax Legomena in Biblical Hebrew* [SBLDS 74; Chico, CA: Scholars, 1984] 107) translates "split"; so also J. Greenfield ("Lexicographical Notes I," *HUCA* 29 [1958] 203-28), who relates *btq* to *ptq*, which can mean "to cut, sever limbs" (220-21). The Akkadian *bitqu* and *batāqu* both can refer to cutting through or dividing, especially to opening water sluices or dikes (*CAD* 2. 161-65, 277-79). If these derivations are correct, then the woman is either being hacked to pieces, or sliced up the middle. Given the violently phallic imagery of the latter possibility, it is perhaps the more consistent with the sexual revenge being described.

ff   Reading *wtrgzy* with the versions as a Hiph'il.

gg   *hʾ*. Possibly equivalent to *hnnh*; cf. Gen 47:23.

hh   Emending *wlʾ* to *hlʾ*; cf. v 56, where the same phenomenon occurs.

ii   Reading, with some Greek mss, Syriac, and Vulgate, a plural in place of *ʾḥwtk*, to agree with *gʿlw*.

jj   Reading *qṭn* for *qṭ*, with LXX, *mikron*.

kk   Reading *gʾwn* as a construct (cf. Greenberg, *Ezekiel 1-20*, 289). While awkward in English, the phrase "the pride of abundant food" is consistent with the notion, found elsewhere in Ezekiel (34:29; 36:30), of famine as a disgrace.

ll   Translating *kʾšr rʾyty* in the sense of "according to what I saw (with a causal nuance)," following C. Gaenssle (*The Hebrew Particle ʾšr* [Chicago: University of Chicago, 1915] §160).

mm   Lit: "she was not as a report in your mouth." The sense could be that Sodom, having been punished, was not mentioned (as bad luck?), but this seems to go against the tradition of celebrating the defeats of one's neighbors. More likely *wlʾ* should be emended, as in v 43, to *hlʾ*, giving the opposite sense, that is, did you not talk about Sodom?

nn   Lit: "not from your covenant." The meaning is unclear, as "your covenant" could refer either to Jerusalem's (broken) covenant (v 59, and see 17:13), or to Yahweh's covenant with her (vv 8, 60, 62). If *mn* is read to mean "deriving from" (GKC §119z; Williams, *Syntax*, §319), then a contrast is made between Yahweh's covenant, which will be fulfilled, and Jerusalem's, which has become meaningless. Such a contrast would be consistent with the emphatic "*I* will remember/establish my covenant" of vv 60 and 62.

B. *Ezekiel 23*

¹The word of Yahweh came to me saying, ²Mortal, there once were two women, daughters of one mother. ³They prostituted themselves in Egypt; they were prostitutes[a] in their youth. There their breasts were squeezed and there their virginity was taken.[b] ⁴And their names were Oholah (the elder) and Oholibah, her sister. They became mine, and bore sons and daughters. As for their names, Samaria is Oholah and Jerusalem is Oholibah. ⁵And Oholah became a prostitute in spite of me,[c] and lusted after her lovers, for Assyria[d] [who] arrived[e] ⁶dressed in purple, governors and prefects, all of them desirable, choice young men, riders on horseback. ⁷And she bestowed her prostitutions on them, on all of the choicest Assyrians; and with all the idols of everyone for whom she lusted, she defiled herself. ⁸She had not given up her prostitutions since Egypt, when they had laid her in her youth and had taken her virginity, and spilled out[f] their prostitution on her.

⁹Therefore I handed her over to her lovers, to the Assyrians after whom she had lusted. ¹⁰They exposed her nakedness and took her sons and daughters, and her they killed with the sword. She became a byword[g] among women, and they passed judgments[h] against her.

¹¹And her sister Oholibah saw, but her lust became more degenerate than her [sister's], and her prostitutions worse than her sister's whoredoms.[i] ¹²She lusted for the Assyrians, governors and prefects arriving impeccably dressed, riders on horseback, all of them desirable men in their prime. ¹³And I saw that she had defiled herself; the two of them had gone the same route.

14But she added to her prostitutions when she saw men carved on the wall, the figures of Chaldeans[j] etched in red coloring, 15girded with belts about their waists, billowing turbans[k] on their heads, all with the appearance of officers[l]—the likeness of Babylonians, natives of Chaldea. 16And she lusted for them, to feast her eyes [on them],[m] so she sent messengers to them in Chaldea. 17And the Babylonians came to make love to her[n] and defiled her by their prostitution. And after she had defiled herself with them she was revolted[o] by them. 18When she had exposed her prostitutions and exposed her nakedness, I became revolted by her, just as I had been revolted by her sister.

19But she multiplied her prostitutions, remembering[p] the days of her youth when she was a prostitute in the land of Egypt. 20She lusted for their services,[q] whose members were like a donkey's and whose ejaculation like a horse's. 21You revisited the perversion of your youth, carrying on your lovemaking since Egypt, because of your young breasts.

22Therefore, Oholibah, thus says Lord Yahweh, "Look—I am arousing your lovers against you, at whom you were revolted, and am bringing them against you from every direction: 23the Babylonians and all the Chaldeans, Pekod and Shoa and Koa,[r] all the Assyrians with them,[s] all of them desirable, choice young men, governors and prefects, officers and men of rank,[t] riders on horseback, all of them. 24They will come against you, stallion, chariot, and wheel,[u] with an assembly of peoples; shield and buckler and helmet, they will set against you on every side. And I will appoint them to bring justice[v] so that they sentence you with their judgments. 25I will lay my jealousy upon you and they will deal with you in rage. They will cut off your nose and ears; what remains of you[w] will fall by the sword. They will take your sons and daughters, and what remains will be consumed by the fire. 26They will strip off your clothes and take away your treasures. 27I will put an end[x] to your perversion and to your whoring[y] since the land of Egypt. You will lift your eyes to them no longer and will remember Egypt no more."

28For thus says Lord Yahweh, "Look—I am handing you over to those you hate, to those at whom you were revolted. 29And they will deal hatefully with you and take all that you own and abandon you stark naked; your whorish nakedness[z] will be exposed.[aa] Your perversion and your prostitutions[bb] 30have brought[cc] these things upon you, your whoring[dd] after nations with whose idols you defiled yourself.

31You have gone the way of your sister, and I will put her cup into your hand." 32Thus says Lord Yahweh,

"You will drink your sister's cup,
>   which is deep and wide (she is laughed at and mocked);ee
>   it contains much.
33You will be filled with drunkenness and grief.
A cup of desolation and despair
>   is the cup of your sister Samaria.
34You will drink it and drain it,
>   and chew its dregs.ff
Then you will tear out your breasts—

for I have spoken," declares Lord Yahweh. 35Therefore thus says Lord Yahweh, "Because you forgot me and tossed me behind your back, therefore, you, bear the consequences of your perversion and your prostitutions."

36Then Yahweh said to me, Mortal, would you judge Oholah and Oholibah? Then inform them of their abominations. 37For they have committed adultery and blood is on their hands; they have committed adultery with their idols, and even their children whom they bore me they have passed over as food for them. 38This too they did to me: they defiled my sanctuary the same day, and profaned my sabbaths. 39When they had slaughtered their children to their idols, they came into my sanctuary the same day to profane it.

Not only thus did they do within my house, 40butgg they even sent for men coming from far away; a messenger was sent to them . . . and they came, for whom you washed, painted your eyes, and adorned yourself lavishly. 41And you sat on a glorious couch with a table spread before it, on whichhh you put my incense and oil. 42The noise of a carefree crowd was in it.ii . . . And [you sent] to some from a crowd of men brought in drunk from the wilderness. And they put bracelets on the women'sjj hands and a beautiful crown on their heads. 43And I said, "To completekk the adulteries, now she [Oholibah] is committingll her [Oholah's] prostitutions—she also." 44They enteredmm her the way one comes in to a prostitute; thus they entered both Oholah, and [now] Oholibah, the perverted woman.nn

45But righteous men, these will judge themoo with the sentence against women who commit adultery and shed blood—for they are adulteresses, and blood is on their hands.

46For thus says Lord Yahweh, "Bring up a throng against them and hand thempp over to be terrorized and plundered.qq 47And the throng will stone them with stones and cut them uprr with their swords. They will kill theirss sons and daughters and burn theirss houses with fire.

[48]And I will rid the land[tt] of perversion, and all women will be warned not to imitate your[uu] perversion. [49]And they will lay the consequences of your perversion upon you, and you will bear responsibility for your idolatrous sins;[vv] and you will know[ww] that I am the Lord, Yahweh."

Notes

a   The repetition of *znw* is not attested in LXX, Syriac.

b   Lit: "the loves of their virginities were done." Emendation to yield a meaning parallel to that of the preceding line (cf. Zimmerli, *Ezekiel 1*, 471) is unnecessary. The reference is not to further handling of the breasts but to intercourse; cf. LXX, *ekei diepartheneuthēsan*.

c   Lit: "under/in place of me"; cf. 16:32. She has had sex with others in place of (i.e., instead of) with Yahweh.

d   Both *ʿl* and *ʾl* are used after the verb *ʿgb* here, and cf. vv 7 (*kl ʾšr ʿgbh*) and 9 (*ʿl*). The significance of the different prepositions in this instance is unknown (cf. note t on 16:28).

e   Reading *qrwbym* as participle with Syriac (cf. Keil, *Ezekiel*, 1. 323).

f   Only here does the expression, *špk tznwt* appear with a masculine subject. In this case, the "showering forth" apparently refers to ejaculation (cf. the noun *špkh*, which BDB takes as referring to the "male organ [as fluid duct]"; 1050a).

g   Lit: "She became a name." Cf. 36:3.

h   Emending *špwtym* to *šptym* with mss; cf. 16:41.

i   The verse contains the plural of both *tznwt* and *znwnym*. The latter is translated "whoredoms" to distinguish it from the former.

j   Reading the qere, *kśdym*.

k   Hapax: from *tbl*, "to dip." Apparently the headgear billowed, fluttering and "dipping" as the officers approached.

l   *šlšym*. This term may specify an officer of the third rank, or a military unit of three men (see D. G. Schley, "The *šališîm*: Officers or Special Three-Man Squads?," *VT* 40 [1990] 321-26).

m   Hiphʾil participle. Lit: "as an exhibit for her eyes."

n   Lit: "came to her to a bed of lovemaking."

o   Lit: "to be dislocated," as in Gen 32:26, of Jacob's thigh. As a metaphor of relationships, "alienated" or "repulsed." In this context emotional estrangement is a metaphor for political revolt.

p   Lit: "to remember."

q   The only occurrence of the masculine form of "concubine," but with the 3mpl possessive suffix: "their concubinage." Given the description of the Egyptians in the second half of the verse, the object of the woman's lust may be understood to be sexual services.

r   The identity of these peoples is uncertain. While Pekod is mentioned in Jer 50:21, it may be that the names are fanciful (cf. Eichrodt, *Ezekiel*, 328), puns on *pqd*, "to muster; punish," *šwʿ*, "cry," and perhaps *yqʿ*, "to dislocate; tear away" (cf. vv 17, 18, 22).

s   Reading *ʾtm* for MT *ʾwtm*, with mss.

t   Lit: "summoned/invited." Perhaps these are "commissioned" officers. Occurring in place of the difficult *qrwbym* of vv 5 and 12, it is easily explained as a scribal error, as attested by LXX.

u   Emending, with Reider ("Contributions to the Scriptural Text," *HUCA* 24 [1952/3] 85-106), from *hsn* to *hṣn*. The resulting list—stallion, chariot, and wheel—describes the attacker synecdochaically; description of weapons is substituted for description of the one using the weapons. The lack of the particle *b* is therefore not relevant; the expression is the equivalent of the English expression "smite them hip and thigh." For a discussion of other possibilities, see Zimmerli (*Ezekiel 1*, 475).

v   Lit: "I will put justice before them."

w   Lit: "your rear/latter part." Cf. the anatomical usage in Ezek 8:16. The exact meaning here is uncertain and must depend on what kind of "ending" might plausibly be cut off by a sword and burned in the fire. The possible reference to Oholibah's anatomy, which would continue the imagery of her nose and ears being cut off, breaks down in the second half of the verse, when "your end" evidently refers to the people remaining after the sons and daughters are taken. LXX renders "remnant."

x   Lit: "I will make a sabbath." Probably ironic in context.

y   *znwtk* is an anomalous form, found here and in 43:7, 9. Some mss read *tznwt*, a solution preferred by Zimmerli (*Ezekiel 1*, 476), but emendation is unnecessary. The form *tznwt* is itself unique to Ezekiel, and there is no reason not to attribute to him a second anomalous form of the root *znh*, especially considering that the form *znwtk* appears three times. LXX does not distinguish between *tznwt* and *znwnym* (cf. v 11), and so is of no use in this regard.

z   Lit: "the nakedness of your prostitutions." In the context of public exposure of an adulteress, an accurate translation might be, "your unfaithful genitalia," though the English "nakedness" retains the euphemism of the Hebrew.

aa   Emending *wnglh* to *wnglth* (cf. Zimmerli, *Ezekiel 1*, 476).

bb   *wzmmtk wtznwtyk* must either be taken as in apposition to *ʿrwt znwnyk*, leaving the subject of the following verse uncertain, or read as the beginning of v 30 (cf. Zimmerli, *Ezekiel 1*, 476).

cc   Reading *ʿśw* for *ʿśh*, with mss.

dd   The *b* of *bznwtk* is taken as an instrumental *b* (GKC §119o, p); Oholibah's prostitution has been the means by which she has brought about her destruction.

ee   *thyh lšhq wllʿg* is unattested in LXX and some versions; perhaps a late addition?

ff   Or, "You will gnaw its sherds" (see Driver, "Ezekiel," 155). If *ḥrś* is translated "sherds," a step is left out of the story, namely the breaking of the cup into sherds. If BDB is correct in relating the root to the Arabic *kherash*, "irritation" (360), then Oholibah may be commanded to chew "the gritty part," that is, the dregs. The Akkadian *ḥarṣu*, a term used "of beer and soda" (*CAD* 6. 115b) and *ḥarṣu*, "barley cleaned or treated in a special way" (hops?), also would point to Oholibah's chewing some remnant of the drink, rather than the cup itself. This would make for a natural, if unpleasant, sequence of events: drink it, drain it, chew the dregs.

gg   Verses 39b-40a serve as a comparative introduction to what follows; see BDB 65a,3 for discussion of *hnnh* . . . *ʾp ky* as "how much more" (cf. GKC "not to mention...," §154a.1.c).

hh   *ʿlyh* refers to *šlḥn* rather than to *mṭh*. Although the feminine suffix may be an error, *šlḥn* regularly takes the fpl ending, *šlḥnwt*, and so the use of the feminine suffix might have been acceptable.

ii   Lit: "in her." This presumably refers to Oholibah as "her" = the city, since the crowd cannot be in the woman.

jj   Lit: "their" (f).

kk   The entire verse is difficult; *BHS* suggests emendation to follow LXX, *hlʾ kʾlh nʾpw*; Driver's suggestion ("Ezekiel," 155) that the initial *l* be understood as an exclamatory particle is not without merit, but he unnecessarily resorts to reading the abrupt ending of the verse as due to Yahweh's horrified lack of words; Zimmerli (*Ezekiel 1*, 479) sees here "radical corruption," and does not translate the verse at all. The present translation takes *lbblh* as a form of *blh*, "to wear out through use" or (in Piʿel) "to complete." The rest of the verse can be translated without emendation.

ll   Reading the kethib.

mm   Emending *wybwʾ* to *wybʾw*, with mss.

nn   Repointing *ʾšt* as a construct rather than with Zimmerli and Driver ("Linguistic Problems," 175) as "an unusual plural formation" (*Ezekiel 1*, 479).

oo   The 3mpl form here could reflect the tenor of the metaphor; that it is the people of Jerusalem and not two women only who will be attacked. More likely, the form reflects a grammatical preference for 3mpl over 2fpl (cf. GKC §103b; Rooker, *Biblical Hebrew*, 79 n44).

pp   Again, 3mpl for the expected 3fpl; see note oo, v 45.

qq   Lit: "for terror and for plunder."

rr   While *qhl* can take a singular or plural verb (cf. Ezek 16:40; 1 Kgs 8:14), it is rare for it to govern both in one sentence. The peculiar placement of the subject may influence the choice of verbal forms. On the phenomenon of a collective noun governing both a singular and plural verb in a single sentence, see GKC §145g.

ss   3mpl; see note oo, v 45.

tt   Lit: "I will cause a sabbath of perversion from the land."

uu   A return to 2fpl; the mention of "all women" and "your" perversion bring the
     narrator back into the metaphorical vehicle.
vv   Lit: "the sins of your idols." Presumably the idols are not capable of sinning.
     Oholibah's and Oholah's sins of idolatry are therefore intended.
ww   2mpl. Although this may be an instance of the preference for mpl over fpl
     forms, more likely this is a departure from the metaphorical vehicle to address
     the concluding warning to Ezekiel's intended, male audience.

III. THE DISTINCTIVENESS OF EZEKIEL'S MARRIAGE METAPHOR
RELATIVE TO THOSE OF EARLIER PROPHETIC BOOKS

Ezekiel's use of the marriage metaphor in chaps 16 and 23 differs
markedly from that of the earlier prophets on whose work Ezekiel's is
evidently dependent. The metaphor in Ezekiel is distinctive with respect
to its literary style (length, coherence, and detail), its content (both the
metaphorical actions of the woman and their historical referents), and its
placement in the book (in the middle rather than at the beginning).

These differences in the form of Ezekiel's metaphor relative to earlier
prophetic works suggest a different function for the marriage metaphor
as it is used by Ezekiel. The book of Ezekiel is dominated by Ezekiel's
concern with the fate of the temple, and with the question of whether
Yahweh can have a dwelling among the people without risking defilement as a result of their sins. Focusing on the destruction of the
Jerusalem temple, first the inevitability of destruction, and then on its
aftermath, the book of Ezekiel is structured to reflect the changing
relationship between Yahweh and the temple. Chapters 1-24 recount and
justify Yahweh's abandonment of his dwelling; chaps 25-39 promise a
renewed relationship and describe the preparatory cleansing of the land;
and chaps 40-48 relate Ezekiel's vision of a new and purified temple to
which Yahweh returns, and in which he pledges to remain.[7]

In the personification of Jerusalem as a woman Ezekiel finds a powerful metaphor for the relationship between Yahweh and his temple. The
concern over the temple that governs the shape of Ezekiel as a whole also
governs the use of this metaphor: Ezekiel recasts the adultery metaphor
to focus on the pollution that precipitates Yahweh's abandonment of the
Jerusalem temple. Ezekiel's distinctive concern for the purity of
Yahweh's "holy place" critically influences his use of the marriage

---

[7] For further discussion of the relationship between the structure and content of
Ezekiel, see J. Blenkinsopp, *Ezekiel* (Louisville: John Knox, 1990) 5-6.

metaphor as regards its style, content, placement, and function within the book.

A. *Differences in Style*

Stylistically, the marriage metaphor in Ezekiel differs from previous treatments in length, in coherence, and in degree of detail. Ezekiel devotes 112 verses to the depiction of the unfaithful wife, making this by far the most sustained of his narrative metaphors, as well as far surpassing the length of the personifications of Hosea[8] and Jeremiah.[9] More important than sheer length, however, is the conceptual coherence of Ezekiel's metaphor. In Jeremiah the marriage metaphor is interspliced with address to and about (male) Israel and Judah, and consequently cannot be read as a unity. In Hosea the metaphor seems to govern all of chaps 1-3 (39 verses), but the constant changes in the metaphor's tenor make for a more impressionistic than coherent depiction of Yahweh's unfaithful wife.[10] Ezekiel, by contrast, devotes two lengthy chapters exclusively to telling "Jerusalem her abominations" (16:2) and to predicting and justifying her consequent punishment. The result is a vivid and compelling narrative focused on the unfaithful woman Jerusalem.

The amount and type of detail included in Ezekiel's depiction of the unfaithful wife also surpass those of either Hosea or Jeremiah, both at the level of the vehicle and of the tenor. At the level of the vehicle, the woman in Ezekiel 16 is provided a history of her gory birth and childhood (vv 1-8), after which her clothing (vv 10-14), her preparations for her lovers (vv 15-29), and her punishment (vv 35-43) are all described at length. The lavish description in Ezek 23:5-24 of the equipage and sexual endowments of Jerusalem's lovers is similarly without precedent in the other prophets.

At the level of the tenor, Ezekiel is unique in his use of the marriage metaphor to provide a comprehensive (and largely comprehensible) survey of Israelite and Judean history. Beyond their mention of Israel's early

---

[8] Thirty-nine verses of Hosea, if all of chaps 1-3 are included, seem to personify Samaria or the land as Yahweh's wife.

[9] Though it is difficult to determine what should count as personification in Jeremiah, the total number of verses in which Jerusalem or the nation are presented as female cannot exceed sixty verses.

[10] The "intrusion" of Ezekiel's "referent" (tenor) noticed by Greenberg (*Ezekiel 1-20*, 25) seems minor when compared with the jumbling of vehicle and tenor in the marriage metaphors of Hosea and Jeremiah.

days in the wilderness (Hos 2:16-22; Eng 2:14-20; Jer 2:2),[11] neither Hosea
nor Jeremiah exploits the potential of the woman's biography to serve as
a vehicle for depicting the nation's history. Though both Hosea and
Jeremiah use the metaphor as a vehicle for commenting on the politics of
their day (as, e.g., in Hos 3:4-5; Jer 2:18, 36), neither clearly makes extensive or consistent use of the metaphor to depict specific historical events.
Ezekiel, however, in 16:23-29, and especially in 23:5-21, thoroughly re-
views Israelite and Judean alliances, both past and present, as part of his
accusation of adultery against Jerusalem. Ezekiel further distinguishes
within the metaphor between the charge of idolatry and the charge of
inappropriate foreign alliances,[12] a distinction that is either lacking or
unclear in both Hosea and Jeremiah. On the whole, Ezekiel's representations of Jerusalem the wife display far greater unity and depth of detail
than do those of the earlier prophets.

The marked stylistic differences between Ezekiel's use of the marriage metaphor and those of Hosea and Jeremiah is probably due to the
fact that Ezekiel apparently used Hosea and perhaps Jeremiah as sources
for his own reworking of the metaphor. Beginning with models of how
this metaphor could be employed as a rhetorical tool, Ezekiel had the
opportunity to refine and develop the metaphor. In addition, the effect
for stylistic clarity and coherence of Ezekiel's status as a *writing* prophet
cannot be overestimated.[13] The book of Ezekiel has long been noted for
the elegance and complexity of its structure;[14] Ezekiel's authorial sensibil-
ity is evident in his focused and rhetorically effective use of the marriage
metaphor.

Neither the fact that Ezekiel began from an already existing core of
prophetic oracles against Yahweh's unfaithful wife, nor the unity and
direction that might be expected in a writing prophet, however,
sufficiently accounts for Ezekiel's decision to move the marriage
metaphor from its ancillary role in Hosea and Jeremiah into the literal

---

[11] It is interesting that in chap 16 Ezekiel transforms Hosea's and Jeremiah's images of the faithful bride in the wilderness into an image of Jerusalem's utter helplessness and near-death in the wilderness. Both Hosea and Jeremiah depict the
woman as actively participating in the early stages of relationship with Yahweh,
whereas Ezekiel presents Jerusalem only as passive or rebellious.

[12] The two offenses are presented as separate in 16:15-22 and 16:23-34, while in
23:5-35 Ezekiel claims that Jerusalem's idolatry is the result of her foreign liaisons.

[13] For an analysis of the specific features of Ezekiel as a writing prophet, see Davis,
Swallowing the Scroll, chaps three and four.

[14] Cf. H. H. Rowley, *Men of God: Studies in Old Testament History and Prophecy*
(London: Thomas Nelson, 1963) 169-71.

and conceptual center of his own prophecy. The crucial difference in the style of Ezekiel's representation of the adulterous wife stems from the different symbolic role played by the marriage metaphor in Ezekiel's theology. For Ezekiel, the exiled priest, Jerusalem represents above all the temple, and it is the fate of the temple—its pollution, destruction, and envisioned restoration—that motivates Ezekiel's writing and gives his rendering of the story of Jerusalem's infidelity its particular clarity and power.

B. *Differences in Content*

Ezekiel's reworking of the marriage metaphor in light of the imminent destruction of Jerusalem and its temple results in significant differences in the metaphor's content from those of Hosea and Jeremiah. Ezekiel departs from earlier versions in his account of the origins, the sins, the punishment, and the envisioned restoration of Yahweh's wife, in each case reflecting the greater severity of Jerusalem's offenses and its consequent pollution.

1) *Origins*

Ezekiel's depiction of Jerusalem's origins differs from the depictions in Hosea (2:17; Eng 2:15) and Jeremiah (2:2), first, in asserting Jerusalem's native foreignness. Both Hosea and Jeremiah recall the time when the city/nation was "a bride" as if she had had no previous life. Consequently, the woman is presented as having no identity other than as Yahweh's wife. This sense of the ontological "givenness" of the marital relationship is consistent with the ancient Near Eastern conceptual metaphor of the marriage between the god and the city; even though the relationship's "beginning" is remembered, the marriage may now be assumed rather than having to be posited. Ezekiel "deconstructs" this given, depicting Jerusalem as not only foreign, "other" from her birth, but as outcast from even her own family. Her marriage to the god is depicted as a reflection of Yahweh's kindness, and the contingency of her status is thus emphasized.

Ezekiel also deletes the "honeymoon" stage from Yahweh's marriage as depicted by both Hosea and Jeremiah—the period of the woman's initial fidelity.[15] Though Yahweh is evidently proud of his bride (16:14), she neither "responds" as in Hosea (2:17; Eng 2:15) nor "follows" as in

---

15 Jerusalem's initial fidelity is likewise assumed in Isaiah's use (1:21, 26) of the epithet "faithful city" to denote the city's status before her "fall" into prostitution.

Jeremiah (2:2). Instead, in Ezekiel 16 the woman is depicted as first passive in relation to Yahweh, and then actively rebellious, while in Ezekiel 23 she is "unfaithful" even before her marriage to Yahweh (v 3; cf. 20:7-8).[16] Ezekiel's deletion of Yahweh and Jerusalem's happy past is consistent with his depiction of Jerusalem as inherently other, unclean and unworthy, and of the marriage as an exceptional kindness by Yahweh.

Ezekiel does adopt one feature of Jerusalem's origins as depicted by both Hosea and Jeremiah: the sisterhood between Israel north and south. Jeremiah, apparently playing on Hosea's plea to Israel not to entice Judah to infidelity (Hos 4:15), weaves a story (3:6-11) in which unfaithful Israel is divorced by Yahweh, after which her sister Judah heedlessly proceeds to imitate her behavior. Yahweh concludes that even Israel is better than "deceitful Judah" and asks her to repent and come home (vv 12-13). Ezekiel, apparently influenced by Jer 3:6-11, changes "Judah" and "Israel" to "Jerusalem" and "Samaria" and gives two separate accounts of the sisters' parallel infidelities. In 16:44-63 Ezekiel adds Sodom, a third sister, and depicts a Jerusalem who is so bad as to make her wicked sisters look righteous by comparison (16:44-63). In 23:1-35 an extensive narrative is devoted to describing how Judah witnesses her sister Samaria's infidelity and punishment, but succeeds in outdoing her sister's depravity.[17] Ezekiel, having apparently suppressed Hosea's and Jeremiah's accounts of the wife's initial fidelity, thereupon expands upon their comparison between the infidelities of South and North.

2) *Sins*

Like the women of Hosea and Jeremiah, Ezekiel's Jerusalem is accused of both idolatry and inappropriate foreign alliances. The distinctiveness of Ezekiel's portrayal lies in (1) his attention to the cultic and legal implications of Jerusalem's transgressions, (2) the consistency with which he distinguishes between cultic and political infidelity, and (3) the lurid intensity of his language. Relentlessly focusing on Jerusalem's worsening depravity, Ezekiel presents a woman whose perversion is without remedy.

---

16   Hosea does, like Ezekiel, refer to the woman's youth in Egypt (2:17; Eng 2:15), but for Hosea Egypt is the place from which the faithful bride is brought during the period of her initial fidelity, not the scene of her "youthful prostitution."

17   The idea that Judah has outdone even those (like Sodom and Samaria) known for their evil is also raised in passing in Jer 2:33, where Yahweh accuses the woman (either Judah or Jerusalem) of having "instructed evil women."

In 16:15-22 Ezekiel straightforwardly depicts Jerusalem engaging in her "prostitution" with idols. Using vocabulary drawn from the Exodus description of the tabernacle, Ezekiel tells how the clothing, food, and gold with which Yahweh endowed his bride are returned to their cultic function, as the woman builds a high place, forms images, clothes them, and offers them a "pleasant aroma."[18] In addition to his depiction of the woman's idolatry, Ezekiel also posits a connection between foreign over-lords and foreign gods, portraying idolatry as the inevitable consequence of affairs with foreign "men": "She profaned herself with all the idols of everyone for whom she lusted" (23:7).[19]

Ezekiel's unambiguous portrayal of Jerusalem's idolatry and foreign alliances is a departure from both Hosea and Jeremiah. The earlier prophets repeatedly accuse the woman of "infidelity," but only imply the nature of the infidelity committed. Jeremiah indicates Jerusalem's idolatry merely by its location: infidelity "on every high hill and under every lush tree" (Jer 2:20; 3:6; cf. 13:27). Hosea's marriage to Gomer (1:2) is not explained as, but only intimated to mean, either cultic or political infidelity. Prefiguring Ezekiel's description of Jerusalem (16:15-22; 23:40), Hosea suggests Israel's idolatry most strongly in his portrayal of the woman's transfer (2:10; Eng 2:8) of Yahweh's gifts of produce, silver, and gold to, and her self-adornment (2:15; Eng 2:13) for, her lovers. In Hosea, however, at exactly those points (2:8, 13) where "the baalim"[20] are explicitly mentioned, it is impossible to tell whether the woman is offering herself and her goods to idols or to the "lords" to whom she pays tribute of both produce and money. It is possible that Hosea intentionally conflated Israel's infatuation with foreign powers and her dalliance with their gods (punning on the word "baal"), but the subtley of the interplay is difficult for (at least) the modern reader to follow.

Just as his depictions of Jerusalem's idolatry are clearer and more fully developed than those of either Hosea or Jeremiah, so also are Ezekiel's accusations of "infidelity" with foreign men. In both chaps 16 (vv 23-34) and 23 (vv 12-21) Ezekiel names the nations to whom Jerusalem has "prostituted herself," leaving no doubt as to the identity of

---

[18] On the connection between the woman's clothing and the appurtenances of the tabernacle, see Chapter Four.

[19] In this Ezekiel echoes the opinion of Exod 34:15 (cf. Num 25:1-2) that making a covenant with another nation will involve the people in "prostitution" with their gods (and cf. Cogan, *Imperialism and Religion*, 44, on the probable necessity for vassal states to participate in the cult of the suzerain power).

[20] Or "*the* baal," in 2:10.

these "lovers." Hosea, in contrast, only hints that Israel's "lords" may include other sovereign states,[21] while Jeremiah mentions Jerusalem's dependence on both Assyria and Egypt (2:18, 36), but nowhere labels this dependence as "infidelity." The verb *znh* seems to be used in Jeremiah exclusively of infidelity with idols.[22]

Ezekiel is similarly alone in accusing Yahweh's wife of child sacrifice, a charge brought in both 16:20-22 and 23:37-39. Though Jeremiah repeatedly accuses the people of offering up their children (7:31; 19:5; 32:35; cf. Ezek 20:25), he never includes this accusation in his personification of woman Jerusalem. Ezekiel here conflates vehicle ("mother" Jerusalem) and tenor (the actual children of the city) to produce a truly horrifying effect.[23] The picture of "our mother" handing over her children to her hungry lovers confirms that this "adulteress" is not merely unfaithful, but deeply and uncontrollably perverse.[24]

Ezekiel is also unique in explicitly accusing the personified city of covenant violation (16:59) and of pollution of the sanctuary (23:38-39), both offenses that defile Yahweh's name and dwelling, and thus contribute directly to his abandonment of the temple.[25] Ezekiel's detailed

---

[21] In 8:9 Hosea refers to Ephraim's "lovers" who "go up" (*ʿlh*) to (or "against") Assyria. Whatever the identity of these lovers, their action of "going up" to or against Assyria suggests that they represent nations.

[22] In Jer 4:30, however, Jerusalem is shown adorning herself (cf. Hos 2:15; Eng 2:13; Ezek 23:40) "in vain," because her "boyfriends" (*ʿgbym*; cf. Ezek 23:7, 9, 11-12, etc.) have turned upon her. Though the woman is nowhere depicted as "prostituting herself" with foreign nations, in context the former boyfriends who seek her life can only be political allies.

[23] This crossover between the vehicle of the personified city and the tenor of the city's children was apparently standard, as shown by the depictions in Nah 3:10 and Isa 47:8-9 (cf. *ANET*, 556-59) of cities bereft by the murder of "their" children. Ezekiel simply extends this peculiarity of the received metaphor, contradicting the commonplace of the nurturing mother to describe a city with a different attitude toward her offspring.

[24] At the level of the tenor, literal *fathers* would in fact have offered their children as sacrifices. The metaphorical transfer of the act to "mother" increases the horror of the act in several ways. First, the image works against the commonplace of mother as a nurturer. Second the metaphor depicts the mother usurping the prerogative of the father; the woman is taking the fruits of her sexual obligation to her husband and transferring them to idols, who as "lovers" at the level of the vehicle, are the husband's sexual competitors. Finally, Yahweh is offended by the woman's actions, both as dishonored God and as dishonored husband.

[25] All sins in Israel, no matter where committed, polluted the outer altar of the temple, but unrepented sins polluted the holy of holies itself. Child sacrifice to idols, of which Ezekiel accuses the people (16:20-22; 23:37-39; but cf. 20:25, in which the sacrifices are made to Yahweh) would incur simultaneously the pollutions associated

and impassioned condemnations of the woman Jerusalem reflect his historical situation, especially his preoccupation with the defilement and impending fall of the temple. Delivering Yahweh's accusations on the eve of the city's destruction,[26] Ezekiel builds a thoroughly damning case against the woman Jerusalem, emphasizing the abominations (*twʿbwt*; 16:2, 22, 47, etc.), pollution (*ṭmʾ*; 23:17, 30, 38), bloodguilt (16:36, 38; 23:37, 45), and perversion (*zmmh*; 16:27, 58; 23:29, 48, etc.) that justify Yahweh's rejection of his wife.

3) Punishment

The punishment prescribed for the woman in Ezekiel is based on that described in Hosea and Jeremiah (and cf. Nah 3:5-6), but is characteristically expanded and intensified. In Hosea Yahweh divorces his wife (2:4; Eng 2:2), takes back the provisions he had given her, and exposes her before her helpless lovers (2:11-12; Eng 2:9-10). He also takes revenge upon the faithless land (2:13-14; Eng 2:11-12), destroying its produce. In Jeremiah 2-3 the woman's punishment is merely implied in Yahweh's prediction that Egypt will fail her as badly as did Assyria.[27] Only in Jer 13:26 does Yahweh threaten to expose the woman for her adultery. Ezekiel's depiction of the woman's punishment, comprising 16:35-43, 53-59 and 23:22-34, 45-49, describes at length the removal of Yahweh's gifts and the exposure of the woman, first before her lovers (16:37) and then by them.[28] In addition, the woman is mutilated, burned, and sliced open, her children killed, and her houses burned. The language of violence against the woman and of pillage in the city are mixed indiscriminately.

---

with bloodshed and idolatry. If the sacrificers then also entered the sanctuary "that same day" (23:39), they would add to this the strong contamination adhering to those who had had contact with corpses (cf. Ezekiel's objection in 43:7 to the gravesites of kings adjoining the sanctuary). On the pollution of the temple, see J. Milgrom ("Israel's Sanctuary: the Priestly 'Picture of Dorian Gray'," *RB* 33 [1976] 390-99); and also T. Frymer-Kensky ("Pollution").

The breaking of the oath was likewise a highly polluting offense, defiling the name of Yahweh (Lev 19:12; and see Milgrom, *Cult and Conscience*, 13-22).

[26] On the use of forensic language in these chapters, see Hals, *Ezekiel*, 105-07; Zimmerli, *Ezekiel 1*, 336; Greenberg, *Ezekiel 1-20*, 273-74.

[27] Yahweh also implies in Jer 3:1 that he has divorced the city.

[28] The role of the foreign nations in depictions of the exposure of the "adulteress" varies widely. Ezekiel seems to combine some elements of scenario in Hos 2:12 (Eng 2:10), in which the lovers stand by helpless, with elements of the scenario in Nah 3:5, in which foreign nations form the scornful witnesses to the exposure, and then expands upon the comment of Jer 4:30 that those for whom the woman lusted now seek to kill her.

A telling difference between Yahweh's punishment in Ezekiel and that in the earlier accounts occurs in Ezekiel's ending to chap 23. Following a series of threats against the city dating back centuries, the end has finally come. "Bring on the mob," commands Yahweh (v 46), initiating the woman's punishment, rather than merely threatening it. Moreover, the punishment that earlier prophets conceived of as a corrective measure, Ezekiel recasts as the woman's imminent death.

4) *Restoration*

Ezekiel's sensitivity to the gravity of Jerusalem's sins and the reality of Yahweh's rejection may account for a final discrepancy in content between Ezekiel 16 and 23 and earlier personifications of Samaria or Jerusalem; unlike Hosea and Jeremiah, in Ezekiel Yahweh's promises of restoration are minimal. Hosea (2:16-25; Eng 2:14-23; 3:5) speaks passionately of the lengths to which Yahweh will go to reclaim his ex-wife, and predicts that these efforts will be successful. Jeremiah (3:1, 11-13, 19) holds out less hope for the metaphorical woman, but promises restoration to the *literal* Judah and Jerusalem in passages (3:15-18, 22-25; 4:1-4) interwoven with the personification so as to give the impression that Yahweh's pleas have been effective.[29]

Ezekiel offers no such hope. The only positive result of the punishment foreseen in chap 23 is that Jerusalem will recognize Yahweh (v 49). The situation in chap 16 is only marginally better; Yahweh promises that he will establish another covenant with Jerusalem,[30] and that he will cleanse (*kpr*) her (vv 60, 63)—but with the result that Jerusalem's shame will be deepened. Recognizing Yahweh, she will shut her mouth forever (v 63).

C. *Differences in Placement and Function*

The thoroughness with which Ezekiel has reworked the metaphor of Hosea and Jeremiah is also evident in his different placement of the metaphor within the book. Whereas the personification of the land and city is concentrated in the beginning of both Hosea and Jeremiah, Ezekiel's addresses against the personified city are placed in the midst of his accusations against Jerusalem (chap 16), and at their climax (chap 23). The earlier prophets use the figure of the unfaithful woman to set the

---

[29] Even the brief personification of Jerusalem in Isa 1:21, 26 includes the promise that after the purification of her officials, she will again be called "the faithful city" (v 26).

[30] Cf. the new covenant and rebetrothal in Hos 2:20-22 (Eng 2:18-20).

stage for their prophecy; appearing at the beginning of Hosea and Jeremiah, the metaphor provides an effective introduction to the themes of the people's depravity and of Yahweh's desire for their repentence. In Ezekiel's case, the metaphor is employed only after the time for pleading has passed. Only when he has seen the continuing abominations in the temple and has heard that Yahweh has doomed it for destruction does Ezekiel begin his harangue against woman Jerusalem. Rather than urging her repentance, Ezekiel recounts Jerusalem's abominations in order to pronounce her sentence.[31]

Beginning from the metaphor of the nation/city as Yahweh's wife in Hosea and Jeremiah, Ezekiel reshapes it in accordance with the concerns governing his own prophecy—the defilement and destruction of the Jerusalem temple. The marriage metaphor is especially suited to depict the defilement of Yahweh's temple. If the city is a woman, then the temple is her vagina, and the offense of Jerusalem's granting illicit "access" to foreign men and competing gods becomes plain, both as a legal transgression and as a personal injury to the husband. In light of the impending destruction of the temple for its extreme pollution, Ezekiel exploits the marriage metaphor's latent potential to depict highly offensive defilement.[32] Focusing on female sexual pollution as emblematic of all pollution, he transforms the marriage metaphor from the strong but ancillary image of Hosea and Jeremiah into a symbol of the central problem of the book.

Because the woman is able by her infidelity so powerfully to compromise the honor of Yahweh, her uncleanness is particularly threatening, and the need to punish her urgent. The reunion envisioned in Jeremiah and especially Hosea between Yahweh and his wife also

---

[31] Greenberg (*Ezekiel 1-20*, 299) observes that the impulse for Ezekiel's dramatic extension of the marriage metaphor "came from theodicy. The imminent destruction of the 'last remnant of Israel' was a catastrophe that demanded a correspondingly enormous sin to justify it."

[32] The problem motivating Yahweh's departure from the temple in Ezekiel is defilement of the holy place, rather than idolatry or foreign alliances per se. For this reason, not only those sins that can obviously be depicted as illicit sexual activity (the woman's allowing foreign men and idols into her "holy place") are depicted as "prostitution," but also child sacrifice (23:37-39) and oath violation (16:59). Because all serious offenses defile the most holy place, they become, symbolically, *sexually* polluting within the terms of the metaphoric vehicle. Thus even sins that are not analogous to literal adultery (that do not involve male figures in competition with Yahweh) become, within the metaphor, as shaming as the sins of infidelity, since they cause Yahweh's wife to be polluted. Yahweh's humiliation is thus deepened by the application of the marriage metaphor to various kinds of temple pollution.

becomes problematic for Ezekiel. If Yahweh's temple is, symbolically, a female body, then that temple is always in risk of pollution, either through menstruation or through illicit sexual activity. Ultimately, the metaphor of Jerusalem as wife is itself a problem, always threatening to transform Yahweh's marriage into a marriage between the Holy and the unclean. Ezekiel therefore depicts Yahweh as ultimately driven to destroy his hopelessly polluted temple. Moreover, just as Yahweh destroys the temple, so also must he preside over the death of his metaphorical wife (16:40), not only to vindicate his dishonored name, but to remove the potential for *future* defilement that the city's feminine persona represents.

IV

THE CITY AS YAHWEH'S WIFE IN EZEKIEL 16 AND 23

Ezekiel's personifications of Jerusalem as Yahweh's wife in chaps 16 and 23 contain elements in common with the earlier personifications of Hosea and Jeremiah. Ezekiel, however, has shaped the metaphor of the city as Yahweh's wife to reflect his distinctive concerns regarding the purity of the Jerusalem temple and the historical situation on the eve of the destruction of Jerusalem and its temple. Ezekiel's condemnation of the woman is therefore lengthier and more impassioned than those of the earlier prophets, so as to justify Yahweh's abandonment of the holy city. Exploiting the commonplaces of pollution and "otherness" associated with the female body, Ezekiel shapes his personification to highlight the woman's sexual pollution, which becomes a symbol of the pollution of the city's "holy place." Defining the woman as persistently defiled and defiling, Ezekiel justifies Yahweh's exclusion of Jerusalem from the realm of his possessions and his protection.

This chapter will focus on the metaphor of Jerusalem as Ezekiel's wife as it appears in Ezekiel 16 and 23. The metaphor will be explicated at the level of both tenor and vehicle, and both historical reconstruction (of the tenor) and literary analysis (of the vehicle) will be undertaken. Especially, the rhetorical force of this metaphor will be explored—its assumptions, its logic, and its implications.

In chap 16 the story of the rise and fall of "foundling Jerusalem" is told in terms of a power struggle between Yahweh and his wife. In vv 1-14, Yahweh is depicted as the one in control, and the result for Jerusalem is growth and beautification. In vv 15-43, Jerusalem takes control, causing her own descent into shame and finally, destruction. This story of Yahweh's nurture and Jerusalem's degradation is shaped chiastically, tracing first Jerusalem's ascent from a state of blood-covered rejection to the "perfection" gained from Yahweh's attentions, and then Jerusalem's slide back into a state of rejection and bloody death.

Throughout the story of Jerusalem's rise and fall, the woman's nakedness and clothing will be shown to symbolize her shame and honor, respectively, reflecting her status as either "owned" (and therefore clothed) by Yahweh, or rejected (and therefore naked). The exposure of Jerusalem's bloody, naked body, both in her infancy and in her punishment as an adulteress, is metonymous for her defilement and rejection.

Ezekiel 23 continues the focus of chap 16 on Jerusalem's body as a symbol of her self-disposition. In addition to nakedness or clothing as symbols of inclusion or exclusion (rejection), security or vulnerability, the language of "looking" and "seeing" is employed to symbolize Yahweh's struggle for control of Jerusalem and her sister, Samaria. Jerusalem's offenses now include her ogling of potential lovers, an act Yahweh punishes by exposing *her* to public view. In chap 23 the power struggle culminates, not as in chap 16 in a prediction of Jerusalem's downfall, but in Yahweh's actual call to muster the troops to destroy the city.

Both Ezekiel 16 and 23 use the metaphor of the wife's adultery as a vehicle for relating the history of Jerusalem and its political alliances. While in some places this depiction of Jerusalem seems almost allegorical, a point for point pairing of the woman's actions with the city's history, in other places the connection between tenor and vehicle is obscure. This obscurity seems at times due to the modern reader's lack of knowledge of the metaphor's original historical context, but at times the vehicle seems simply to take over; the woman Jerusalem acts "on her own" and not as a reflection of any specific historical situation. This relative "independence" of the metaphorical vehicle from its historical tenor heightens the sense that it is not only, or most truly, the city that is guilty, and therefore punished, but the woman herself, Yahweh's (metaphorical) wife, whose actions have made the city's punishment inevitable.

I. EZEKIEL 16

A. *Jerusalem as Unclean Other: 16:1-43*

Ezekiel's personification of Jerusalem in chap 16 can be divided into two main sections:[1] vv 1-43 and vv 44-58. Verses 1-43 form the core of the narrative, while vv 44-58 provide little more than variations upon themes from the preceding section.[2] The narrative metaphor of 16:1-43 influences the tone and content, not only of chap 16, but of all Ezekiel's charges against the woman in both chaps 16 and 23. Ezekiel 16:1-43 forms the base upon which the rest of chaps 16 and 23 is built.[3]

Ezekiel focuses the story of Jerusalem's infancy on the question of the girl's inclusion or exclusion. Jerusalem begins life excluded, "other" in terms of her family membership, her national identity, her community status, and her ritual purity. The daughter of an Amorite and a Hittite (v 3), the girl is born in the land of Canaan, but outside the community of Israel. Nor is she included within the community of her own people; she is exposed in the countryside at birth. The infant's physical expulsion simultaneously represents her legal abandonment. Ezekiel's claim that she has been thrown out while still in her birth blood not only places upon her the stigma of blood pollution, but signifies that her parents

---

[1] So, e.g., Greenberg, *Ezekiel 1-20*, 292; Eichrodt, *Ezekiel*, 202; Zimmerli, *Ezekiel 1*, 333.

[2] Those who divide Ezekiel into "authentic" and "secondary" material consistently consider vss 44-58 "secondary" (so Hölscher, *Hesekiel*, 96; Irwin, *The Problem of Ezekiel: An Inductive Study* [Chicago: University of Chicago, 1943] 160; Zimmerli, *Ezekiel 1*, 333). These scholars are correct in their assessment of the secondary importance of the section; its plot is subsidiary, and its emotional impact slight. This analysis, however, will argue that the two sections are integrated (as is the coda, vss 59-63). Greenberg (*Ezekiel 1-20*, 25, 292-306) has shown that Ezekiel's oracles frequently take the form of an A section, followed by a B section in which the themes of the A section are further developed, and concluding with a brief "coda" section in which the themes of A and B are integrated. Talmon and Fishbane ("The Structuring of Biblical Books: Studies in the Book of Ezekiel," *ASTI* 10 [1976] 129-53) similarly acknowledge Ezekiel's structural complexity without positing a second (or third) author. While it remains possible that an editor was responsible for reweaving Ezekiel into the highly integrated whole it appears to be (on which integration, see the comments of H. H. Rowley, *Men of God*, 169-71), the work of such an editor would have been so extensive that he or she would in effect be the author of the book.

[3] Interestingly, although chap 16 was banned from public reading in the synagogue (*Meg.* 4:10) because of its unsavory depiction of "mother" Jerusalem (*b. Hag.* 131), there is no recorded discussion of banning the reading of chap 23. Chapter 16 is consistently treated as the heart of Ezekiel's accusations against Jerusalem.

have rejected her "from birth," consigning her to "the ownerless domain."[4] Yahweh passes by (v 6) and sees the infant, expelled, exposed, and covered with unclean blood. She is entirely outside the boundaries of the ordered world and on the brink of the ultimate "exclusion," death. Yahweh, however, calls her back from near-death, commanding her, "Live." Malul points out that Yahweh's taking charge of the infant "in her blood" represents his legal adoption of her "from birth," and therefore his complete authority over her.[5] The command to "live" is not, however, known to be part of the adoption formula, and so must be otherwise accounted for. The juxtaposition of the command, "Live," with the stipulation "in your blood" is problematic. Although there is no biblical parallel to the phrase, "live in your blood," the expression does find a near-opposite in the concept of *dying* with one's blood on one. The image of dying with one's blood on one is common, both within Ezekiel (18:13; 33:4-5; cf. 3:18, 20; 33:6, 8) and in the legal corpus (e.g., Lev 20:9-15), and denotes dying a deserved death,[6] ordinarily, through capital punishment.[7] Rather than incurring guilt on the killer,[8] the shed blood is said to rest on the victim, symbolizing his or her own responsibility for the death. The command, "In your blood, live," while not an exact verbal parallel, is a conceptual reversal of the "death sentence." Jerusalem, cast out to die in her blood, is kept from death by Yahweh's command, "In your blood, live." The command, emphasizing Jerusalem's state of disgraced near-death, also draws attention to the distance between the power of the pure, male god and the helplessness of the dying, defiled girl.

Yahweh's command rescues the infant from death, but the divine call to live "in [her] blood" does not relieve Jerusalem of her excluded

---

[4] Meir Malul ("Adoption of Foundlings in the Bible and Mesopotamian Documents: A Study of Some Legal Metaphors in Ezekiel 16.1-7," *JSOT* 46 [1990] 97-126). Malul argues on the basis of Mesopotamian records that the rejection of the infant describes, not simply physical abandonment, but the parents' legal renunciation of any claims to the infant. Exposing her while still in her birth blood, the parents claim never to have given the infant legal recognition as their own (100).

[5] Having been found in her birth blood, she is both legally and symbolically adopted "from birth" ("Adoption of Foundlings," 106).

[6] See H. G. Reventlow, "'Sein Blüt komme über sein Haupt'," *VT* 10 (1960) 311-27; K. Koch, "Der Spruch, 'Sein Blut bleibe auf seinem Haupt'," *VT* 12 (1962) 396-416; B. Kedar-Kopfstein, "*dām*," in *TDOT* III, 234-50.

[7] See, e.g., Lev 20:9, 11, 12, though occasionally (e.g., Ezek 33:4, 5) the offender dies from other causes, a kind of "divine capital punishment."

[8] As, for example, is suggested in Gen 4:11; Jonah 1:14; Lev 17:11.

status. Rather, Yahweh's action moves her from an excluded into a liminal state. Included in the community of the living and legitimated by Yahweh's adoption, the girl nonetheless lives "in her blood"; she remains unclean,[9] and so excluded from full membership in the community.[10]

The infant multiplies "like the sprouts [ṣmḥ] of the field" (v 7). The image of Jerusalem "multiplying" abandons the figure of Jerusalem as a growing girl in favor of a metaphor that reflects the nation's numerical growth.[11] The tenor of population growth is represented through the vehicle of spreading vegetation. The comparison between Jerusalem and the "sprouts of the field," however, also maintains the connection between the girl and the external realm (she is like something "of the field," śdh, the place in which she lay abandoned). The vehicle of a growing girl (who does not "multiply like sprouts") is abandoned only briefly, however, and the image is immediately resumed in the following phrase: "you grew up, and acquired the finest adornments; your breasts were formed and your hair sprouted [ṣmḥ]." The use of ṣmḥ in both the vehicle of vegetable fertility and the vehicle of female puberty creates a verbal bridge between the two images. The "sprouting" of field cover is implicitly compared to the sprouting of the girl's pubic hair.[12] The effect of this momentary shift of metaphoric vehicles, and of the verbal link between them, is to reinforce the connection between the growing girl and the wild and uncultivated realm without. Even under Yahweh's protection, the girl remains a (literal) outsider, a thing of "the field."[13] As if to emphasize the girl's continued status as outsider, Yahweh notes that the pubescent girl remains stark naked, exposed to every gaze.

After the girl has reached puberty, Yahweh passes by again (v 8) and notes the naked girl's sexual maturity. It is striking that having

---

9 Kedar-Kopfstein ("dām," 246) cites the interpretation of Yahweh's command, "In your blood, live," as meaning, "In spite of the blood that still defiles you, you shall live."

10 T. Frymer-Kensky ("Pollution," 399-414) discusses the connection between the boundary between clean and unclean, and that between life and death. Malul ("Adoption of Foundlings," 102, 106) also describes both impurity and "the field" into which the girl is thrown as "the ownerless area, . . . the domain outside the law." See also G. Andre, "ṭāmē," in TDOT V, 331.

11 Cf. Davidson, Prophet Ezekiel, 102-03.

12 Cf. the similar image used by Inanna, who describes her pubic hair as "lettuce" waiting to be "watered" by her lover (T. Jacobsen, The Harps That Once . . ., 74).

13 This is especially interesting given that the girl Jerusalem is, throughout the narrative, a metaphor for a city. This insistence on Jerusalem's origins outside the walls inverts the association of the city with inclusion and security, redefining the city in terms of exclusion and vulnerability.

"adopted" the infant in v 6, Yahweh has left her to grow up feral and naked in the field. Her continuing naked vulnerability, while apparently inconsistent with her adoption by Yahweh, furthers the narrative emphasis on both Jerusalem's vulnerability and her shockingly evident sexuality. Exposed at birth to the elements, Jerusalem's sexual "readiness" is exposed in her adolescence. As at her birth, the naked girl is depicted as the helpless (and, as it turns out, bloody; v 10) object of Yahweh's appraising gaze.[14] Yahweh covers her, marries her,[15] and cleanses her of her blood,[16] completing the legitimation he began in her

---

[14] Repeatedly in both chaps 16 and 23, Jerusalem is described being exposed sexually before a male audience. Yahweh, the male god, tells his surrogate, Ezekiel, to describe Yahweh's act of gazing at the naked body of the woman to the (male) people. Ezekiel, the narrator, in turn passes this image on to the implied (male) reader of the text.

At the climax of chap 16 Jerusalem is exposed by Yahweh before her former lovers, thus creating a combined audience of the woman's husband and his male peers (the foreign nations), and Ezekiel and his male peers (the readers). The effect of this multilayered exposure of the woman is strikingly similar to that achieved in cinema in which a male hero's gaze controls the spectator's view of women. The spectator is allowed to identify with the main male, "so that the power of the male protagonist as he controls events coincides with the active power of the erotic look, both giving a satisfying sense of omnipotence" to the spectator (L. Mulvey, "Visual Pleasure and Narrative Cinema," *Screen* 16 [1975] 6-18, 12).

[15] Whether or not marriages were sworn either ordinarily or in special circumstances, and whether or not the "spreading the garment" constituted marriage, the combination in v 8 of Yahweh spreading the skirt, swearing and entering a covenant, and declaring that Jerusalem is "his," may be understood to constitute marriage. Note that in Ruth 3:13 Boaz does swear an oath, but the question of whether or not he spreads his skirt, either figuratively or literally, is left open. Boaz does promise that he will see to it that Ruth is redeemed, and this in itself may constitute "spreading the skirt," if spreading the skirt means only "offering protection." If, however, spreading the skirt is part of a marriage agreement, Boaz may only promise that he will "spread the skirt" if the other redeemer does not.

[16] The word "blood" is in the plural form, which could designate either her birth blood (cf. Lev 12:4) or her menstrual blood (cf. Lev 20:18). Irwin (*Problem*, 161) dismisses the possibility that Yahweh cleanses the woman of her menstrual blood as "so much disgusting absurdity," apparently overlooking the disgusting absurdity of the alternate possibility; that the girl has been left from infancy until adolescence in her birth blood (cf., e.g., Greenberg, *Ezekiel 1-20*, 278). In either case the image is disturbing, the more so because it casts Yahweh simultaneously in the roles of father, husband, and mother or female servant. (See M. Malul, *Studies*, 161-79, on ancient Near Eastern traditions of anointing or cleansing the bride prior to the wedding. This action, though sometimes performed by the prospective father-in-law, is never performed by the future husband.) Malul ("Adoption of Foundlings," 98n) is probably correct that the two forms of unclean blood have "coalesced" in the author's mind.

infancy. He then outfits and feeds her, and makes her "perfect in beauty" (v 10-14). Once perfected by Yahweh, Jerusalem's fame spreads to the nations, making her the object of admiring, rather than scornful, gazes.

The clothing in which Yahweh dresses his bride reflects Ezekiel's focus on Jerusalem as the location of the temple. The woman's clothing is more elegant than any other described in the Bible. In fact, the woman is clothed in material (*tḥš*) mentioned elsewhere *only* as the covering for the tabernacle and its cultic paraphernalia (e.g., Exod 25:5; 26:14; 35:7, 23; Num 4:6, 8, 10). Jerusalem's clothing includes *rqmh* and *šš* (v 10). The root *rqm* is most commonly used to describe the priestly garments and the curtains of the wilderness tabernacle (Exod 26:36; 27:16; 28:39; 35:35; 36:37; 38:18, 23; 39:29), and is often used in conjunction with *šš*, the fabric of the priestly vestments and tabernacle curtains (e.g., Exod 25:4; 26:1, 31, 36; 28:5, 6, 8). Outside of Ezek 16:10, the two roots are used together exclusively to describe the materials and furnishings of the tabernacle (Exod 26:36; 27:16; 28:39; 35:35; 36:37; 38:18; 39:29). The woman who is "fit to be queen" (v 13) is adorned with the same materials that adorn Yahweh's holy place,[17] and is fed *slt* and *šmn* (v 13), offerings prescribed for the tabernacle (e.g. Lev 2:7; Num 6:15; 7:13, 19; 8:8).

Throughout her rise from bloody near-death to cleansed and ritually adorned perfection, Jerusalem has remained passive while Yahweh has been active, passing by, gazing, covering, swearing, taking, cleansing, and adorning. In vv 15-34 the situation is reversed. Yahweh maintains control only by virtue of his role (through Ezekiel) as the narrator; within the narrative Jerusalem is the active party, and Yahweh is passive.

Against the theory that the plural always indicates "violently shed blood," see Kedar-Kopfstein, "*dām*."

The blood washed off by the bridegroom could also be the blood of first intercourse. If this were the case, then the sexual and marital significance of the "spreading the skirt" and "entering a covenant" in v 8 would be confirmed. There is, however, no evidence as to the husband's responsibilities regarding the blood of first intercourse (if this is what is meant by the "signs of virginity," then Deut 22:15 suggests that the woman's parents continue to exercise a role in this regard).

[17] This association between the clothing of Yahweh's wife and her symbolic identity as the temple/tabernacle is made explicit in the Targum: "I clothed you in embroidered garments . . . and I put costly shoes on your feet. And I consecrated priests from among you that they may serve before Me in linen headgear, and the high priest in colorful vestments. . . . And I placed My tabernacle in your midst, set with gold and silver and a curtain of linen and colored cloth and embroidery" (S. Levey, ed. *The Targum of Ezekiel* [The Aramaic Bible 13; Wilmington, DE: Michael Glazier, 1987] 63).

The structure of 16:1-43 is chiastic;[18] vv 1-14 tell the rise of Jerusalem from exposed infant to pampered queen, and vv 15-43 describe her decline, to end in the state in which she began, in naked and bloodied abandonment. Each step of Jerusalem's rise is matched with a step in her decline.

Jerusalem's infidelity (*znh*) is described in vv 15-22 as idolatry;[19] the gifts given by Yahweh in v 13, gold, silver, and fine clothing, Jerusalem gives to "male images," offering them Yahweh's food and incense as a "pleasant aroma." Starting from the pinnacle of perfection in v 14, Jerusalem systematically divests herself of the privileges granted her by Yahweh. Fine food and clothing, the last gifts given by Yahweh, are the first to be given away. The gifts given to Jerusalem in 16:10-14, and now given away to her lovers, are not the ordinary food and clothing of even the most honored woman, but the construction materials and offerings (*slt* and *šmn*) prescribed for the wilderness tabernacle. The "perfection" Jerusalem reaches in v 14 reflects the presence of Yahweh's sanctuary. Thus, when in vv 15-22, Jerusalem reallocates Yahweh's gifts, she uses them in a manner dictated by their original function. The food and clothing continue to be used as cult paraphernalia, while the identity of the cult is changed. Jerusalem's adornment in *rqmh* and *tḥš* in vv 10-14 identified her as bearer of the sanctuary; in vv 15-22 Jerusalem's use of her food (temple offerings) and clothing (temple furnishings) in encounters with "other gods" specifically violates her function as Yahweh's cult center.

Prior to dressing Jerusalem as his sanctuary in vv 10-14, Yahweh had cleansed her of the unclean blood that had defiled her since birth (v 9). In vv 20-22, having removed the signs of her cultic identity, Jerusalem continues to mirror in her decline the steps of her ascent, defiling herself again with unclean blood. Earlier her mother's (uterine) blood and her own menstrual blood had clung to her; now she is again polluted by blood, blood tangentially associated with her own body—she sheds the

---

[18] Talmon and Fishbane ("The Structuring of Biblical Books") explicate a similar use of chiastic structuring in Ezek 13:2-23 (though no analysis of chiasm in Ezekiel 16 has been published to date).

[19] Jerusalem's idolatry is described in sexual terms; she prostitutes herself (*znh*) with "every passerby," even making "male [phallic?] images" (v 17) with which to prostitute herself. The vocabulary of literal, cultic activity, however, is used along with the figurative vocabulary of sexual activity. Thus the "high places" and "incense" employed by the woman represent, simply, high places and incense, blurring the distinction between tenor and vehicle.

blood of her children. Offering her children to her idols, she brings pollution and bloodguilt upon herself.[20]

Having enumerated Jerusalem's cultic offences, Ezekiel moves on to chronicle the next phase of her decline (vv 23-34). The story of Jerusalem's adoption by and marriage to Yahweh (vv 6-14) took place in two parallel sections, one depicting Jerusalem's infancy (vv 6-7) and one her adolescence (vv 8-14). Each section was introduced by the announcement that Yahweh "passed by" the young Jerusalem. The story of Jerualem's decline in vv 15-43 is similarly divided into two sections marked by the "passing by" of men, in this case, not Yahweh but Jerusalem's illicit lovers (vv 15, 25). Jerusalem's degradation is described in v 15 and again in v 25 as infidelity with "every passerby." The two phases of infidelity correspond to the two phases of Jeruslem's youth (vv 1-7, 8-14), when Yahweh was the passerby to whom she was available.

Jerusalem first prostitutes herself on the high places (vv 15-22) through her idolatry. She next builds public platforms (vv 24-25) on which to prostitute herself, again with "every passerby." Now the passersby are not gods, but foreign nations: Egypt, Assyria, and Chaldea. The depiction of Jerusalem's infidelities with Egypt, Assyria, and Chaldea is clear and detailed enough to suggest that Ezekiel is referring to specific incidents in Jerusalem's history, rather than to foreign alliances in general. In particular, Yahweh's claim that he diminished Jerusalem's "portion" (hq; v 27), handing her over to the Philistines because of her liaison with Egypt, fits the situation following Hezekiah's rebellious alliance with Egypt in 705, after which Sennacherib gave Judean territory to the loyal Philistines.[21] Judah then resubmitted to

---

[20] Both idolatry (Jer 7:30; Ezek 5:11; 2 Chron 36:14) and corpse contamination (Num 19:13, 20; Ezek 9:7) are said to pollute the temple, as does the sacrifice of children to Molech. In fact, corpse pollution and child sacrifice would involve Jerusalem in two of only three activities that are specifically said to pollute the sanctuary (D. Wright, *The Disposal of Impurity: Elimination Rites in the Bible and in Hittite and Mesopotamian Literature* [SBLDS 101; Atlanta: Scholars, 1987] 19; cf. Frymer-Kensky, "Pollution," 406). The third action cited as polluting the sanctuary is "sexual impurity" (Lev 15:31). The use in Ezek 16:15-22 of the sexual metaphor thus allows the prophet to combine an accusation of sexual pollution (at the level of the vehicle) with the charges of idolatrous child sacrifice (at the level of the tenor), with the result that the woman Jerusalem, the site of Yahweh's holy place, is accused simultaneously of all three types of temple pollution.

[21] See *ANET*, 288. Sennacherib claims that having defeated Hezekiah, he "reduced his country, but . . . increased the tribute" demanded from the Judean monarch. Within the marriage metaphor, Yahweh's diminishing Jerusalem's allotted "portion" may signify his withdrawal of material support from his unfaithful wife. (Cf.

Assyrian domination (v 28) until Assyria's fall to Babylon.[22] Jerusalem's prostitution with the nations (vv 23-24) corresponds, within the chapter's chiastic structure, to Yahweh's entering a covenant with Jerusalem in v 8. Just as Jerusalem has forfeited (in vv 15-22) her cultic status as Yahweh's most holy place (bestowed in vv 10-14), in her alliances with foreign nations she similarly forfeits her political status (established in v 8) as Yahweh's covenant partner.[23]

In the final section of his condemnation of Jerusalem's political "prostitution" (vv 30-34), Yahweh describes Jerusalem's prostitution as more perverted than that of other women. Playing on the fact that Jerusalem must pay tribute to those with whom she has illicit liaisons, Yahweh mockingly claims that his wife is no common prostitute. On the contrary; ordinary prostitutes are paid by their clients, while Jerusalem must pay hers. The joke portrays Jerusalem as unnatural in every respect, an impression achieved by reversing the role of the metaphor's tenor and vehicle. Throughout most of the narrative metaphor, Jerusalem's cultic and political activities, the metaphoric tenor, govern the use of the vehicle. The political reality, for example, that Jerusalem had alliances with Egypt, Assyria, and Chaldea, governs the portrayal of her sexual partners as these three nations. The vehicle of sexuality is used to make Jerusalem's normal political activities seem abnormal. Likewise, Ezekiel's

---

Greengus, "Textbook Case," who cites situations in which the unfaithful wife forfeits her estate, or is herself sold into slavery. In all cases of adultery, however, the forfeiture of property is in addition to divorce.)

[22] Jerusalem's prostitution with Chaldea (v 29) is problematic. It could be a reference to the treaty with Nebuchadrezzar in 604, but given the prior collapse of Assyria, Jerusalem could not be charged with abandoning Assyria for Chaldea at that time. Alternatively, the move from Assyria to Chaldea could reflect Hezekiah's visit from the representatives of the Chaldean "Merodoch-baladan," reported in 2 Kgs 20:12-15 (Isa 39:1-4). If so, Ezekiel would be presenting the sequence of events as set out in 2 Kings 18-20 (Isaiah 36-39), that Sennacherib withdrew from Judah (2 Kgs 19:35-37; Isa 37:33-38) *before* the visit of Merodoch-baladan (2 Kgs 20:12f; Isaiah 39). This sequence is probably inaccurate, given that Merodoch-baladan's revolt against Assyra came during the reign of Sargon, around 713 (see *ABC*, 75-77; *ARAB* §66; J. H. Hayes and S. A. Irvine *Isaiah, the Eighth-Century Prophet: His Times and His Preaching* [Nashville: Abingdon, 1987] 272), whereas Sennacherib's confrontation with Hezekiah did not occur until 701 (*ANET*, 288).

[23] Despite the almost point for point correspondence between Jerusalem's "prostitutions" and events in Judean history, the specific nature of Jerusalem's offense is not clear. Though it is a commonplace that Yahweh (as king) considered any international alliance a breach in Israel's covenant obligation of exclusive loyalty to Yahweh, in Ezekiel Yahweh also functions as the guarantor of international covenants, whose name is dishonored by their violation (see, e.g., Ezek 17:18-19).

description of Jerusalem's child sacrifice becomes all the more shocking because it is described as the action of a mother. In Yahweh's charge of "abnormal" prostitution, however, Ezekiel reverses the role of tenor and vehicle. Defining *prostitution*, the vehicle, as normal, Yahweh claims that Jerusalem's actual activities (the payment of tribute) do not conform to the norm. Jerusalem is thus described in 16:1-43 as perverse, first, because her actions are like prostitution, and then, in vv 32-34 because, once defined as a prostitute, her actions seem unlike those of a "normal" prostitute.

In vv 35-43 Yahweh sentences Jerusalem to punishment, completing her own abandonment of her once-exalted condition. As in the account of his favor (vv 6-14), so again in his revenge (vv 35-43), Yahweh is active and Jerusalem passive. Yahweh hands her over to her lovers to be exposed (v 37), recapitulating in his rage the reversal Jerusalem herself has accomplished in her promiscuity; because she has become guilty of bloodshed, Yahweh "puts blood" upon her (v 38), and because she has offered her clothes and jewelery to her lovers, her lovers now strip her of clothing and jewels (v 39).[24] Stoning her, burning her houses,[25] and slicing her open with swords, they abandon her just as she was first abandoned, naked and exposed, the bloody and dead or dying object of scorn.

Ezekiel recasts the story of Yahweh's adulterous wife as a two-part story, each part of which takes place in two stages: Yahweh enters by two stages into a relationship with Jerusalem, and Jerusalem passes through two stages of adultery against him. The nature of these two stages is especially clear in the description of Jerusalem's "prostitution." The woman prostitutes herself with two groups of "passersby": gods (vv 15-22) and foreign powers (vv 23-43). Ezekiel, as noted above, departs from the pattern of Hosea and Jeremiah in consistently distinguishing between idolatry and inappropriate foreign alliances in his depiction of

---

[24] The lovers' action is logically inconsistent within the context of the narrative; she has already given away the clothing they supposedly strip from her. Symbolically, however, "poetic justice" (as well as chiastic symmetry) is achieved by portraying the woman's ex-lovers stripping her of the beautiful clothing with which Yahweh had once clothed her, and which she had misused.

[25] The burning of the woman's "houses" is an especially clear example of the "intrusion of referent" (Greenberg, *Ezekiel 1-20*, 287). The woman is punished by having "her," that is, the city's houses burned. Irwin (*Problem*, 160) considers vss 40-42 to have "lost their clue," because the presence of an entire army represents a disproportionate use of force against a single woman, "however bad she may be."

Jerusalem's infidelity.[26] Ezekiel, however, by describing each form of infidelity as taking place with a different group of "passersby," clearly separates Jerusalem's idolatry from its political alliances, and dwells at some length on the horrors of each.[27]

In describing idolatry and foreign dependency as separate offenses, Ezekiel also highlights the two aspects of Jerusalem's relationship with Yahweh that are violated by idolatry and foreign alliances respectively. In idolatry Jerusalem violates the cultic obligation to have no gods before Yahweh (Exod 20:3) and destroys the cultic purity that allows Yahweh to remain present among the people (Exod 33:5; Lev 15:31). In political alliances, Jerusalem violates her covenant obligation to Yahweh as king, simultaneously forfeiting his protection and defiling the divine name.[28]

The chiastic structure of 16:1-43 makes it clear that in his use of the adultery metaphor Ezekiel not only separates these two types of infidelity, but understands these two infidelities as transgressing separate aspects of Jerusalem's obligation to Yahweh. The story of Jerusalem's rise and fall follows this chiasm:

> A. Jerusalem is dying; naked, *bloody*, abandoned (vv 1-5).
>
> B. **Passerby: Yahweh—**
>
>   adopts her, enters covenant of marriage (vv 6-8).
>
> C. **Passerby: Yahweh—**
>
>   washes off *blood*, dresses her as tabernacle (vv 9-14).
>
> C'. **Passerby: Idols—**

---

[26] Jeremiah, for example, mixes the imagery of foreign dependency (e.g., drinking the waters of the Nile and the Euphrates; 2:18) with the language of idolatry (bending over "on every high hill and under every green tree" in 2:20, or naming stone and tree as mother and father; 2:27), but elaborates neither in detail.

[27] It is unclear whether Ezekiel, in distinguishing between cultic and political infidelity, is creating a new conceptual distinction, or merely emphasizing the "adulterous" aspects of each of two recognized types of infidelity. Whereas the metaphoric use of *znh* in extraprophetic texts is confined to cultic violations ("prostituting oneself after other gods"; Exod 34:15; Judg 2:17, and so on), earlier prophetic use of the metaphor need not include idolatry as an aspect of infidelity at all (cf. the "faithful city" of Isa 1:21, whose "prostitution" consists of domestic injustices).

[28] Cf. the covenant made in 2 Kgs 11:17 among Yahweh, the king, and the people, that the people would belong to Yahweh (and cf. the similar agreement made before Yahweh by Josiah, in which the people participate, in 2 Kgs 23:3; and see Weinfeld, "bĕrîth").

> Jerusalem uses clothing and food for idols,
>
> sheds *blood* of children (vv 15-22).

B'. **Passerby:** Foreign men—

> Jerusalem enters into relationships with
>
> foreign powers (violates covenant; vv 23-34).

A'. Yahweh "puts *blood* on" Jerusalem; she is exposed,

> slaughtered, abandoned (vv 35-43).

The chiasm illuminates the premises governing Ezekiel's separation of idolatry from foreign alliances. First, the marriage between Yahweh and Jerusalem is a matter of covenant (section B): similarly, it is covenant that is at issue when Jerusalem enters into relationships with foreign powers (section B'). Second, the marriage between Yahweh and Jerusalem describes the conceptual and topographic exclusivity implied by Jerusalem's status as Yahweh's cult center (section C): she is, physically, *holy* to Yahweh, and it is her trespass against Yahweh's sancta, the ritual objects and sacred space, that Ezekiel expresses as Jerusalem's "prostitution" with idols (section C'). Jerusalem's status as covenant partner and as cult center are both established by Yahweh, when he "passes by" and sees the need of Jerusalem. The violation of both these two statuses occurs when Jerusalem, in her pride, makes herself available to "any passerby." Finally, the chiasm emphasizes the similarity of Jerusalem's end to her beginning: bloody, naked, rejected, and dead or dying.

Ezekiel shapes his metaphorical account of Jerusalem's infidelity to correspond to the two types of trespass of which he considers Jerusalem guilty: violation of covenant (defilement of the sacred name) and trespass against temple sancta (defilement of sacred space).[29] Because all covenants are sworn in the name of the deity, covenant violation is itself a form of trespass against sancta (dishonoring the divine name). Hence, both kinds of trespass contribute to the profanation of the temple and to Yahweh's consequent abandonment. Ezekiel employs the vehicle of marital infidelity to depict two tenors, cultic and political infidelity, which result in Yahweh's dishonor and abandonment of both his covenanted protection of Jerusalem and his residence in its temple. The structure of Ezek 16:1-43 reflects and expresses Ezekiel's understanding

---

[29] J. Milgrom (*Cult and Conscience,* esp. 13-22) describes in detail the relationship between oath violation and sancta trespass proper.

that even as Jerusalem's obligation to Yahweh is twofold, so also is her betrayal. While the rhetoric of Ezekiel's structure is an important aspect of his reuse of the adultery metaphor, the twofold structure of Jerusalem's infidelity does not explain the power of Ezek 16:1-43, how a metaphor that was commonplace by the sixth century is in this passage rendered striking and disturbing. Much of the emotional power of the metaphor derives, not from its logical or rhetorical structure, but from the intensity of its subject matter.[30] Sex and sexual infidelity naturally arouse a range of strong and conflicting emotions. Further, in a world in which male honor is bound to female sexual behavior, female infidelity is both socially and personally threatening to the male.[31] Finally, because the cuckolded husband of the metaphor is no mortal, but Israel's male, warrior god,[32] the entire male community is threatened by its god's loss of honor.

The visceral power inherent in the marriage metaphor itself is, however, also insufficient to account for the particular intensity of this metaphor in Ezekiel. Ezekiel 16 is somehow more offensive than the same metaphor in Hosea and Jeremiah. The metaphor occurs in many forms in the Hebrew Bible, but only Ezekiel 16 was banned by the rabbis from public reading (*Meg.* 4:10). A key element in Ezekiel's uniquely visceral rendering of the marriage metaphor is his focus on the woman and especially on the female body as both defiled and defiling.

Ezekiel exploits fully the unique ability of the female body to exhibit not only the defilement of adultery, but also every type of blood pollution, from menstruation and childbirth to murder. The woman is depicted graphically and repeatedly as unfaithful (and therefore unclean; cf. Ezek 18:6; Lev 18:24). She is also, however, characterized by pollution with every type of unclean blood. At birth she is left in the unclean blood of her mother's womb. Upon reaching puberty, she apparently remains in the impurity of her unwashed menstrual blood, until washed by her husband. Finally, she incurs bloodguilt through the murder of her own children. Horrified at her bloody deed, Yahweh laments, "You did not

---

[30] On the use of the natural emotional force of the marriage metaphor as a rhetorical device, see E. J. Adler, "Covenant as Marriage," 32-42, 70-93.

[31] See, e.g., Pitt-Rivers, *The Fate of Shechem*, 78-83, 161; Brandes, "Wounded Stags," and Wiken, "Shame and Honour."

[32] The intensity of the need to avenge Yahweh's (and thus the community's) honor may also be related to Ezekiel's historical situation. Setel ("Prophets and Pornography," 94-95) discusses possible connections between Judah's (and Yahweh's) military defeat, and the subsequent increased restriction of women as a means of reasserting the male god's (and the male community's) power.

remember the days of your youth, when you were naked and exposed, wallowing in your blood" (v 22). None of these images of the bloody woman has direct precedent in earlier prophetic texts;[33] the insistent focus on the bloody pollution of Jerusalem's body is distinctive to Ezekiel.

Ezekiel's emphasis on Jerusalem's bloodiness is directly related to his concern over Yahweh's abandonment of the Jerusalem sanctuary. Control over the life-bearing power of blood is central to the priestly purity system, since the correct or incorrect handling of blood determines the cleanliness or defilement of the sanctuary, and therefore Yahweh's ability to dwell within it.[34] All shed blood is to be ritually offered, preferably at the sanctuary itself;[35] improperly shed blood pollutes the altar, and this pollution can only be removed by the blood of the sin offering (or in some cases, not at all).[36] Ezekiel's charge that Jerusalem is irremediably polluted with unclean blood explains the necessity for Yahweh to abandon the city.

Ezekiel draws more explicitly than the earlier prophets the connection between the sexuality of Yahweh's metaphoric wife and the sanctity of the Jerusalem temple. Moreover, Ezekiel does not depict Jerusalem as indiscriminately polluted, but polluted specifically by uterine blood.[37]

---

[33] Nahum's cry, "Woe to the bloody city" (3:1), is used by Ezekiel only in passages where Jerusalem is not explicitly personified (24:6; cf. 22:2; and see discussion below). Jeremiah accuses Jerusalem of having "the blood of the innocent poor" on her skirts (2:34). Like Nahum, Jeremiah accuses the city of responsibility for the lives of innocent citizens, an accusation made by Ezekiel outside chaps 16 and 23. Ezekiel's personified Jerusalem is defiled exclusively by blood that is in some sense her own—blood accompanying her birth and blood that has issued from her body.

[34] On ritual pollution as a determinant of Israel's history, see Frymer-Kensky ("Pollution," 399, 409-12).

[35] Although Deut 12:15-16 allows for secular slaughter, Ezekiel seems to subscribe to the rubrics prescribed by Lev 17:1-9, which defines secular slaughter as a form of bloodshed. Ezekiel implicitly contradicts Deuteronomy's instructions to pour out blood on the earth (12:16, 24) by his horror in 24:7 that "the bloody city" has poured out blood without covering it (on the relationship between Ezekiel and the Holiness Code, see A. Hurvitz, *A Linguistic Study of the Relationship between the Priestly Source and the Book of Ezekiel* [Cahiers de la Revue Biblique 20; Paris, Gabalda, 1982]; J. Levenson, *Theology of the Program of Restoration of Ezekiel 40-48* [HSM 10; Atlanta: Scholars, 1986]).

[36] The gravest forms of pollution "cannot be rectified by ritual purification" (Frymer-Kensky, "Pollution," 408; cf. Milgrom, "Israel's Sanctuary"). Ultimately, the point of no return is reached, and purification is of no avail.

[37] The blood of Jerusalem's children is, of course, only symbolically connected with her uterus as their place of origin, though the connection is one Yahweh makes by his charge that in murdering her children, Jerusalem forgets the days when she

Given Ezekiel's sensitivity to the symbolic connection between the womb of Yahweh's wife and the inner sanctum of Yahweh's temple, his graphic depiction of a Jerusalem polluted from within by unclean blood has disasterous implications. At the level of the vehicle, Yahweh's wife is unclean in both her behavior (adultery) and her substance. Intercourse, the penetration of her unclean body, would be an abomination, even if performed by a (merely) clean male;[38] such contact between the Holy One and a bloody woman would be unthinkable. At the level of the tenor, the implications are equally severe. If the sanctuary has become the locus of unclean blood, it is impossible for the Holy to remain within it.

In addition to depicting Jerusalem as characteristically defiled with uterine blood, Ezekiel uses the language of looking and seeing to emphasize the distance in purity and in power between Jerusalem and Yahweh:[39] Yahweh sees—Jerusalem is seen. The act of looking establishes the power of the one who looks over the one seen[40] and creates a boundary between subject and "other." The object of a gaze is by definition "objectified" and is defined de facto as "other." In 16:1-14 Yahweh

---

herself was "wallowing in [uterine] blood," having been left by her own mother to die (v 22).

[38] Cf. Lev 20:18. The abomination of intercourse with a menstruating woman seems to combine reverence for blood as the bearer of life (and, flowing, a sign of death; see J. Milgrom, "A Prolegomenon to Leviticus 17:11," in *Studies in Cultic Theology and Terminology* [SJLA 36; Leiden: Brill, 1983] 96-103; and cf. anthropological studies such as M. Douglas, *Purity and Danger*; A. S. Meigs, "A Papuan Perspective on Pollution," *Man* 13 [1978] 304-18; and P. R. Sanday, *Female Power and Male Dominance: On the Origins of Sexual Inequality* [Cambridge: Cambridge University, 1981]) with male "dread of woman" (on which see, inter alia, K. Horney, "The Dread of Woman," in *Feminine Psychology* [New York: Norton, 1967] 133-46; and H. R. Hays, *The Dangerous Sex: The Myth of Feminine Evil* [New York: G. P. Putnam's Sons, 1964]). Horney observes that "a woman becomes doubly sinister in the presence of the bloody manifestations of her womanhood" (135). That is, when woman is herself perceived as a potentially dangerous "other," menstruation heightens an already present threat.

[39] Distance is thus also established between Jerusalem and both Ezekiel and the reader, who "see" her only through Yahweh's eyes.

[40] On the role of "looking" in establishing subjectivity, and for a survey of the discussion on "the subject," see K. Silverman, *The Subject of Semiotics* (New York: Oxford University, 1983). Cf. also M. Bal, *Narratology: An Introduction to the Theory of Narrative* (Toronto: University of Toronto, 1985) 100-02; T. de Laurentis, *Alice Doesn't: Feminism, Semiotics, Cinema* (Bloomington: Indiana University, 1984); S. Gubar, "Representing Pornography: Feminism, Criticism, and Depictions of Female Violation," *Critical Inquiry* 13 (1987) 712-41; A. Kuhn, *The Power of the Image: Essays on Representation and Sexuality* (London: Routledge & Kegan Paul, 1985); Mulvey, "Visual Pleasure"; K. Silverman, "Masochism and Subjectivity," *Framework* 12 (1980) 2-9.

continually draws attention to Jerusalem's body and to its state of shameful and vulnerable exposure. Her birth is the story of the care *not* given her body when "no eye pitied" her (v 5), and of her disposal (technically, her exposure), naked and bloody, in the field. Yahweh passes by, sees her, naked and polluted "in [her] blood," and assumes the power she lacks, namely, power over her own life. Passing by again, he observes her breasts and pubic hair, exposed to any passerby (including, through the narrative, the reader). The nakedness of Jerusalem metonymically signifies her shame;[41] exposed and despised, she is therefore despicable. Yahweh replaces her nakedness, symbolic of shame, with clothing symbolic of the honor with which she is clothed by virtue of her marriage to him. Only when covered by Yahweh's splendor does the girl become "beautiful," the object of admiring gazes.[42]

Heedless of the days when she was "naked and exposed" (v 22), however, Jerusalem gives away her clothing along with the honor it represents and "exposes her nakedness" (v 36) through adultery.[43] In punishment for her self-exposure, Yahweh gathers the men who were once his rivals, to "see her nakedness" as he uncovers her (v 37).[44] They will also strip her "in the sight of many women" (v 41), completing her shaming and avenging Yahweh's honor.[45] Throughout the passage

---

[41] The shaving (and thus, exposure) of the pudenda (a word derived from the Latin pudere, "to be ashamed") was part of the public shaming of the adulteress in the ancient Near East (cf. Greengus, "Textbook Case," 39-43; Westbrook, "Adultery," 559).

[42] Mulvey comments on the traditional role of the woman as connotating "to-be-looked-at-ness" ("Visual Pleasure," 11), that is, to be looked at by the male.

[43] The phrase in v 36, hššpk nhštk, is obscure, referring to something "poured out" in the woman's prostitution. Greenberg (*Ezekiel 1-20*, 285) relates the noun nhš to the Akkadian nahšati, a "morbid genital outflow [of a woman]." Disparaging reference to the woman's genital excretions would be consistent with the lurid fascination with female bodily fluids that characterizes the passage.

[44] The exposure of Jerusalem by Yahweh before his peers (Jerusalem's other lovers), as "revealed" to Ezekiel, and by Ezekiel to *his* peers (the implied male readers) bears a striking resemblance to the effect achieved by the cinematic technique of the "showgirl," in which a woman performs for, or is otherwise displayed before a group of men within the narrative, so that "the gaze of the spectator and that of the male characters in the film are neatly combined" (Mulvey, "Visual Pleasure," 12). Ezekiel (who, in this case, would have a role analogous to that of the camera) and his audience of readers mimic the power of exposure shared by Yahweh and the crowd of lovers.

[45] The act of exposing Jerusalem before other women serves a double purpose. First, at the level of the tenor, Jerusalem's shame will mean humiliation before other city-states, most notably the "daughters of the Philistines" already mentioned in v 27.

Jerusalem is the object of powerful gazes, whether admired because she is covered by Yahweh's "majesty" (v 14), or the naked object of contempt. Ezekiel's relentless focus on Jerusalem's body as appraised by Yahweh, her ex-lovers, and the implied (male) reader, presents her as simultaneously fascinating and perverse. This emphasis on Jerusalem's shameful exposure to the male gaze heightens the sense of mingled fascination and disgust provoked by the persistence of her bloody uncleanness.

Through his description of Jerusalem's "clothing" in 16:10-14, Ezekiel recasts the traditional marriage metaphor in terms of Jerusalem's status as the bearer of Yahweh's temple. He then further reshapes the traditional depiction of Jerusalem to define her as utterly polluted with unclean blood and as the continual object of men's shaming gazes. The resulting version of the metaphor of Jerusalem's infidelity compounds an already emotionally laden image with both the ritual horror of contact between the holy and the unclean, and a visceral, if less articulated, horror at the bloody otherness of the female body.

Expressing his outrage over the defiled temple in terms of the metaphor of adultery, Ezekiel uncovers the full implications of that metaphor. If the city is a woman, then that woman is a whore. If the temple within that city has been (as in chap 8 Ezekiel sees it has been) defiled from within, then the woman's uterus has itself become the source of defiling pollution. Compounding the horror of the actual pollution of Yahweh's house with horror at the implied pollution of his bed, the marriage metaphor makes the literal pollution of the temple seem all the more repulsive. The emotional force of metaphor adds to the perceived horror of the literal situation.

B. *Jerusalem Shamed: 16:44-58*

Compared with the first half of the chapter, 16:44-58 is surprisingly dry and prosaic. After repeating (v 45) the ignoble ancestry attributed to Jerusalem in 16:3, Yahweh claims that the unfaithful Jerusalem has unfaithful sisters, Samaria and Sodom. The structure and rhetoric of the section are straightforward: Yahweh argues that Samaria and Sodom

---

Second, at the level of the vehicle, the public exposure of the adulteress served not only to transfer shame from the cuckolded husband onto the publicly humiliated wife, but also had an effect on the women: not only were the women "warned" (cf. Ezek 23:48) of the dangers of disobedience; by their participation as spectators, they shared in the objectifying role of the male spectators, identifying themselves with the community and its norms, and thus further excluding the adulteress.

were bad, but Jerusalem is worse, making her sisters look righteous by comparison. Jerusalem must therefore suffer the shame of "justifying" her infamously wicked sisters. Yahweh's claim that Jerusalem is worse than her sisters and must therefore suffer her shame, is repeated with variations three times in vv 46-52, after which Yahweh promises (vv 53-58) to restore all three cities. The promise of restoration follows the logic of the accusation; all three sisters will be restored, but Jerusalem will be ashamed at being the worst of the three. Jerusalem's shame, whether in punishment or in reconciliation, at being worse than those she was accustomed to mocking, is the entire content of the section, hammered home by repetition.

No specific accusation is brought against the woman Jerusalem in 16:44-58. Support for Yahweh's accusation must therefore come from the account of her actions in the first half of the chapter. Loosely based on Jeremiah's conclusion that "faithless Israel is more righteous than deceitful Judah" (3:11), Ezekiel's comparison, with its addition of a third, even more infamous sister, serves simply to elaborate the shame threatened in the preceding section, including Jerusalem's suffering in front of women who are themselves unrighteous (vv 28, 41; cf. 54, 57).

C. *Coda: Covenant, Cleansing, and Shame: 16:59-63*

The coda to chap 16 characteristically draws together elements from both of the larger sections of the chapter.[46] Themes and catchwords from vv 1-43 alternate with those of vv 44-58, but in a way that integrates them into a single argument. Yahweh concludes that he will "do to [Jerusalem] as [she] did" (v 59; cf. v 43), "in showing contempt for the oath by breaking the covenant." Jerusalem's violation of a covenant-oath can only refer to her violation in vv 23-24 (within the vehicle of marriage, through adultery, or at the level of the tenor, through competing international treaties) of the covenant made by Yahweh in v 8. Yahweh's claim in v 59 that Jerusalem has shown contempt for the oath is, however, the first mention that not only Yahweh, but also Jerusalem, was bound by an oath. Only Yahweh swears the oath in v 8, but both in v 59 and implicitly in the depiction of Jerusalem's political infidelity in vv 23-43, Jerusalem is held accountable as a covenant partner.[47] Just as Jerusalem has abandoned her

---

[46] See Greenberg, *Ezekiel 1-20*, 294-95.

[47] If, in cases where no male (the father or brother) had authority to receive a contract for the woman, a marriage could be established by the man swearing an oath to the woman (cf. Ruth 3:13 and see discussion in Chapter Two), then the lack of any mention here of Jerusalem's part in the covenant might constitute an accurate depic-

responsibility of exclusive fidelity to Yahweh, so Yahweh will abandon his responsibility for Jerusalem's preservation and safety.

After Jerusalem's punishment, "remembering" his covenant "in the days of [her] youth," Yahweh will establish an "everlasting covenant" with Jerusalem (v 60). The idea of Jerusalem's restoration is taken from vv 44-58, but the language includes vocabulary from the first half of the chapter. Although Jerusalem has refused to "remember the days of [her] youth" (vv 22, 43), Yahweh will both "remember" and honor the broken covenant of Jerusalem's youth. Only then will Jerusalem also "remember" (v 61) and "be ashamed" at her ascendancy over her two sisters. In vv 61-63 Ezekiel makes a clear connection between the two larger sections of the chapter. Jerusalem will "remember," as she failed to do in vv 1-43, but only when she experiences both the restoration and the shame predicted in vv 44-58. Yahweh will establish his covenant (v 62; cf. v 8), and Jerusalem will duly recognize Yahweh.

Although the "recognition formula"[48] ordinarily signals the end of a section, in this case Ezekiel continues both Yahweh's castigation and the interweaving of themes from the two sections: Jerusalem will "remember and she will be ashamed" (v 62). Jerusalem, he says, will never open her mouth again, when he has "purged" her of her actions (v 63).[49]

Yahweh's final action on Jerusalem's behalf is ambiguous. The verb *kpr* most frequently refers to the ritual purging of sin from the altar, and the usual expression for cleansing the altar on behalf of a group or individual is *kpr ʿl*.[50] The expression *kpr l* with a human object occurs else-

---

tion of a *marriage* covenant in which the man swore to the woman. This type of marriage covenant would have differed in form from a mutually sworn vassal treaty, whether between Yahweh and Israel, or between Israel and a suzerain power.

[48] See Zimmerli, *Ezekiel 1*, 37-38.

[49] In various ancient Near Eastern cultures, "opening of the mouth" (on which, and on the relationship between "mouth opening" and "mouth washing," see V. Hurowitz, "Isaiah's Impure Lips and Their Purification in Light of Akkadian Sources," *HUCA* 60 [1989] 39-89, esp. 48-49 n26 and 50-57; and cf. J. Kennedy, "Hebrew *pithon peh* in the Book of Ezekiel," *VT* 41 [1991] 233-35) was ordinarily a sign of divine status, and occasionally a sign of exceptional human purity. If Ezekiel is alluding to this tradition, then his claim that Jerusalem will no longer "open her mouth" when *he* has cleansed her could be interpreted as a revocation of her divine status (as consort) when he restores her. Such a revocation of the city's personification as the divine consort would be consistent with the striking absence of any personification of the holy city in the restoration of Ezek 40-48. Ironically, it is at the point that the city and temple are destroyed (and Jerusalem's mouth shut) that Ezekiel's own "mouth is opened" by Yahweh (24:27; 33:22).

[50] See J. Milgrom, "Prolegomenon," 97.

where only twice (Deut 21:8; Isa 22:14). In both these cases the expression refers, not to individual expiation via sacrifice, but to Yahweh's cleansing (or, in Isaiah 22, refusing to cleanse) the entire people.[51] The closest parallel to the expression in 16:63 is Num 35:33,[52] a reference to the cleansing of the land. Yahweh's ritual "cleansing" of the woman thus seems to be another allusion to Jerusalem as the locus of the temple. For Ezekiel, the sign of Jerusalem's restoration is not Yahweh's forgiveness of the people per se, but his cleansing of the holy place.

II. EZEKIEL 23

A. *The Two Sisters: 23:1-35*

Ezekiel 16, especially vv 1-43, depicts Jerusalem as initially, and perhaps irremediably, unclean, other, and excluded from the boundaries of cult and community. Simultaneously, Ezekiel's metaphoric depiction focuses on Jerusalem's special identity as Yahweh's covenant partner, and as locus of the temple, Yahweh's "holy place." This contradiction between the unclean "otherness" of the woman Jerusalem and her role as Yahweh's intimate is expressed through a chiastic narrative in which Yahweh rescues Jerusalem from the ownerless domain (the "field"), honors her with "perfection," and makes her "holy" to him, but Jerusalem responds by reverting to her native pollution and shaming Yahweh, who restores his honor by shaming her in return. Throughout the narrative, Jerusalem's nakedness or coveredness serve to represent her honor or shame. Yahweh, despite the temporary dishonor of Jerusalem's infidelity, maintains his position of control through his roles as both narrator and focalizer, watching, describing, and judging the always visible woman Jerusalem. The depiction of Jerusalem's shameful and shaming uncleanness begun in chap 16 is continued in chap 23. The language of looking and seeing, already significant in the earlier chapter, is developed in chap 23 as a means of denoting control or desired control of the other.

Like Ezekiel 16, chap 23 follows the common pattern of opening with a long section setting out the central argument (vv 1-35), continuing with a shorter section that elaborates a theme from the first section (vv

---

[51] On the syntax of *kpr*, see B. A. Levine, *In the Presence of the Lord* (SJLA 5; Leiden: Brill, 1974) 63-67.

[52] *l'rs l' ykppr lddm*, "the land cannot be cleansed of the blood."

36-45), and concluding with a coda that combines elements of the first two sections (vv 45-49).[53] In this case the coda combines not only elements from the main sections of chap 23, but from chap 16 as well.

Chapter 23 is more closely focused on the political history of Israel than is chap 16; a survey of Israel's and Judah's foreign alliances in 23:1-35 is followed in vv 36-45 with a detailed description of a specific, and presumably recent incident of transgression. Together, the account of the women's history of "adultery," plus the charge in vv 36-45 of specific, serious offenses, form the argument in a case brought by Yahweh against Israel, a case in which Ezekiel is called as judge (v 36). Verses 46-49 function as the verdict in the case, announcing the women's punishment.

Ezekiel 23:1-35 expands upon the story of Jerusalem in chap 16, combining themes from both earlier sections of the chapter. Like Ezek 16:44-58, 23:1-35 compares Jerusalem unfavorably with her sister, Samaria;[54] like 16:1-43, 23:1-35 tells of the promiscuous adultery of Yahweh's wife (now, wives). The story of the two sisters in chap 23, however, gives a different account of Jerusalem's youth than does 16:1-43. Whereas both Jerusalem and Samaria are said in chap 16 to be of mixed Amorite and Hittite origin (vv 3, 45), and Jerusalem's youth apparently takes place in Canaan, in 23:3 the women are said to have spent their youth in Egypt,[55] where already they "prostituted themselves."[56] In

---

[53] This division is generally accepted (cf. Zimmerli, *Ezekiel 1*, 480, 492; Wevers, *Ezekiel*, 133, 138), though vss 36-49 are taken as secondary by commentators such as Zimmerli and Irwin, who typically see in the development of an argument the work of a later redactor. The beginning of each section is clearly marked by both an introductory formula and a change in topic.

[54] The passage seems to be based more closely than is 16:44-58 on the comparison of the two sisters in Jer 3:6-11. Sodom, the third sister described in Ezek 16:44-58, drops out of the story, allowing Ezekiel to focus on the parallel histories of the Northern and Southern kingdoms.

[55] Ezekiel depicts the history of Jerusalem as an exact parallel to that of Samaria. The goal of describing the "parallel lives" of the two sisters affects Ezekiel's depiction of the sisters' origins. First, the capital cities, rather than the nation, are said to have been in Egypt, and second, Ezekiel anachronistically retrojects the division of Israel onto the pre-exodus period.

[56] The tenor of this "youthful prostitution," whether idolatry or a political alliance, is ambiguous. Any reference to Israel's youth in Egypt calls up images of the pre-exodus period (cf. Hos 2:17 [Eng 2:15]). Ezekiel elsewhere (20:7-8) accuses Jerusalem of idolatry already in Egypt, an accusation that would support reading the youthful "prostitution" of 23:3 as idolatry. Ezekiel's claim, however, that in this "prostitution" the women's "breasts were fondled and their virginity taken," suggests political, rather than cultic infidelity, first because idols are not generally credited with *actions* in the OT, and especially because in 23:8 (and cf. v 21) Ezekiel says it was the

fact, only *after* their initial prostitution do the two women marry Yahweh.[57]

The women are given symbolic names, Oholah for Samaria and Oholibah for Jerusalem (v 4).[58] Yahweh tells the story of Oholah (vv 5-10) in four parts that can be identified almost point for point with events in the history of Samaria: (1) she prostitutes herself for the Assyrians, whose physical desirability and regalia are described in detail (vv 5-7a); (2) she defiles (*ṭmʾ*) herself with their idols (v 7b); (3) she continues ("did not abandon"; cf. 20:8) the prostitution she has practiced since her days in Egypt (v 8); and (4) Yahweh hands her over to the Assyrians, who expose and kill her (vv 9-10). These four episodes can easily be read as a history of Samaria's vassaldom. Beginning in 841-40, Samaria partici-pated in an alliance with Assyria (1),[59] an alliance which presumably in-

---

Egyptians who fondled the women's youthful breasts. This would suggest that Israel had an early political alliance with Egypt, which could also have entailed her acknowledgment of Egyptian gods.

[57] The claim that the women were sexually used before any alliance with Yahweh is unprecedented in the prophets. Though the claim of primal infidelity is inconsis-tent with the story in chap 16 of Jerusalem's foundling youth, it is entirely consistent with the implication of the story of chap 16 that Jerusalem was bad from the start. The charge that Israel was disobedient from the beginning is also made in the recita-tion of the exodus story in Ezekiel 20, in which Israel is said to have refused to "abandon the idols of Egypt"; that is, Israel's disobedience antedates even the exo-dus.

[58] The names are traditionally translated "She has a tent" for Samaria, and "My tent is in her" for Jerusalem (see Zimmerli, *Ezekiel 1*, 483-84, for a summary of the dis-cussion), referring to the independent sanctuary of Samaria and to Yahweh's pres-ence in the Jerusalem sanctuary. This interpretation is consistent with Ezekiel's depic-tion in 16:10-14 of Jerusalem as Yahweh's sanctuary, furnished not as the temple per se, but as the *tabernacle*. The reference in Ezek 41:1 to the temple building as a "tent" also supports Ezekiel's identification of the Jerusalem temple with the tabernacle.

In both chaps 16 and 23 a metaphorical connection is drawn between the women's "tents" and their sexual organs. This connection is not unique to Ezekiel. Mishnah describes women's sexual organs in architectural terms: within the woman are "a chamber, an ante-chamber, and an upper room: blood in the chamber is unclean; if it is found in the ante-chamber, . . . [it] is deemed unclean, since it is presumed to be from the fountain" (*The Mishnah.* H. Danby, ed.; Oxford: Oxford University, 1933. *Nid.* 2:5). Curiously, the Mishnaic tractate on purity and impurity is named "Oholoth," "tents." M. Bal (*Murder and Difference*, 102, 124) draws attention to the function of the tent of Jael ("blessed among women of the tent") in Judg 4-5 as the woman's private locus which the man enters for the purpose of intercourse. Note also that Rachel and Leah have separate tents (Gen 31:33), apparently their own quarters.

[59] *ANET*, 280-281.

cluded at least minimal participation in the Assyrian state cult (2).[60] Despite this alliance, Samaria under Hoshea participated in a rebellious alliance with (among others) Egypt (3)[61] and was consequently destroyed in 722-21 by Assyria (4).[62]

The story of Oholibah (vv 11-35) mirrors that of Oholah, except that the Southern sister is even worse than the Northern (cf. Ezek 16:44-58; Jer 3:5-11). The story of Oholibah, like that of her sister, consists of four distinct episodes: (1) Oholibah prostitutes herself with the Assyrians (v 12), whose regalia is exactly that described in vv 5-7a; (2) Yahweh says that Oholibah is "defiled" (*tmʾ*) in the same way as her sister (v 13), who had defiled herself with the idols of her lovers (v 7). At this point the parallel course of Oholibah's and Oholah's stories is interrupted by an account of the ways Oholibah was even worse than her sister (vv 14-18). Already prostituted to Assyria, Oholibah sees wall carvings of the Chaldeans and *their* attractive uniforms, and she lusts for, sends for, and defiles (*tmʾ*) herself with them; (3) Oholibah then returns to her sister's route, "remembering the days of her youth" (cf. 16:43), when she prostituted herself with Egypt (vv 19-21); (4) Yahweh therefore hands her over to her lovers (vv 22-35), who will expose and then destroy her.

Identifying the historical referents is more difficult in the story of Oholibah than in the story of Oholah. The initial alliance between Jerusalem and Assyria (1) could have been made at the same time as (and even subsumed under) that between Assyria and Samaria, in which case Jerusalem would naturally have been "defiled" (2) by her "lover's idols" in the same way as Samaria.[63] Jerusalem's next move, however, "expanding her market" by prostitution with the Chaldeans, is open to more widely differing interpretations. Twice in her history Jerusalem

---

[60] See M. Cogan, *Imperialism and Religion: Assyria, Judah, and Israel in the Eighth and Seventh Centuries B.C.E.* (SBLMS 19; Missoula, MT: Scholars, 1974), 44-49 for a review of the discussion on the invocation of the deities in vassal oaths. Cogan argues that the Assyrian vassal oath "implies obligatory recognition of Assyrian gods" (44), but also that "in vassal states the vassal's gods were formally invoked" in the swearing of the oath (48). According to D. Hillers (*Treaty-Curses*, 80) copies of treaties were "deposited in the temple of the national god." Cf. also M. Tsevat, "The Neo-Assyrian and Neo-Babylonian Vassal Oaths and the Prophet Ezekiel," *JBL* 78 (1959) 199-204; and R. Frankena, "The Vassal Treaties of Esarhaddon and the Dating of Deuteronomy," *OTS* 14 (1965) 122-54.

[61] 2 Kgs 17:3-4.

[62] 2 Kgs 17:5-6; *ANET*, 284.

[63] Judah is missing from Assyrian tribute lists until after Tiglath-Pilesar's 734/2 campaign, probably indicating that until that time it paid tribute through Israel (cf. *ARAB* I, §590; *ANET*, 283).

moved from alliance with Assyria to alliance with Babylon, and then to alliance with Egypt. In 714 Hezekiah entertained the ambassadors of the Chaldean Merodoch-baladan, who was at that time gathering support for rebellion against Assyria. When Babylon proved unable to stand up under Assyrian pressure, Hezekiah turned to Egypt, participating in a full-scale rebellion in 705. Following Sennacherib's reprisals, Jerusalem apparently remained loyal to Assyria until the latter fell to Babylonia in 605. Jerusalem then transferred loyalty from Assyria to Babylon a second time, although not in conjunction with rebellion. Within four years, however, the Judean Jehoiakim was part of a rebellious alliance led by Egypt. Thus the "prostitutions" of Jerusalem in Ezek 23:14-21 might refer to either the period 714-705, or the period beginning in 605 and continuing up to Ezekiel's own day.

Several factors support each possible referent. First, the fact that only in 714 and following did Jerusalem actually abandon Assyria for Babylon and then move on to Egypt supports interpretation of the passage as referring to the late eighth century. By the time Jerusalem became a Babylonian vassal in 604, Assyria had already capitulated to Nebuchadrezzar, and the new Babylonian alliance constituted no infidelity, at least not to Assyria.[64] Second, the arrival of the Babylonian emissaries in v 17 is reminiscent of the account of the visit of Merodoch-baladan's representatives as recorded in 2 Kgs 20:12-19 (Isaiah 39). Further, Ezekiel's reference in 16:27 to Sennacherib's gift of Judean territory to Philistia in 701 has already drawn attention to Jerusalem's behavior during this period.

The strongest argument against reading 23:14-21 as referring to events of the late eighth century is the probability that Ezekiel's primary concern was with the events of his own time. Within the passage itself, however, the greatest inconsistency with an eighth century setting lies in the account of the woman's punishment. First, while Yahweh recounts

---

[64] In fact, Assyria had not been the major power in the region for some time; various factors point to Egyptian hegemony in the region. Herodotus claims that Scythians attempting to invade Egypt in approximately 630 were stopped "in Palestine" by Psammeticus I (I, 105), who had also besieged and taken "Azotus" (Ashdod?) around 635 (II, 157). The Babylonian Chronicles record the Egyptians fighting as far east as Gablini in 616 (*ABC*, 91). Nineveh had been destroyed in 612, and when combined Egyptian and Assyrian forces went to meet the Babylonians at Haran in 610, it was the Pharaoh who not only killed the Judean king, but also claimed the authority to choose his replacement (2 Kgs 23:28-35). For a survey of the politics of the period, see J. M. Miller and J. H. Hayes, *A History of Ancient Israel and Judah* (Philadelphia: Westminster, 1986) 381-90.

the punishment of Oholah (vv 9-10) as having already occurred, Oholibah's punishment (vv 22-35) is depicted as yet to come, not as if it had occurred in 701. Moreover, that punishment is to be carried out by a coalition including "all the Assyrians," but apparently headed by the Babylonians (vv 22-23; 28), a scenario fitting Ezekiel's own time better than the end of the eighth century. The marauding army will strip Oholibah of her fine clothing and her treasure (v 26; cf. v 29, "all that you own"), a fate not experienced by Oholah, but which (in light of chap 16) suggests the looting of the Jerusalem temple. All these aspects of Oholibah's punishment fit the situation of the early sixth century better than that of the late eighth.

Neither historical scenario matches all the details of Ezekiel's account, though each is strongly suggested. A third possibility is that Ezekiel has intentionally combined elements from both episodes of Jerusalem's political history, to draw an implicit connection between past and present. What begins as a depiction of events under Hezekiah ends as an account of current events.[65] Jerusalem's eighth century infidelity (apparently alluded to both in 16:27 and here), though ancient history by the time of Ezekiel, was considered relevant to the events of the day. The incident was remembered vividly enough to be recorded by the editors of both Isaiah and 2 Kings, who cite the Babylonian king's representatives' inspection of the temple treasury as the reason for the looting of the temple by Babylon a century and a half later (2 Kgs 20:15-17; Isa 39:4-5).[66] Ezekiel may have intentionally spliced his prediction of Judah's coming punishment onto an ambiguous account reminiscent of her eighth century infidelities, in order to emphasize the parallel, whether a causal connection or simply a similarity, between the visit of Merodoch-baladan's men in 714 and the upcoming looting of the temple. The resulting narrative highlights the similarities between the two periods, and it is precisely the apparent similarities between the events of Hezekiah's time and those of recent years that make Ezekiel's "true" referent impossible

---

[65] The technique is similar in its use of time to the use of geography in Amos 1-2. Amos "circles" Israel, condemning its neighbors one by one, before finally zeroing in on Israel itself as the chief object of Yahweh's wrath. In Ezekiel 23 the unexpected conclusion is not the move to "this nation," but to "this era." Ezekiel himself uses a similar technique in chap 18, where he engages his audience in a theoretical discussion of the rewards and punishments due to past generations, before accusing his present audience of choosing their own death through their unjust actions.

[66] The claim of 2 Kings and Isaiah 39 that because the Babylonians had *seen* the treasure, they would later take it, fits the motif in Ezekiel 16 and 23 of "looking" as a means of control.

to determine. In both cases Jerusalem transfers her loyalty from Assyria to "a Babylonian from Chaldea" (v 15),[67] and from him to Egypt. The implications of this comparison between the revolt of 705 and the revolt in Ezekiel's own time are twofold: first, that the events of the present are implied to be the final outcome of Jerusalem's long history of infidelity, and second, that the punishment only partially imposed by Assyria in 701 is about to be completed by Babylon.

Ezekiel concludes the survey of Oholibah's prostitution and punishment with the prediction that Oholibah will be forced to drink the cup of her sister Samaria (vv 32b-34). The transition from the prose historical survey to the poetic "song of the cup" is accomplished by means of a brief chiasm (vv 29-31) that both summarizes the point of the survey and introduces the idea of Samaria's punishment as a "cup." Yahweh tells Oholibah that the nations will punish her "because [she] whored with the nations and dirtied [herself] with their idols." He then says, "You have followed your sister; therefore I will put her cup in your hand." This summary of Oholibah's offenses and punishment follows an ab:a'b' pattern, in which "a" and "a'" represent Oholibah's punishment, and "b" and "b'" represent its cause. She will (a) be punished by the nations, (b) *because* she was a prostitute to them and their idols; (b') *because* she has imitated her sister, (a') her sister's "cup" will become hers. The chiasm thus points backward to Oholibah's encounters with the nations, then forward to her punishment with Samaria's "cup."

As in the story of Jerusalem in 16:1-43, so also in the story of Oholibah in 23:11-35, the language of looking and seeing plays an important role. Rather than functioning primarily to establish Jerusalem as an object and as "other," as in Ezekiel 16, however, in Ezekiel 23 Jerusalem herself participates in ogling and objectifying, thus usurping and implicitly challenging the omniscient and objectifying gaze of the males. After telling of the prostitutions and punishment of Oholah, Ezekiel begins the account of Oholibah's history by saying, "Oholibah saw" (v 11). Oholibah has seen her sister's actions and their consequences, but ignores what she has seen of Oholah and prefers what she sees before her: "attractive" Assyrian men, equipped with the visible signs of their pres-

---

[67] Living in Babylon, Ezekiel would certainly have distinguished between Babylonia and Chaldea, and have known that both Merodoch-baladan and Nebuchadrezzar were, though kings of Babylon, of Chaldean descent (see J. A. Brinkman, *A Political History of Post-Kassite Babylonia 1158-722 B.C.* [AnOr 43; Rome: Pontificium Institutum Biblicum, 1968] 260-67).

tige.[68] Next she sees, not men, but red-tinted pictures of men, likewise dressed in impressive regalia. Aroused by the pictures, she longs to "feast her eyes" on the men themselves,[69] and sends for them. Next, she turns to the Egyptians, whose prowess is not displayed through their dress, but more directly (and crassly), through their *undress*; they have large penises.[70] Jerusalem has gone from being the naked or lavishly dressed object of men's gaze (in 16:1-43) to being, in chap 23, through her own gaze, a sexual objectifier of men. Yahweh responds (vv 22-29) as he did to Jerusalem's earlier prostitutions; gathering the men Oholibah has used, he restores them to their status as active agents, and changes them from his rivals into his allies. Yahweh's newly recruited allies will then punish Oholibah and return her to her status as the object of men's actions and men's gazes. Under Yahweh's direction, the men mutilate Jerusalem and expose her to public gaze, lest she "lift up [her] eyes" (v 27) again to gaze on the well-endowed Egyptians.

Ezekiel 23:1-35 retells the story of Jerusalem, taking from chap 16 the themes of Jerusalem as the more debauched sister of Samaria, and of the city's history as a history of promiscuous adultery. Whereas the metaphor of 16:1-43 describes Jerusalem's degradation as a return to the pitiful state in which she began, 23:1-35 focuses on the consistent willful-ness of the woman's infidelity. The comparison between Samaria's his-

---

[68] Whereas in 16:1-43, Jerusalem's clothing (or more often, nakedness) was of cen-tral concern, and functioned metonymically to express her status, here it is the cloth-ing and equipment of the men that are obsessively described. Uniforms, horses, chariots, and weapons are metonymic symbols of "phallic" authority (see Silverman, *Semiotics*, for a discussion of phallic symbolism, and of metonomy; and Bal, *Murder*, 120, for a discussion of chariots as metonymous for male power of office). In light of the feminine symbolism of tents in Ezekiel and generally, and the phallic authority conveyed by the chariot, it is appropriate that Yahweh, in Ezekiel 10-11, abandons his "tent," but rides and displays his "chariot," while remaining himself hidden from the objectifying gaze.

[69] Yahweh's depiction for Ezekiel of Jerusalem eyeing the wall-engravings of the Babylonians is reminiscent of the old men in the temple, each eyeing his pictures in secret, and all of them seen by Ezekiel, who stares through a peephole while Yahweh asks, "Do you see?" (8:8-13). The association between Oholibah's action and that of the men in the temple emphasizes the connection between Oholibah's lust for the Babylonians and the people's defilement of the temple.

[70] Ezekiel's simile that the Egyptians' penises are "like those of asses" (v 20) is sometimes interpreted as denigration of the abnormal lust of the "foreigners" (see, e.g., Wevers, *Ezekiel*, 136). More likely, the comparison is intended to insult Jerusalem (and may even reflect some jealousy of the Egyptians' endowments), depicting *her* lust as abnormal, even bestial (cf. Lev 18:23; 20:15-16, which prescribes the death penalty for bestiality).

tory and Jerusalem's makes it plain that, having seen Samaria's actions and their consequences, Jerusalem has knowingly chosen to continue in her sister's way. Jerusalem's history of infidelity is constructed so as to blur the distinction between the offenses of the distant and the more recent past, so that the implied comparison between Jerusalem's serial infidelities of the eighth century and her current liaisons highlights faithlessness as the persistent pattern of Jerusalem's life. The cumulative effect of the negative comparison between Jerusalem and Samaria, and the broad array of historical evidence adduced of Jerusalem's infidelity, is to confirm that Jerusalem has earned, and cannot escape, the approaching punishment.

The emotional overtones of 23:1-35 differ from those of Ezek 16:1-43. Whereas the earlier passage focused on Jerusalem's *body*, and especially its bloodiness, as an object of pollution, in 23:1-35 the focus is on the similarly defiling perversity of Jerusalem's *actions*. In 16:1-43, Jerusalem is portrayed as an outcast and bloody object, polluted but passive, from her birth; in 23:1-35, she is said to have spent her youth in willful prostitution. No longer the unclean object of men's stares, in chap 23 Jerusalem actively "defiles herself," lusting for the men at whom *she* stares. The theme of Jerusalem's defiling insatiability, while stemming from chap 16 (cf. 16:28, 29, 33), in chap 23 is depicted as the dominant motif of Judean history. The life of Jerusalem becomes a case study in abnormal lust. The emphasis in 23:1-35 on the consistency, the willfulness, and the remarkable excesses of Jerusalem's infidelity will provide the background for the more detailed portrayal in 23:36-45 of one specific case of Jerusalem's lustful defilement, and for Yahweh's ultimate call for her destruction.

B. *The Temple as Brothel: 23:36-45*

Section two of chap 23 (vv 36-45) is the final scene in the story of the woman Jerusalem.[71] Unlike previous depictions of the woman (16:1-43;

---

[71] Following the pattern of 23:1-35, the story is presented as the judgment against "Oholah and Oholibah" (v 36), both Samaria and Jerusalem. The inclusion of Samaria as a party to Jerusalem's continuing infidelity is anachronistic and confusing. Nor is the inclusion consistent; vv 40b-41 are addressed directly to one woman, presumably Oholibah, and vv 42-44a refer to the same woman in the third person. It is possible that Ezekiel is distinguishing between native Judeans and Northern immigrants as Oholibah and Oholah respectively, or that Samaria was sufficiently recovered to be an ally of Jerusalem in its second rebellion against Babylon. No records exist of the membership of the 592 coalition against Nebuchadrezzar, but the existence of an

23:1-35) that begin with a rehearsal of the woman's misdeeds and lead up to a prediction of her judgment, 23:36-45 begins (v 36) and ends (v 45) with references to Jerusalem's condemnation and is immediately followed by Yahweh's call to muster the avenging horde (v 46). Preceded by the survey in 23:1-35 of Jerusalem's adulterous history, 23:36-45 focuses on what seem to be her most recent and perhaps most serious "abominations," presented as the concluding evidence in her trial.

In v 37 Yahweh accuses Oholah and Oholibah of "adultery and bloodshed," and then explains the metaphor: "they have committed adultery[72] with their idols, and offered them as food the children they had borne me." The women's "adultery and bloodshed" represent the cultic offenses of idolatry and child sacrifice.[73] Verses 38-39 follow the same pattern as v 37: a twofold accusation, followed by a clarification of the charge. In v 38 Yahweh accuses the women of defiling ($tm^{\jmath}$) the sanctuary "that same day" and profaning (hll) his sabbaths.[74] He explains that having sacrificed their children to the idols, they entered the temple precincts[75] the same day, profaning it. If the day of combined child sacri-

---

"army of Samaria" in Nehemiah's time (Neh 4:2) supports the possibility that Samaria was already a factor in regional politics in Ezekiel's day.

[72] The women are accused of literal adultery, $n^{\jmath}p$, rather than znh, which denotes adultery only figuratively (cf. the combined accusation of "adultery and bloodshed" in 16:38). On the distinction between $n^{\jmath}p$ and znh, see Adler, "Covenant as Marriage," 312.

[73] Like 16:1-43 (and unlike 23:1-35), the passage begins with a depiction of idolatry, which includes child sacrifice, and only then moves on to describe illicit political alliances.

[74] "Profaning Yahweh's sabbaths" does not necessarily refer to violation of the commandment to hallow the seventh day (Exod 20:8-11). For the argument that the "sabbath" was a festival observed on the new and full moons of each month, see M. Fishbane, *Biblical Interpretation in Ancient Israel* (Oxford: Oxford University, 1985) 145-51. Gnana Robinson (*The Origin and Development of the Old Testament Sabbath* [Beiträge zur biblischen Exegese und Theologie 21; Frankfurt: Peter Lang, 1988]) argues for a post-exilic association of the sabbath with the seventh day, but believes it to have been a monthly festival in the late pre-exilic and exilic periods, centering around sanctuary festivities.

[75] $mqd\check{s}y$ can refer either to the temple proper, or to the entire temple complex, all of which was holy, and any of which would suffer corpse contamination from the presence of people who had that day performed human sacrifice. In 20:26 Yahweh claims that he had misled the people into sacrificing their children to *him*, thus defiling $tm^{\backprime}$ them. Jeremiah also attests indirectly to the practice of child sacrifice to Yahweh. After acknowledging (and condemning) the *fact* of child sacrifice (Jer 7:31; 19:5; 32:35), Yahweh three times denies responsibility for it: "I neither commanded nor decreed [it]; it hadn't entered my mind!" Apparently the sacrificers themselves claimed, as does Yahweh in Ezek 20:26 (and cf. Exod 22:29), that Yahweh had in fact

fice and temple worship were a Yahwistic holy day, then all aspects of Ezekiel's accusation, child sacrifice outside the temple, subsequent defilement of the temple, and profanation of Yahweh's sabbath, could easily have been components of a single ritual observance.[76]

In vv 39b-42 Yahweh goes on to describe the defiling observance within the temple: "For here is what they did inside my temple [byty]!" (v 39).[77] Whereas in 16:1-43 Ezekiel separates his portrayal of idolatry (vv 15-22) from that of political infidelity (vv 23-34), here he depicts Jerusalem's political infidelity as part of, or at least carried on in conjunction with, her defiling religious observance.[78] The ensuing description of the women's rendezvous in the temple is obscure.[79] The women send for "men from afar," whom Oholibah, adorned,[80] receives at a "seat of glory [mṭh kbwdh]," before which are placed Yahweh's incense and oil (v 41). The women also send[81] for a less noble group of drunken men from the wilderness. A rowdy party ensues, and the men array the women in bracelets and crowns.

---

commanded the sacrifice of children (see also M. Smith, "A Note on Burning Babies," *JAOS* 95 [1975] 477-79; W. Robertson Smith, "Moloch," *Encyclopaedia Brittanica* [9th ed.; New York: Henry Allen, 1889] 695-96; D. Edelman, "Biblical Molek Reassessed," *JAOS* 107 [1987] 727-31; G. Heider, *Cult of Molech*; J. Day, *Molech: A God of Human Sacrifice in the Old Testament* [Cambridge: Cambridge University, 1989]; and S. Olyan, *Asherah*, 11-13).

76 If, as Ezek 20:26 suggests, the child sacrifices were offered to Yahweh, then a Yahwistic holy day might be the appropriate time for such sacrifice, with accompanying worship at the temple. In that case, Ezekiel's condemnation of such observance as "idolatry" would be a polemical means of expressing his opinion that such worship was deviant.

77 The combination of *whnnh* and *kh* points forward to the scene in vv 40-42 inside Yahweh's "house" (contra, e.g., Zimmerli, *Ezekiel 1*, 478; Eichrodt, *Ezekiel*, 318). Having charged in v 38 that the women had "entered my sanctuary to defile it," Yahweh then proceeds to elucidate just what it was that took place "in the house."

78 The depiction of idolatry in 16:15-22 and especially in 23:26-39a conflates the metaphoric tenor and vehicle. The vocabulary describing "high places," the offering of a "pleasant scent," and so on, is the literal vocabulary of worship. While the depiction of Jerusalem as a woman remains metaphorical, that of her idolatry (unlike foreign alliances, which are always described in sexual terms) is mostly literal. The woman represents the city, but her idolatry represents, simply, idolatry.

79 Most commentators virtually pass over vv 39-43 because of the garbled state of the text and the obscurity of the referent (cf. e.g., Wevers, *Ezekiel*, 139; Eichrodt, *Ezekiel*, 333; Zimmerli, *Ezekiel 1*, 492; and Hals, *Ezekiel*, who does not comment on these verses at all).

80 *ʿdyt ʿdy*; cf. 16:7.

81 See notes on translation to 23:42 in Chapter Three.

After describing the scene, Yahweh decries Oholibah's actions as completing her imitation of Oholah's adulteries (vv 43-44).[82] He explains that now Oholibah, like Oholah before her, has been "entered" the way one would enter a prostitute. Yahweh's explanation in v 43 relies, not on the legal aspect of the adultery metaphor (that the city, like an unfaithful woman, has broken a covenant), but on the physical analogy between the topography of the sacred city and the anatomy of a woman's body. Oholibah has been "entered" by men to whom she should have denied access. In light of Yahweh's claim in vv 37-39a that people had entered the sanctuary to profane it, and the description in v 41 of Oholibah entertaining her lovers with Yahweh's incense at a "seat of glory," Yahweh's charge is clearly that it is the temple that has been entered. Because of its central location, the concern for its purity, and its exclusive dedication to Yahweh, the temple serves as a symbolic uterus. Thus when foreign men enter the temple of the woman called "My Tent is in Her," the offended divine husband charges that she has been entered "as one enters a prostitute," that is, sexually.[83]

Ezekiel's depiction of Jerusalem's illicit rendezvous with foreign men in the temple precincts serves as the conclusion and culmination of Yahweh's accusations against woman Jerusalem. Following a survey of Jerusalem's history of political infidelity (including her "defilement" [ṭmʾ] with the idols of all her lovers), Yahweh shows Ezekiel exactly what has taken place: "For here is what they did inside my temple!" (v 39b). He then paints a detailed vignette of an encounter within the temple or temple complex.

Given the placement of vv 39b-44 at the end of the historical survey and immediately before the announcement of the siege of Jerusalem (24:1-2), it is reasonable to suppose that the passage describes an actual and recent event,[84] one Ezekiel considered Jerusalem's ultimate affront to

---

82   The text is corrupt, but see translation, Chapter Three.

83   Ezekiel's metaphor is mixed at this point, but effective. When Oholibah receives her lovers in the temple, she is depicted as *herself* inside as well, presumably preparing to allow the men access to her body. When Yahweh claims in v 43 that Oholibah has been entered "as one enters a prostitute," the entire city is the woman's body; she is no longer in the temple, but the temple in her, the private part that is particularly Yahweh's possession.

84   The difficulty of modern commentators in identifying Jerusalem's guests may attest to the authenticity of the depiction. If Ezekiel were depicting current events, the intended audience would already know the principle actors' identities, and so would require fewer clues than in the passages where Jerusalem's more distant past is portrayed.

Yahweh. Within the framework of the dates in Ezekiel, chap 23 forms the end of a section whose beginning is dated to August 591 (20:1) and precedes a section dated to January 588.[85] Whether or not the events described metaphorically in 23:39b-44 occurred during precisely this period, the event seems to have been both recent and significant enough to stand as the climax of Jerusalem's infidelity.

Although the details of the event portrayed metaphorically by the temple rendezvous can not be reconstructed with any certainty, several factors point to Jerusalem's reception of Egyptian officials (the "men from afar"), and also of representatives from smaller nation-states in the region (the rabble from the wilderness) to form a rebellious alliance, as the occasion described as adultery in 23:39b-45. First, according to Jeremiah 27-28, Jerusalem had already in 594[86] been the site of an international gathering that included many of Judah's neighbors, to plot revolt against Nebuchadrezzar. In 593, Zedekiah had been summoned to Babylon, probably to swear renewed loyalty to the Babylonian king. This visit occurred in the same year as Ezekiel's opening vision. In the following year Pharaoh Psammeticus II made a tour of Palestine. His entourage included priests, some of whom were apparently left behind after he returned to Egypt.[87] An Egyptian royal entourage would have

---

[85] On the probable substantial accuracy of the dates in Ezekiel, see K. S. Freedy and D. B. Redford, "The Dates in Ezekiel in Relation to Biblical, Babylonian, and Egyptian Sources," *JAOS* 90 (1970) 462-85; Zimmerli, *Ezekiel 1*, 9-10, 72-75; Greenberg, *Ezekiel 1-20*, 8-11.

[86] Or perhaps in 597, on which dating see J. H. Hayes and P. K. Hooker, *A New Chronology for the Kings of Israel and Judah, and Its Implications for Biblical History and Literature* (Altanta: John Knox, 1988) 95-96; and N. Sarna, "The Abortive Insurrection in Zedekiah's Day (Jer 27-29)," *EI* 14 (1978) 89-96.

[87] Rylands Papyrus IX (*Catalogue of the Demotic Papyri in the John Rylands Library* [F. L. Griffith, ed.; 3 vols.; Manchester: The University Press, 1909] 3. 95-98) relates the woes of an Egyptian priestly family who are suing to retrieve a hereditary temple position. The position had been lost when the author's grandfather had been "duped" into going with Psammeticus to Palestine. The priest was to be among those bearing "the bouquets of the gods." Upon his return he found that his position had been usurped, and that Psammeticus was on his deathbed. The Pharaoh was thus unable to hear his complaint, and subsequently died before a formal suit could be lodged. This account suggests that Psammeticus' agenda in Palestine included worship, and that this worship was not a one-time event, but involved stationing priests in Palestine (Psammeticus did not die until more than three years after his visit to Palestine; see J. H. Breasted, *Ancient Records of Egypt: Historical Documents from the Earliest Times to the Persian Conquest* [5 vols.; New York: Russell & Russell, 1905-1907] 1. 75). Such a long stay in Palestine would also explain how the priest's position could have been taken over in his absence.

constituted at least an implicit invitation to revolt, and the presence of Egyptian priests who were subsequently stationed in Palestine, strongly suggests that the rebellious pact was sworn in 592 with accompanying ritual formalities and continuing diplomatic relations. Ezekiel's vision of the abominations in the temple is also dated to 592 (Ezek 8:1), the year of Psammeticus's visit.

If the Egyptians had entered the temple or temple complex along with their priests in 592 in conjunction with their inciting Zedekiah to rebellion, this could be the event described in 23:36-45 as people's entering the temple "to profane it." The "men from afar," received for an adulterous liaison with Oholibah, would then be the Egyptians.[88] If the temple debauchery of 23:36-45 depicts the formation of the rebel alliance of 592, then the "men from among the rabble, brought in drunk from the wilderness" (v 42) would be the representatives from the surrounding, and less highly regarded desert nations such as Moab and Edom.[89]

---

[88] Ezekiel's narrative metaphor of the eagle and the vine in chap 17 asserts that Zedekiah will be punished for his alliance with Egypt because the rebellious alliance is a breach of Yahweh's covenant (17:18-19), that is, the covenant with Nebuchadrezzar, which was sworn in Yahweh's name (cf. 2 Chron 36:13, which reports that Zedekiah was made to swear "in the name of God"). The language of 17:18, "he showed contempt for the oath by breaking the covenant," is identical to Yahweh's summary of the woman Jerusalem's offenses in 16:59. Thus the "prostitution" of Jerusalem is specifically connected with Zedekiah's breach of the covenant with Babylon in favor of Egypt (see M. Tsevat, "Vassal Oaths"; Zimmerli, *Ezekiel 1*, 364-66; and the discussion in Davis, *Swallowing the Scroll*, 98-99). J. Milgrom (*Cult and Conscience*) notes that in Ezek 17:20 Yahweh calls Zedekiah's oath violation "the trespass [*mʿl*] which he committed against me" (cf. Lev 26:40). The violation is a "trespass" (*mʿl*) because it violates a sanctum, the name of Yahweh (19-20).

Ezek 44:6-8 also supports the possibility that it was the Egyptians who are depicted in 23:36-45, entering and profaning the temple. In 44:6-8 Yahweh accuses "the rebellious ones" of admitting foreigners to his sanctuary (*mqdšy*; cf. 23:38) to profane (*ḥll*; cf. 23:38) his temple (*byty*; cf. 23:39a). The foreigners (reading with MT, "they") are specifically accused of breaking "my covenant," a term used elsewhere in Ezekiel only in 16:59 and 17:18-19, where it refers to the covenant with Nebuchadrezzar. Further, Yahweh claims that the foreigners were put in charge of objects or rituals (*lšmry mšmrty*; v 8) in the temple or temple precincts (*mšmrty*). The vocabulary in 44:6-8 suggests that it refers to the same situation as 23:36-44, and the events depicted are consistent with those of both 23:36-44 and the evidence of Rylands IX Papyrus.

[89] It is possible that *ʾnšym mrb ʾdm* in v 42 is mispointed, and should be read "men from the rabble of Edom" rather than the awkward "men from a crowd of people." Edom is mentioned in Jer 27:3 as among those attending the rebellious conclave of 594 (or 597), but the makeup of the alliance of 592 and following is unknown. Ezekiel is particularly harsh in his condemnations of Edom, mentioning this power in four separate oracles (25:12-14; 32:29; 35; 36:1-7). Edom is also the only power besides the

Yahweh concludes his final accusation against Jerusalem as he began it, with a prediction of judgment and another mention of the two women's crimes of adultery and bloodshed, repeated as in 23:37: they will be sentenced for adultery and bloodshed, "because they are adulteresses, and blood is on their hands" (v 45). In 23:36-45 Ezekiel follows up the survey of the misdeeds of Israel, North and South, with an account of one instance of Oholibah's corruption. He moves from expounding the lessons of history to examining the most recent example of Jerusalem's infidelity, an offense whose consequences she is about to undergo.

C. *Coda: The Call to Arms: 23:46-49*

The conclusion to chap 23 interweaves elements, not only from both preceding sections of chap 23, but also from chap 16. The final judgment[90] against the woman Jerusalem (23:46-49) serves as a conclusion to both chapters in which the city is personified. The passage contains the "standard" elements of judgment against the woman as predicted in earlier passages (16:37-41; 23:9-10, 22-29): Yahweh assembles a throng (*qhl*; 16:40) who uncover (16:37, 39; 23:10, 26, 29), stone (16:40), and hack (16:40; 23:10) the woman, kill her children (cf. 23:10, 25), and burn her houses (16:41). The woman will thus be prevented (*šbt*; 16:41; 23:27) from further infidelity, be shamed before other women (16:41, 57; cf. 16:27;

---

enigmatic Magog (chaps 38-39) singled out for condemnation after the fall of Jerusalem is reported in 33:21. Edom may even be the nation represented as "Sodom" in 16:44-58. Although Moab and Ammon are the two nations associated with Sodom in Genesis 19, it is Edom who is said to be Israel's sibling (Genesis 36; Num 20:14; Deut 23:7). Yahweh's admonition to Jerusalem in 16:56-57, that though she had used "Sodom" as a byword, now she herself was the object of gossip for Edom and its neighbors, could be understood to say that the relationship between Jerusalem and Edom ("Sodom") had been reversed. The theme of Jerusalem as the object of gossip is taken up again in the oracle against Edom in 36:3 (on relations between Edom and Judah in this period, see J. Bartlett, *Edom and the Edomites* [JSOTS 77; Sheffield: Journal for the Study of the Old Testament, 1989] 151-57).

[90] The root "judge" (*špt*) has two senses in Ezekiel 16 and 23; the verb means "to sentence," as in 23:36, and the noun may denote either the sentence (or verdict?) passed, or the punishment prescribed in that sentence (e.g., 23:10). Thus in 23:25, the men "sentence" Oholibah to undergo their "punishments," and in 23:45 righteous men will "sentence" the women to the "punishment" against adulteresses and the "punishment" against bloodshedders.

23:10),[91] bear the consequences of her misdeeds (16:43, 52, 58; 23:35), and recognize the authority of Yahweh (16:62).[92]

The passage is unique, however, in that it depicts the two women (Samaria and Jerusalem) punished simultaneously, despite Samaria's having been "destroyed" in 23:9-10. It is also unique in that, rather than being a prediction of judgment (or, as in the case of 23:9-10, an account of an already accomplished judgment), 23:46-49 is a *call* to judgment. Yahweh summons the throng, commanding that they begin the long-threatened destruction. Yahweh's call for the troops to muster is followed immediately by his command to Ezekiel in 24:2 to record "this day" as the day the siege of Jerusalem began. Ezekiel moves in chap 23 from a survey of the historical background of Jerusalem's infidelity (vv 1-35) to an explication of her most recent and critical betrayal. Having offered evidence of Jerusalem's past and continuing guilt, he is then commanded to set in motion the punishment to which she has been sentenced.

III. CONCLUSIONS

The metaphor of the city as Yahweh's wife, already powerful as employed by Hosea and Jeremiah, is reshaped by Ezekiel into a virtually obsessive investigation of Jerusalem's sexual impurity. Influenced both by his anguished revulsion at the pollution of Yahweh's temple, and by its quickly approaching destruction, Ezekiel rereads and retells the story of the woman Jerusalem as a story of female sexual pollution and of male disgust and revenge.

This depiction of Jerusalem's infidelities in Ezekiel 16 and 23 is pornographic writing in the most literal sense of the word. In chaps 16

---

[91] Zimmerli (*Ezekiel 1*, 492) interprets the "warning to all women" of v 48 as a literal warning against adultery to "individual women." Given Ezekiel's identification in 16:27, 57, of the witnessing "women" as the daughters of the Philistines and Edomites, there is no reason not to read v 48 as a warning to other city-states against "infidelity" to sworn covenants.

[92] The "recognition formula" is in 2mpl form (as are three of the possessive endings in vv 46-47). Although this is the form in which the formula most frequently occurs, the formula ordinarily conforms to the number and gender appropriate to the context (e.g., in 13:21; 25:7; and within the adultery metaphor, 16:62). The inconsistency of gender in 23:49 is an instance of the "intrusion" of the (male) referent, but the intrusion may be intentional; as he calls forth the army against his people, Yahweh abandons the personification of Jerusalem, and confronts the implied (male) audience directly with the purpose of their punishment.

and 23 Ezekiel is commanded by Yahweh to make known the prostitution of Jerusalem and her sister, Samaria. Accordingly, each chapter is presented as a prostitute's biography. Annette Kuhn notes that "'pornography' . . . referred originally to writings about the lives and activities of prostitutes,"[93] a definition that exactly describes Ezekiel 16 and 23. The prophet's narrative metaphors about Jerusalem also qualify as pornography in the modern sense. The legal definition of Dworkin and MacKinnon designates as pornography "the graphic sexually explicit subordination of women through pictures and or words,"[94] criteria by which Ezekiel's depictions could well be defined as pornographic.

Jerusalem is defined as the defiled and defiling other, the constant object of the objectifying gaze. Yahweh makes Ezekiel audience to his verbal display of Jerusalem's nakedness, a display Ezekiel in turn provides for his audience. In punishment for her sexual defilement, and, in chap 23, for her own attempt to make men the object of her gaze, the woman will be punished "for her own good" before an audience of hostile men.

With Yahweh's call for the city's destruction in 23:46-49 the metaphor of Jerusalem as Yahweh's wife has run its course. The personified city has proven to be an utterly unacceptable consort to the god. Her restoration, hinted at in Yahweh's promises of 16:59-63, will never come to pass; rather, the elimination of the marriage metaphor will be an apparent precondition for the renewed and sustainable purity of Yahweh's new house in Ezekiel 40-48.

---

[93] *Power of Image,* 24.
[94] Cited in J. Dolan, "The Dynamics of Desire: Sexuality and Gender in Pornography and Performance," *Theatre Journal* 39 (1987) 156-74, 157.

V

The Woman Jerusalem: Her Role in the Book of Ezekiel

I. INTRODUCTION

The central concern of the book of Ezekiel is arguably the status of Yahweh's temple and of the city Jerusalem as the bearer of that temple. The structure of the book reflects this concern. Ezekiel's oracles of judgment against Jerusalem lead up to the destruction of the temple after chap 24, and his oracles of promise beginning in chap 25 build toward the final vision of the temple restored in chaps 40-48. Similarly, the visions in chaps 1, 10, and 43 of the divine chariot depict Yahweh's catastrophic abandonment of the polluted temple and his ultimate return to the purified temple that will be his eternal dwelling.

Because pollution of the temple made Yahweh's residence there impossible, the sanctity of the temple and the city in which it was located were of critical importance. The book of Ezekiel reflects upon this problem in the specific context of the Babylonian destruction of the Jerusalem temple. For Ezekiel, temple pollution was directly responsible for the fall of Jerusalem; accordingly, the establishment of a new and undefiled temple and city was necessary for the return of God to the people of Israel.

Personification of the city as the wife of the god, an image familiar both from its roots in ancient Near Eastern tradition and from its use by earlier biblical prophets, provided Ezekiel with a powerful metaphor with which to describe the pollution of the Jerusalem temple. In addition to exploring the legal and physical analogies between marital and cultic/political infidelity (violating obligations of exclusivity by allowing outsiders access), Ezekiel exploits particularly vividly the potential for defilement associated with the female body. Specifically, the taboo surrounding uterine blood[1] is used to emphasize his horror at the defilement of the sanctuary. The symbolism of the temple's central location, its sanctity to Yahweh, and its function of regulating the life-bearing power of blood, create a strong association between the city's temple and the woman's uterus.[2] Based on the analogy between temple and uterus, Ezekiel depicts the woman Jerusalem as defiled through both her own uterine blood and her illicit sexual activity. The status of the woman as defiled and consequently defiling is used to account for Yahweh's revulsion at and rejection of his consort.

Although Jerusalem is explicitly personified as a woman only in chaps 16 and 23, the critical role played by the city in Ezekiel raises the question of the relationship between the abandoned "woman" of Ezekiel 16 and 23 and the abandoned city that provides the focus of the entire book. Given Ezekiel's exceptionally powerful use of the adultery metaphor in chaps 16 and 23, does this metaphor in any way influence his portrayal of the city elsewhere in the book?

In examining Ezekiel's depictions of Jerusalem, it is important to note that the portrayal of the city does not follow the pattern that might

---

[1]   On the social connection between menstrual taboos and control of female sexuality, see F. W. Young and A. A. Bacdayan, "Menstrual Taboos and Social Rigidity," *Ethnology* 4 (1965) 225-40; Sanday, *Female Power*, esp. 91-112. M. N. Powers ("Menstruation and Reproduction: An Oglala Case," *Signs* 6 [1980] 54-65) argues that in the Oglala rituals such taboos emphasize the menstruating woman's reproductive *power* rather than her defilement, and Meigs ("Papuan Perspective," 309) notes that menstrual fluids are "of course" considered "the most dangerous and polluting of all substances."

[2]   On the symbolism of temple as womb, see Neumann, *The Great Mother*, 8-9, 46; M. Eliade, *Patterns in Comparative Religion* (Cleveland: World, 1963) 377. J. S. Ackerman ("Satire and Symbolism in the Song of Jonah," in *Traditions in Transformation: Turning Points in Biblical Faith* [B. Halpern and J. D. Levenson, eds.; Winona Lake: Eisenbrauns, 1981] 213-46) points out the function of the temple as a symbolic womb in Jonah (236).

be expected, given the structure of the book as a whole.
Ezekiel is divided into oracles of doom (chaps 1-24), oracle
(chaps 25-39), and the vision of the new city/temple (chaps
chaps 1-24, Jerusalem is prominent as an object of conde
Though the city is central to the oracles of doom, however, after ─ announcement of the siege and impending fall of Jerusalem in chap 24,
mention of the city virtually ceases. Rather than being the object of
Ezekiel's oracles of promise beginning in chap 25, Jerusalem, once destroyed, is all but forgotten. Ezekiel's oracles of restoration (chaps 25-39)
are directed to the "sheep" (34:11-31), the mountains (36:1-15), and the
"house" of Israel (36:22-37:28), but never to the city of Jerusalem. Even in
the vision of chaps 40-48 depicting Yahweh's return to his holy city, the
city is never referred to by the name "Jerusalem." People, land, and
temple are restored, but Jerusalem is excluded from the vision of future
reconciliation.[3] The oracles of chaps 1-24, containing virtually all references to Jerusalem within Ezekiel, must therefore form the primary basis
for comparison between Jerusalem the wanton wife of Ezekiel 16 and 23
and Jerusalem the unpersonified city in Ezekiel. Although Jerusalem is
never explicitly called a woman outside of chaps 16 and 23, the city of
chaps 1-24 is depicted in much the same vocabulary used to describe the
woman of chaps 16 and 23 (e.g., znh, dmym). Moreover, vocabulary
specifically relating to women, but not found in chaps 16 and 23 (e.g.,
nddh) is also applied to the city in these oracles. Thus Ezekiel's identification of Jerusalem as a woman, while explicit only in the personifications of chaps 16 and 23, seems not to be confined to these two chapters.
Rather, Jerusalem's feminine persona is implicit throughout the condemnations of chaps 1-24. The role of the city's status as Yahweh's symbolic
wife in Ezekiel 1-24 is confirmed by Ezekiel's final sign-act (24:15-27),
the death of his own wife as a sign of the city's fall.

In Ezekiel 25-39, the chapters following Ezekiel's announcement of
the siege of Jerusalem (24:2), the vocabulary of female defilement ceases,
with the single exception of Yahweh's reminiscence that the people of
Israel used to be "like a menstruating woman" (36:18). The restored temple-city of chaps 40-48 is not personified as a woman, nor are any explicitly feminine images used of the city. The new city, while fulfilling sym-

---

[3] After the announcement of its destruction in 36:38, Jerusalem is mentioned by
name only once, in a simile comparing the flocks of the restored cities of the future to
those of Jerusalem in the past (36:38). The absence of Jerusalem from the second half
of Ezekiel is seldom if ever noted. Zimmerli (Ezekiel 2, 327, 546-47) actually calls the
restored city of Ezekiel 40-48 "Jerusalem."

bolically feminine roles as the home and exclusive property of the god and the locus of life-bearing blood, is always described in literal language, as a set of buildings and not as a wife. The city's fidelity is therefore guaranteed, if only because infidelity has been made impossible; the "woman" Jerusalem has become, literally, an object, and so incapable of further disobedience.

II. JERUSALEM IN EZEKIEL 1-24:
THE IMPLIED PROSTITUTE

Although Jerusalem is not personified in Ezekiel outside of chaps 16 and 23, much of the vocabulary and imagery used to depict the city throughout Ezekiel 1-24 is consistent with her personification in chaps 16 and 23. That is, many feminine images are repeated throughout the first half of the book, suggesting an implied or latent personification of Jerusalem. The most basic of these images is the personification implied in the prophet's direct address to the city, using second person feminine forms. In order to determine the extent to which Jerusalem may be considered to be personified outside of chaps 16 and 23, the passages in which Ezekiel directly addresses the city will be examined for vocabulary and imagery that may be considered "feminine" or that is typical of that used to describe the woman Jerusalem of chaps 16 and 23.

A. *Ezek 5:7-17*

Ezekiel first mentions Jerusalem in 4:7, 16, in conjunction with his sign-act of laying siege to a model of the city. The city is not, however, described at any length, and no identifiably feminine imagery is used.

In 5:5-17 Ezekiel reports Yahweh's first address *to* the city. In v 7 Yahweh addresses the city using second person masculine plural forms, but in v 8b, with the announcement of the city's punishment, he for the first time addresses the city directly as a single, feminine entity (using second person feminine singular forms). The very use of direct address implies personification of the city, and both the grammatical gender of the Hebrew word ʿyr and the wider cultural tradition dictate that the personified city be female. Yahweh tells Jerusalem he will perform "punishments" (*mšptym*; cf. 16:38, 41; 23:24, 25) within her,[4] "the likes of which I have never done and will never do again" (cf. 16:16).

Having accused Jerusalem of injustice and announced her punishment, in v 11 Yahweh names Jerusalem's crime: she has defiled his sanctuary (*'t-mqdšty tm'th*) by her abominations (*tw'bt*; cf. 16:2, 22; 23:36). Though no explicitly feminine imagery is used, Yahweh addresses Jerusalem as a woman, whom he holds responsible for polluting Yahweh's holy place. Yahweh describes the aftermath of Jerusalem's punishment in the same terms as the aftermath of the woman's punishment in chap 16; Yahweh's "anger will be spent" and he will "be satisfied" (cf. 16:42). The language of rage spent and satisfied that has such strong sexual overtones in the context of chap 16 is here used in a more neutral context. As in 16:57, Jerusalem will become an object of contempt (*hrph*; v 14) "in the sight of every passerby" (*l'yny kl-'wbr*; cf. 16:6, 8, 15, 25). Themes that in chaps 16 and 23 seem intimately tied to the personification of Jerusalem as a woman—Jerusalem's pollution of Yahweh's sanctuary, Yahweh's "satisfaction" at her punishment by the united male community, the gossip over the public exposure of Jerusalem, and her openness to the gaze of "every passerby"—already in chap 5 form part of the "story" of Jerusalem. In this context the narrative metaphors of chaps 16 and 23 can be seen, not as exceptional depictions of the city, but as one end of a continuum of personification within Ezekiel.

It is important, in comparing Ezekiel's depiction of Jerusalem as a woman in chaps 16 and 23 with depictions of the city in the rest of the book, to note the limits of such comparison. A mere overlap between the vocabulary of Ezekiel 16 and 23 and that used to describe Jerusalem in the rest of the book does not prove that Ezekiel consistently thought of the city as a woman; it is virtually inevitable that the prophet would use similar vocabulary in his various recitations of the city's wrongs. However, Ezekiel's use of direct address to the (grammatically) feminine city, together with his consistent use of images that imply a feminine identity for the city (it is difficult, for example, to picture a "nation" exposed to every "passerby"), reflect strong continuity in his conception of the city as a feminine entity. Both the culturally accepted persona of the city as a woman and the specific prophetic tradition on which Ezekiel

---

4 The placement of the punishments "within" (*b*) Jerusalem does not fit with the metaphor of the city as a woman. However, the same phrase is used of the "woman" in 16:41.

drew would have contributed to Ezekiel's understanding of Jerusalem as implicitly female.[5]

B. *Ezek 6:8-10*

In this passage, Ezekiel does not address the city, but the people, using the root *znh* to describe their infidelity. He predicts that the exiles will "remember" him (*zkr*; cf. 16:61) only after he has broken their "whoring heart that strayed" and blinded their "eyes that went whoring after other gods." Remembering their "abominations" (*tw*‍*bt*; cf. 16:2, 22, 58), they will despise themselves and recognize the authority of Yahweh (cf. 16:63). Here the language of prostitution and vocabulary typical of chap 16 is applied to the people rather than to the personified city. Interestingly, 6:8-10 refers to the period after the fall of the city, that is, after Ezekiel ceases to personify the city as a woman. Ezekiel claims that after the city has fallen, the (male) populace will remember that they *used* to behave "like prostitutes" and will therefore repent. As will be seen below, such usage is consistant with 36:17 and 43:7, 9 in which *nddh* and *znh* respectively are used to characterize the people's behavior before the fall of the temple.

C. *Ezek 7:19-22*

This passage follows the description in 7:14-18 of panic during the siege of Jerusalem. In v 19 Yahweh goes on to relate the scorn with which people will treat their silver and gold; because it cannot save or even feed them, they will throw it into the streets "like a *nddh*." They will treat it thus "because it was the occasion [lit: stumbling block] of their evil." Treating the silver and gold "like a menstruating woman" is a metaphor for the urgency and revulsion with which people will separate themselves from it (cf. Isa 30:22), presumably the opposite of their usual attitude toward money. The role of silver and gold as the occasion of the people's sin (*ʿwn*) is not immediately apparent. Although greed could have been the cause of dishonesty, or wealth a source of inordinate pride, these are never cited by Ezekiel as the cause of the city's destruction.[6] In

---

5 Even in modern English-speaking countries in which cities are not commonly personified, the conceptual metaphor of the city's feminine persona persists. Hence, when personified, a city is "she," not "he."

6 In Ezekiel the city is destroyed because Yahweh has abandoned it, and it is abandoned because the temple is polluted (see Milgrom, "Israel's Sanctuary," 81-82). According to Wright (*Disposal*, 19; and cf. Milgrom, "Israel's Sanctuary," 77), only three crimes are "explicitly described as defiling the sanctuary": corpse contamination (Num 19:13, 20), "sexual impurities" (Lev 15:31), and "offering children to

v 20, however, Yahweh explains the reason gold and silver are the source of the people's downfall; they have used "its splendid ornament" [*sby 'dyw*] for vanity, making the images of their abominations from it."[7] For this reason, says Yahweh, he will make it like a *nddh* to them.[8] The gold and silver of Jerusalem that had been "its" splendid ornament, but was made into idols, would be the gold and silver of the temple. In 16:17 Yahweh tells of the woman Jerusalem taking her gold and silver treasures and making them into idols.[9]

Yahweh's threat to make "it" like a *nddh* to the people is further explained in v 21. He will give "it" to foreigners, who will "profane" (*hll*) it. The referent of "it" is unclear at this point. Because the gold and silver are temple sancta, the verb "profane" could be used of them. If, however, temple treasures had been made into idols, they would be profaned already. "It" could also refer to the temple itself, in which case Yahweh's threat to make it "like a menstruant" would be especially severe.[10] The temple was not only protected from contact with the unclean, but also was the place where blood was employed as a purifying agent. The image of the temple becoming "like a menstruant" is shocking, both because of its implied juxtaposition of holy with unclean and because of its juxtaposition of the most clean (holy) *blood* with the most unclean.

Molech" (Lev 20:3). All of these crimes are attributed to the woman Jerusalem, with the exception that the child sacrifice is not specifically said to be an offering to Molech. Frymer-Kensky ("Pollution," 406-08) lists murder, sexual impurities, and idolatry as the three crimes that pollute the *land* and in extreme cases cannot be ritually purified.

[7] The phrase *mkswl 'wn* is also used to describe idols in 14:7.

[8] Cf. Isa 30:22, in which the gold and silver coverings of the idols become "like a *nddh*" to the people.

[9] The term *'dy* is also used only here and in depictions of the woman Jerusalem: in 16:11 and 23:40 it is used of the ornaments of the woman, both times in conjunction with other vocabulary suggesting her cultic role; and the phrase *'dy 'dyym* (16:7) refers to the signs of puberty. Calvin observes (*Commentaries*, 1. 264) that in his time some took *sby 'dyw* to refer to the temple, though he disagrees (265).

The fact that the gold and silver have been made into idols also explains why Yahweh would note contemptuously in v 19 that it could neither "save nor feed" the people. Although gold and silver would in any case become useless in a siege, gold and silver that had (as idols) been looked to for supernatural protection would be rendered useless, either as money or as an idol.

[10] Cf. the use of feminine imagery to describe the (raped) temple in 1 Macc 2:7-12: "Her temple has become like a man without honor; her glorious vessels have been carried into captivity. Her babes have been killed in her streets. . . . All her adornment has been taken away; . . . behold, our holy place, our beauty, and our glory have been laid waste; the Gentiles have profaned it" (RSV).

In v 22 Yahweh refers more explicitly to the temple, predicting the desecration of the holy of holies: he will allow men to enter and profane his "private place."[11] In the context of a description of the city, Yahweh's private place that will be "profaned" by foreign men would logically be the temple. Interestingly, although *spwn* is grammatically masculine, it is modified in v 22 as if it were feminine; the men will enter and profane "her."[12] It is also possible that this female entity that will be treated "like a menstruant" and "profaned" by foreign men is the city itself rather than the temple, since *'yr* is grammatically feminine. Whether city or temple, however, the image strongly suggests the feminine sexuality of Yahweh's "private place."

The imagery of 7:19-22 is provocative; the "splendid ornament" "made into idols," seems to be the temple ornaments or treasury, and the feminine "private place" profaned by foreign men evokes both the holy of holies and its symbolic status as the womb of Yahweh's wife.[13] The temple is, however, never mentioned explicitly, nor its feminine persona specified. Were it not for Ezekiel's strong personifications in chaps 16 and 23, such allusions might seem insignificant. In light, however, of the personification of Jerusalem as the longest and most highly developed metaphor in Ezekiel, the presence in chap 7 of obliquely sexual imagery to describe the polluted temple points toward an already implicit personification that will be fully developed only in later chapters.

D. *Ezek 22:1-5*

In Ezek 22:1-5 the prophet again addresses the city using words and phrases associated with the woman Jerusalem but does not expressly personify the city as a woman. Chapter 22 begins with Yahweh's question to Ezekiel, "Will you judge, will you judge the bloody city?" This request, *htšpṭ htšpwṭ*, is identical to Yahweh's call to judge Oholibah in 23:36 (cf. 20:4), though the epithet "bloody city" does not appear either in chap 16 or in 23. Jerusalem is not called "bloody" in Ezekiel before 22:2,

---

[11]   *ṣpwny* could also be translated "secret" or "precious" place.

[12]   The identity of the "hidden place" as the holy of holies was widely accepted among the ancients, including Jerome (*PL*, 25. 73) and Theodoret (*PG*, 81. 878, 935). Calvin cites this as the view of "expositors," but disagrees, maintaining that the land is the place hidden under God's protecting care (*Commentaries*, 1. 267). Keil (*Ezekiel*, 1. 108) cites the scholarly consensus that the hidden place is the holy of holies, though he believes that "the temple-treasure is primarily intended."

[13]   Ezekiel's only other mention of foreign men (*zrym*) who defile (*ḥll*) his possession is in 44:7, where the men are explicitly said to have defiled the sanctuary (*mqdšy*).

but the epithet, "bloody city" (*ʿyr hddmym*), does appear in earlier prophetic literature, where it forms part of the personification of the woman Nineveh (Nah 3:1). The only blood attributed to Jerusalem in Ezekiel before chap 22 appears in chap 16,[14] where the city is not said, but rather shown, to be bloody: weltering in unwashed placenta (vv 4, 6), befouled with blood at her marriage (v 9), shedding the blood of her children (vv 21-22), and judged with "the blood of rage" (v 38).

The combination of the call to judge with the epithet, "bloody city," connects this passage with the depictions of the woman Jerusalem in chaps 16 and 23. First, Yahweh's command to "inform her of all her abominations" (v 2) is identical to the opening of chap 16 (v 2). Second, Yahweh's request that Ezekiel both judge and announce abominations appears only once more in Ezekiel, in the judgment of Oholibah in 23:36. Third, the charge brought against the bloody city in 22:3-4—bloodshed and idolatry[15]—is identical to the charge against Oholah and Oholibah in 23:37-39.

In addition to these verbal parallels, the use of the verb *ʿsm* to describe the city's bloodshed in v 4 is also suggestive. Only trespasses against sancta constitute *ʾšm*,[16] and the offering of child sacrifice to Molech is one of the few forms of bloodshed that is also a sancta trespass.[17] Given the proximity of 22:1-5 to 23:36-45, and the use of the identical call for judgment, it is possible that the *ʾšm* of which Jerusalem is accused in 22:4 is the child sacrifice described in 23:27-39 (and cf. 16:20-22).[18] In punishment Jerusalem will be made an object of contempt (*ḥrph*) before surrounding nations, as she was in 16:57 (and cf. 5:14).[19]

---

14 Blood symbolizes the watchperson's guilt in 3:18; the crimes of the land are called "bloody" in 7:23; and the Ammonites' blood is mentioned in 21:32. The only connection between blood and Jerusalem before 22:2 and outside chap 16 is the "bloody plague" predicted in 14:19.

15 In 23:37-39 the women's idolatry is called "'adultery' with their idols."

16 See Milgrom, *Cult and Conscience*, 1-21.

17 Wright, *Disposal*, 19.

18 Ezekiel makes one other unambiguous reference to child sacrifice, in 20:25-26. In this passage Yahweh claims that the sacrifice was made to *him* (Molech is not mentioned in Ezekiel), a situation that would be ironically consistent with Yahweh's repeated denial in Jeremiah that he had ever requested such offerings (7:31; 19:5; 32:35), a denial that would only be necessary if the sacrifices were in fact being offered to Yahweh.

19 In 22:6-16 the city continues to be addressed with feminine singular verb forms, but the crimes discussed have more in common with those described in chap 18 than with those of chaps 16 and 23. Only v 8 is directly connected with accusations against the personified city. Yahweh charges, "You have had contempt for my holy things

Ezekiel's use of the identical phrases to address Jerusalem as those used in 16:2 and 23:36,[20] and the direct address to Jerusalem as "bloody," give Jerusalem a quasi-personified status (cf. 7:19-22, discussed above) in 22:1-5. The close connection in both language and content between 22:1-5 and 23:36-39 affirms the conceptual link between Jerusalem the adulterous wife and the less fully personified Jerusalem already implied here by the use of second person address.

E. *Ezek 24:3-14*

Ezekiel 24 follows immediately upon Yahweh's call for Oholibah to be destroyed (23:46-49), and begins (vv 1-2) with the announcement of the siege of Jerusalem. At the outset, the juxtaposition of this oracle with the call for Oholibah's destruction and the announcement of the siege implies that the siege of the city is the punishment of Yahweh's wife. The announcement of the siege of Jerusalem is followed in vv 3b-5 with the "song of the pot." The pot is a metaphor for Jerusalem under siege, while the meat within it represents her citizens, who are made to feel the heat (cf. 11:3-12). The song is followed by two "woe" oracles (vv 6-8, 9-14), which continue to depict Jerusalem as a pot but change the focus of the metaphor from the meat inside the pot to the filth of the pot itself.

After the opening "song of the pot" Ezekiel announces "woe to the bloody city, the pot" (v 6).[21] The expression, "bloody city," as in 22:2,

---

and profaned my sabbaths." The accusation is essentially the same as that in 23:38, where the women are accused of defiling the sanctuary and profaning Yahweh's sabbaths. "Contempt" (*bzyt*) is the word used in 16:59 of Jerusalem's attitude toward her vassal oath (cf. 17:16, 18-19). Here, contempt for sancta parallels defilement of the sanctuary in 23:38. Given the strong verbal similarities between 22:1-5, 8 and 23:36-39 and the proximity of the two passages, it is possible that they were written at virtually the same time, 22:1-5 setting out Yahweh's arraignment of the city, and 23:36-39 elaborating this same arraignment within the context of the adultery metaphor.

[20] The repeated request, *htšpwt*, occurs with slight variation in Ezek 20:4, where, as here, it is combined with the command to "make known abominations." In 20:4, however, those being judged are the elders of Israel (*htšpt ʾtm*), and the abominations are the abominations of their ancestors (*twʿbt ʾbwtm*). Ezekiel clearly differentiates between the judgment against the elders (masculine plural) for the abominations of their ancestors (masculine plural), and the judgment in 16:2; 22:2; 23:36 against Jerusalem (feminine singular) for "her" abominations. This grammatical distinction demonstrates the consistency with which Ezekiel conceives of the city as a feminine entity (rather than, say, as a group of male inhabitants), in contrast to the *people* of Israel, of whom he conceives as a group.

[21] The phrase, *ʾwy ʿyr hddmym* (vv 6, 9) is identical to the "woe" directed against the woman Nineveh in Nah 3:1.

refers to Jerusalem, which is addressed as "the pot." The connections among "blood," the "city," and the "pot" are left for the reader to supply. The bloody city, already addressed in 22:2, and suggested to be female both in earlier prophetic tradition (Nah 3:1) and by the description of the bloody Jerusalem in Ezekiel 16, is here further identified as a pot. Pots, like cities,[22] are a common symbol of the female body,[23] and the apposition here of "pot" with "bloody" evokes the persona of Jerusalem the menstruant.

In v 6 the "bloody" pot/city is further designated as "the pot whose ḥlʾh is in it/her." The noun ḥlʾh literally means "disease,"[24] and this pot's internal "disease" is identified in v 7 as "her blood" that is "inside her."[25] The metaphoric juxtaposition of the image of an indelible "disease" clinging to the inside of a pot, with the image of the bloody city's internal

---

[22] See Chapter One.

[23] Neumann (Great Mother, 29-39, 46-49, 120-46) discusses at length the use of vessel symbolism to depict the woman, and claims that the "central symbol [of the feminine] is the vessel" (39; see also L. Mumford, The City in History: Its Origins, Its Transformations, and Its Prospects [New York: Harcourt, Brace and World, 1961] 12-13). The noun syr, "pot," may be grammatically either masculine or feminine. Interestingly, in the "song" (see e.g., Zimmerli, Ezekiel 1, 496-97), the pot starts out grammatically masculine (v 3b), but immediately changes gender (v 4), and remains grammatically feminine throughout vv 4-14, allowing Ezekiel to address the (feminine) pot or the (feminine) city interchangeably.

[24] Cf. 2 Chron 16:12 (= 1 Kgs 15:23), in which Asa is said to be "diseased" (ḥlʾ) in his "feet." Nowhere else is the noun applied to an inanimate object, nor is the related noun, tḥlʾym (see, e.g., Jer 14:18; Deut 29:21). J. L. Kelso ("Ezekiel's Parable of the Corroded Copper Cauldron," JBL 64 [1945] 391-93; and cf. D. I. Block, "Ezekiel's Boiling Cauldron: A Form-critical Solution to Ezekiel xxiv 1-14," VT 41 [1991] 12-37) argues that the word literally means "disease," and draws the connection between the "disease" of the pot and the pollution of the Jerusalem temple. See also W. H. Brownlee, "Ezekiel's Copper Cauldron and Blood on the Rock" (in R. A. Coughenour, ed., For Me to Live: Essays in Honor of James Leon Kelso [Cleveland: Dillon/Liederbach, 1972] 21-43), who understands the pot to be an iron cauldron, whose "corrosion" would be rust-red, and therefore a "congruous figure of speech," representing blood. Kelso relates the pot's condition to the corrosion known in modern times as "copper disease," but there is no evidence that the language of disease was used to describe this condition in antiquity. Rather, Ezekiel's usage should be understood as metaphorical.

[25] Ezekiel's description of the "disease" as a visible object (cf. "leprosy"; Lev 13:47-59) suggests a translation such as "infection" or "pus." Given the metaphorical application of the term to describe something to be scoured from a pot, words like "scum" or "filth" might be appropriate. For purposes of this analysis the word "disease" will be used (cf. Zimmerli, Ezekiel 1, 494, 500), as it most strongly conveys the metaphor and its unsettling quality.

pollution suggests the by-now familiar image of the repulsive uncleanness of uterine blood. Mary Douglas notes that although vessels may
serve as either male or female symbols, a "male" vessel is one in danger
of losing its precious contents, while a "female" vessel is in danger of
admitting the impure.[26] Thus, a bloody, defiled pot is a strong symbol of
the female body. Moreover, the use of the word "ḥlʾh" to describe the
pot's bloody interior suggests that the blood "in her" is not only unclean,
but diseased, and thus doubly polluted.[27]

In v 7 Yahweh apparently reveals the tenor of the metaphor; the unclean blood "in her" is bloodshed. The blood "in her" was poured out on
the bare rock, in violation of the law (Lev 17:13) stipulating that blood
must either be offered upon the altar or covered over with dust.[28] In v 8
Yahweh goes on to claim that it was he himself who set the blood on the
rock in order to provoke himself to revenge.[29] Images of the pot, its
"disease," the defiled woman, and actual bloodshed within Jerusalem,
are conflated in an oracle that, despite, or perhaps partly because of its
garbled imagery, is strangely powerful and disturbing.

In vv 9-14 Yahweh begins a second "woe" oracle against "the bloody
city," continuing the identification of the bloody city as the "diseased"
pot and describing his repeated and unsuccessful attempts to purify it.
When all attempts at cleansing fail, Yahweh calls (vv 10-11) for the fire to
be stoked and the pot heated to glowing so that its pollution (ṭmʾ) might

---

[26] *Purity and Danger*, 126.

[27] Kelso ("Ezekiel's Parable") suggests that Ezekiel is likening the city specifically
to one of the temple vessels which, when permanently corroded, could be used for
neither sacred nor profane purposes, but had to be melted down. Kelso's reading, if
correct, would support the theory that Ezekiel habitually depicts the condition of the
city in terms of the purity of the temple, which in turn he associates with the purity
or impurity of the female body. The woman is so indelibly defiled with the unclean
blood within her that she (her uterus) is like one of the unclean temple vessels that,
when unable to be purified, must be destroyed.

[28] See Milgrom, "Prolegomenon," 101; and cf. Deut 12:24.

[29] Yahweh's claim of divine entrapment is logically parallel to that of 20:25-26,
where Yahweh claims to have commanded the Israelites to offer him their children,
with the goal that he might "horrify" them. These parallel claims that Yahweh misled
the people into bloodguilt may both refer to child sacrifice, that bloodshed of which
"the bloody city" is most commonly accused in the book of Ezekiel (16:20-22; 23:36-
39; cf. discussion of 22:3-4 above). The evidence of both Ezek 23:39, that the people
sacrificed children *before* entering the temple precincts, and Jer 32:34-35, that the children were sacrificed in the "valley of Ben Hinnom," is consistent with the accusation
that the sacrificed blood was shed "on the bare rock," or at least in the open air, outside the temple compound.

be melted and its "disease" consumed.[30] In v 12 Yahweh relates the failure of these efforts as well: "The great quantity of its/her 'disease' would
not come out by burning."

The syntax of v 13 is difficult. If the word ḥlʾth, the final word of v
12, which is untranslatable as part of that verse, is read as the first word
of v 13, the resultant phrase is, "Her [the pot's] 'disease' through your
pollution is perversion." The female addressee is apparently still the
bloody city (or pot), Jerusalem. The meaning of the phrase is far from
clear, except that the pot's disease is identified as Jerusalem's pollution, a
pollution acquired through (sexual) perversion (zmmh).[31] The role of the
pot as a feminine symbol is affirmed by the connection between the
"disease" of the pot and the sexual pollution of the city. Yahweh then
explains to Jerusalem (vv 13b-14) his judgment against her, using the
imagery of the defiled pot: "Because I cleansed (ṭhr) you but you would
not come clean from your pollution, you will not be cleansed again until
I have spent my rage upon you" (cf. 16:42). Yahweh's unsuccessful
scouring apparently refers to his frustrating attempt to clean the pot, but
the uncleanness is no longer called ḥlʾh, nor is the cleaning described as
burning. Rather, Yahweh uses the vocabulary of the cult, of ritual
cleansing and defilement, to describe his attempt to purify the pot.
Because her defilement is beyond purification (ṭhr),[32] she will not be
cleansed again. If Yahweh is referring here to the defilement and ritual
cleansing of the temple, the prediction that she will never again undergo
cleansing could be a prediction that the temple will be destroyed before
the next Day of Atonement. The diseased and sexually defiled "pot," the
life-bearing vessel in the belly of the city, will not survive long enough to
undergo yet another attempt at purification.[33]

---

[30] Neumann (Great Mother, 236) cites a Tibetan ritual text that connects woman's
uterus with a "cauldron, in which are enacted all the torments of purification by fire."
Ezekiel's attempt to cleanse the pot by burning provides a curious parallel to this image.

[31] "zmmh" refers specifically to sexual offences (see S. Steingrimsson, "zimmah,"
TDOT IV, 89-90; and cf. Lev 18:17; 20:14; Judg 20:6). The term is used twice of literal
sexual offences in 22:9, 11, eleven times of the woman Jerusalem in Ezekiel 16 and 23,
and here. Keil (Ezekiel, 1. 347), leaving the final ḥlʾth as part of v 12, translates v 13a,
"In thine uncleanness is (there lies) zmmh, i.e. an abomination deserving of death."

[32] The city's defilement was both serious and the result of intentional sin. If, as is
the case in chaps 16 and 23, the sins described here include idolatrous child sacrifice,
they also constitute violations against the temple sancta. On intentional defilement of
sancta, see Milgrom, Studies in Cultic and Levitical Terminology, 49-50.

[33] If this is a prediction of the city's rapid fall, it is, of course, inaccurate, since the
city did not fall until 586. It would not, however, be the only inaccurate prediction in

Ezekiel combines imagery of Jerusalem as a "pot," as full of unclean blood, as diseased, and as sexually polluted. The resulting image—a bloody and defiled cookpot—is a bizarre but forcible allusion to Jerusalem as a defiled woman. In 24:1-14 Jerusalem the "disease"-laden pot, Jerusalem the sexually perverse woman, and Jerusalem the blood-shedding city, are conflated in a single image. Symbolically, the "pot" becomes a defiled womb. Ezekiel uses both the metaphor of the unclean pot and imagery associated with the woman Jerusalem to illustrate Yahweh's rage and despair over the city's persistent defilement, and his decision that she must be destroyed.

F. *Ezek 24:15-24*

In Ezekiel's last recorded sign-act, his own wife's death is seen as a symbol of the destruction of Yahweh's holy city. Ezekiel's sign-acts often place him in the role of Yahweh,[34] and it is therefore grimly appropriate that his own wife's death should signal the demise of the city he identifies as Yahweh's "wife."

Yahweh announces to Ezekiel (v 16) that he is about to "take away" the "delight of [Ezekiel's] eyes" by pestilence.[35] The word *mḥmd*, a source of desire or delight, is used to describe sexual pleasure in Cant 5:16, and otherwise most commonly refers to the treasures within the Jerusalem temple.[36] Yahweh plays on this twofold meaning of *mḥmd*; he is about to take away both objects of Ezekiel the priest's desire, the woman and the temple. For Yahweh, these two objects of desire are the same, since the temple *is* Yahweh's symbolic "wife." Like Ezekiel, Yahweh will lose both temple and "wife" at once. Ezekiel, who earlier challenged Yahweh's interference in his life (4:14; 20:49), apparently accepts this decision without objection. The prophet simply informs the people of what he has

---

the book (cf. Ezekiel's unfulfilled prophecy in 26:7-14 that Nebuchadrezzar would capture Tyre).

[34] E.g., setting his face against Jerusalem (4:7) and the mountains of Israel (6:2) as a sign of Yahweh's opposition; bringing up destroyers against the city (5:1-3); cf. Zimmerli, *Ezekiel 1*, 28-29; G. Fohrer, *Die Symbolischen Handlungen der Propheten* (Zurich: Zwingli, 1968) 35, 76-77.

[35] *bmggph*. The word often designates diseases sent as punishments from God (e.g. Num 14:37; 1 Sam 6:4; 2 Chron 21:14). The death of the woman as divine punishment accords with her role as a symbol of the city Yahweh has decided to destroy. Curiously, it is not stated whether or not the *actual* woman, Ezekiel's wife, has done anything to deserve death as divine punishment.

[36] E.g., in 2 Chron 36:12; Isa 64:10 (Eng 64:11); Lam 1:10, 11; 2:4; and cf. its use in Hos 13:15 to describe the treasury of Samaria.

heard, after which his wife dies and he obeys Yahweh's command to refrain from the outward signs of mourning.[37] The people ask the meaning of the sign,[38] and Ezekiel reports Yahweh's interpretation.

Ezekiel's speech in vv 20-24 is unique in being presented as an actual report of Ezekiel's oracle to the people, rather than as a command from Yahweh containing the words Ezekiel is (later) to address to the people. Ezekiel's speech is also unique in the role confusion it displays between Yahweh and Ezekiel. Ezekiel begins (v 21) by quoting Yahweh, who explains the death of Ezekiel's wife as a sign that Yahweh will profane his sanctuary.[39] The people are then told (vv 22-23) that they will do "as I have done." The speaker changes abruptly from Yahweh to Ezekiel; the people will do as Ezekiel has done, in refraining from the rites of mourning. In the following verse the speaker again changes without notice. "Thus," the speaker continues (v 24), "will *Ezekiel* be a sign for you"; the prophet changes from speaking of himself in the first person to reporting Yahweh's speech about him.[40] The confusion between Yahweh and Ezekiel in the oracle both reflects and compounds the sense that the roles of Yahweh and Ezekiel are the same. Both god and priest are to lose both spouse and temple.

Given the profusion of both explicit and oblique depictions of Yahweh's wife in chaps 1-24 as polluted, unfaithful, and sentenced to death, it is remarkable that Ezekiel makes no accusation of infidelity against his own wife.[41] Her role as a symbol of Jerusalem's fall might in itself be expected to call her fidelity into some question, but Ezekiel refrains from commenting on his own wife, recording instead the defilement of Yahweh's wife and the violent and justified rage of her divine husband.

---

[37] It may be that Ezekiel is here acting the role of the high priest, who is forbidden the outward signs of mourning (Lev 21:10-11). This symbolic role would compound the association of Ezekiel with Yahweh, and of his wife with Yahweh's wife, namely, the temple (to which he as high priest would, like Yahweh, have privileged access).

[38] The sign-act of 24:15-24 is the only account of a dialogue between Ezekiel and the people. In 11:25 Ezekiel reports that he "told all this" to the people, but he is neither quoted as actually speaking to them, nor is their response mentioned (cf. 24:18).

[39] Yahweh does not refer to his sanctuary as the delight of his own eyes, but the delight of the *people*'s eyes. Thus, they are to emulate Ezekiel, who in turn is emulating Yahweh, in their response to the loss of their delight (cf. 1 Macc 2:12).

[40] This alternating voice makes it impossible to determine whether vv 25-27 are meant to be a continuation of Yahweh's *reported* speech, or a separate communication from Yahweh to Ezekiel, though the recognition formula in v 24 implies (but does not necessitate; cf. 37:6) the end of the speech unit.

[41] Like the woman Jerusalem herself, Ezekiel's wife never speaks.

III. THE REAL WOMEN IN EZEKIEL

Although Ezekiel's wife is the only actual woman mentioned as an individual in the book, groups of women appear in two passages in Ezekiel (8:14-15; 13:17-23), and hypothetical women are used as examples of defilement in two additional sections (18:6, 11, 15; 22:10-11). Nowhere in these passages is the vocabulary of defilement and infidelity that describes the woman Jerusalem in chaps 16 and 23 applied to these women. Though in all four passages the women's activities are condemned, their crimes differ markedly from those of the personified city.

A. *Ezek 8:14-15*

In 8:14-15, in the context of his vision of the temple abominations, Ezekiel sees a group of women weeping for Tammuz. This is the third of four "abominations" shown Ezekiel, following his vision of the elders in their "rooms of pictures" (vv 10-13), and preceding a vision of the men turning their backsides to the temple (v 16). Although the women's actions serve as an example of Israel's "abominations," they are mentioned only briefly, as one among several examples of illicit conduct. Neither Ezekiel nor his divine guide comments concerning the women except to note that Ezekiel will see "still worse abominations" (v 15).

B. *Ezek 13:17-23*

In 13:17-23 Ezekiel is told to prophesy against the female false prophets. These women are straightforwardly depicted as counterparts to the male false prophets Ezekiel condemned in 13:1-16. Like their male counterparts, the women are said to "make up" their prophecies (v 17; cf. 13:2). They are also said to sew ritual or magical garments for the people, in order to "hunt them down" as prey. Like the women weeping for Tammuz, the female false prophets receive no special notice as women, but rather, receive the same condemnation as their male counterparts.

Remarkably, although both the women weeping for Tammuz and the female false prophets are condemned specifically for cultic offenses, neither group is accused either of polluting the sanctuary or of being themselves polluted. Nor is the language of sexual infidelity applied to their activity; they are not said to engage in illicit sexual activity, nor does Ezekiel employ images of female sexual defilement (e.g., *znh, nddh, zmmh*) to describe them.[42] Unlike his condemnations of Jerusalem, whether in chaps 16 and 23 or elsewhere in chaps 1-24, Ezekiel's accusations against actual women condemn their ritual activity directly, with no suggestion that as women they are defiled or defiling. Both groups of women are depicted as the female equivalent of their male counterparts, the sun worshipers (8:16) and the male false prophets (13:1-16).

C. *Ezek 18:6, 11, 15; 22:10-11*

In chaps 18 and 22 women are not actually condemned; rather, they are mentioned as the occasion of male transgression. In his discussion of sin and responsibility in chap 18, Ezekiel includes among the acts of the "unrighteous man" sexual intercourse with a menstruating woman (*nddh*) and "dirtying" (*ṭm'*) his neighbor's wife through sexual intercourse (vv 6, 11, 15; and cf. 22:10-11). The two types of women described in these passages are both sexually forbidden: one because she is menstruating; the other because she is the sexual property of another man. The women's sexual status also makes them "unclean"; one is a *nddh*, a virtual byword for uncleanness, and the other becomes unclean (*ṭm'*) through illicit intercourse. In the list of things a righteous man does not do, intercourse with forbidden women serves as an example of defiling contact with the realm of the unclean.

Unlike the Tammuz worshipers and female prophets Ezekiel condemns in chaps 8 and 13, the forbidden women in chaps 18 and 22 *are* depicted in terms of their sexual defilement. In fact, they are little more than symbols of defilement. This portrayal of women as metonymous for defilement has more in common with Ezekiel's portrayal of the woman Jerusalem in chaps 16 and 23 and of the city and temple throughout chaps 1-24 than with his descriptions of actual women. Two factors account for the marked difference between Ezekiel's account of the Tammuz worshipers and the false prophets and his depiction of women in chaps 18 and 22. First, the women in chaps 18 and 22 are not actual, but hypothetical women. Specifically, they are examples of forbidden women, those who have power to make men unclean.[43] Second, the context in which these unclean women appear is a catalogue, not of *their*

---

[42] The only metaphor used to describe the female false prophets is one drawn from a world of presumably male endeavor; they are hunters, tracking down the people (or possibly, they are animals of prey).

[43] The menstruating woman is forbidden *because* she is unclean, while the married women, because she is forbidden, *becomes* unclean through illicit intercourse. Both pollute the male who transgresses the sexual boundary.

pollution, but of *men*'s lawlessness. In context they represent, not a type of woman, but a type of potential transgression by males; along with the oppressed poor and the victim of usury, the women are used as examples of the men's debasement. Unlike the women worshiping Tammuz and the female false prophets, these women are not condemned, because their sexual activity is not considered as their own activity, but as that of the unrighteous man. Sexual contact with defiled (and therefore defiling) women is simply one among many types of crime that the evil man commits and the righteous man avoids. The sexually dangerous women of chaps 18 and 22 are not culpable moral agents, but symbols of potential *male* defilement, a boundary separating the evil man from the righteous.

D. *Conclusions*

Ezekiel's representations of both female false worshipers and hypothetically defiled women are significant for analysis of his depiction of the woman Jerusalem. First, the lack of any language suggesting defilement or illicit sexuality in the condemnations of the actual women argues against the possibility that Ezekiel thought of women only in terms of their potential or actual sexual defilement. Ezekiel's focus on Jerusalem's defilement as specifically "sexual" defilement may therefore best be understood as stemming from his obsession with temple pollution, and from his projection of that pollution onto the figure of the personified city.

Second, Ezekiel's use in chaps 18 and 22 of women to symbolize *male* defilement is telling. Ezekiel describes male sexual transgression exclusively in terms of *female* uncleanness. Thus the evil man approaches "a woman who is a *nddh*" or he "pollutes" his neighbor's wife (rather than himself!) through intercourse. The male "crosses the boundary" between law and lawlessness, which is also the boundary between the clean and the unclean. Although it is the male who transgresses the law and the boundary it defines, the world outside the boundary, the "other" world, is symbolized by the forbidden woman. The woman's uncleanness symbolizes the male's transgression.

Ezekiel's use of female sexual pollution in chaps 18 and 22 as a symbol of male transgression parallels his depiction of Jerusalem throughout chaps 1-24. The transgressions of all Jerusalem's inhabitants are represented by female sexual uncleanness. Just as the unjust man of chap 18 has intercourse with either a *nddh* or with a married woman, so the city is depicted either as a *nddh* (7:20) or as an unfaithful wife. The metaphoric connection between the sanctity of the temple and the sexuality of the personified city becomes the occasion for Ezekiel's translation of various acts of male transgression into instances of female sexual pollution.[44]

IV. AFTER THE FALL: EZEKIEL 25-39

After the report of the death of Ezekiel's wife in 24:15-24, Ezekiel's condemnations of the woman Jerusalem cease. Chapters 25-32 contain a series of oracles against the surrounding nations, a standard prophetic device used for announcing salvation to Israel.[45] Following the oracles against the foreign nations in chaps 25-32, in 33:1-20 Ezekiel reports a second commissioning by Yahweh, after which he hears that Jerusalem has fallen to the Babylonians (33:21-22). The remainder of chaps 33-39 consists largely of oracles of promise to Israel, predicting the cleansing of the land and restoration of the nation.

After the fall of the city Jerusalem is never again mentioned by name. The oracles of salvation and restoration scrupulously avoid mention of Jerusalem, and marital and sexual imagery is entirely absent from the descriptions of Israel's future.[46] Instead, Yahweh promises that "the mountains of Israel" (36:8-15), "my people" (37:13), or "Judah" and "the house of Israel" (37:16) will be renewed and restored. The "everlasting covenant" once promised to the woman Jerusalem (16:60-62) is now promised to the people as a whole (37:26-27). The language of covenant ("I will be their God and they will be my people"; 37:27) associated elsewhere with the marriage metaphor (Hos 2:20-22 [Eng 2:18-20]; Isa 54:10; Ezek 16:8) is here employed exclusively in its literal, political, and cultic senses. The new covenant will establish the kingship of David, the obedience of the people, and peace (vv 24-26). Even Yahweh's presence in a new sanctuary (*mqdš*; v 26), a sanctuary identified explicitly as the tabernacle (*mškn*; v 27), is portrayed without the use of the marriage metaphor and with no reference to Jerusalem.

While Jerusalem itself is not mentioned in Yahweh's promises of restoration, the language and imagery used to depict Jerusalem in chaps 1-24 does appear once in chaps 33-39, in 36:17-21. In a promise to the

---

[44] Sanday (*Female Power*, 92-94) argues that a society's "sense of danger is projected onto the female body," providing "a stage on which to control the dangerous forces" faced by that society.

[45] See Hayes, "Oracles Against Foreign Nations."

[46] On the contrast between this and the restoration envisioned by other prophets see Chapter Three.

mountains of Israel, Yahweh gives a synopsis of Israel's former behavior: "When the house of Israel lived in their own land, they polluted (*tm*ʾ) it by their ways and actions; their behavior in my presence was like the pollution of a menstruating woman (*ktm*ʾ*t hnddh*). So I spilled out my rage onto them because of the blood they had spilled out on the land, in polluting it with their idols" (vv 17-18).

Yahweh's claim is striking. The sins of bloodshed and idolatry, both capital crimes, are said to result in pollution "like that of a menstruating woman." Although menstrual pollution is a strong contaminant, it is not the same category of offense as bloodshed and idolatry, both of which pollute both the holy of holies and the land itself.[47] Nor is menstruation a crime, let alone a capital offense. Yahweh's comparison of two such incommensurate forms of pollution may be partially explained as an instance of Ezekiel's use (7:19; cf. Isa 30:22) of the term *nddh* as a symbol of uncleanness itself, perhaps of especially repugnant uncleanness. If Ezekiel were using *nddh* simply as a generic term for pollution, then Yahweh's comparison in 36:17-18 would amount merely to a claim that idolatry and bloodshed had made the people "disgustingly unclean."

Such an explanation, however, while superficially plausible, ignores the implications of both the term *nddh* and the accusation of "bloodshed and idolatry" within Ezekiel. When Ezekiel says in 7:19 that the people will treat their gold and silver "like a *nddh*," he uses the word as a metaphor for uncleanness. He goes on, however, to explain in vv 20-22 that because its gold and silver have been used for idolatry, he will cause his own "private place" to be profaned, making *it* "like a *nddh*." Ezekiel goes from using *nddh* as a byword for uncleanness, to the shocking implication that the temple itself will be like a *nddh* as a result of its idolatry (here using synecdoche within the metaphoric vehicle; the temple, as metaphoric uterus, is not a *nddh*, but a *nddh*'s uterus). The connection between menstrual impurity and the idolatrous temple suggests the feminine persona of the city and the symbolism of the temple as uterus. The temple rejected as a *nddh* is the uterus of the city described as a blood-covered prostitute in chaps 16 and 23 and the "bloody city whose blood is in her" of 24:6-7 (cf. 22:2-4). The *nddh* of the book of Ezekiel is Jerusalem.

In addition to the images of "bloody Jerusalem" evoked by the term *nddh*, Yahweh's claim that in their idolatry the people have poured out blood on the land (v 18) has a clear antecedent in the actions of the

---

[47] Only "murder, sexual abominations, and idolatry—pollute both the people and the land" (Frymer-Kensky, "Pollution," 408).

woman Jerusalem: the sacrifice of her children, identified in 16:20-22 and 23:36-39 as "bloodshed and idolatry." In 22:3-4 also "the bloody city" is condemned for idolatrous bloodshed, and in 24:7 "the bloody city" is accused of pouring this blood on the rock uncovered. Ezekiel persistently connects the city's bloody (menstrual?) uncleanness with the defilement caused by her child sacrifice. The defilement caused by Jerusalem's child sacrifice is central to Ezekiel's explanation of the city's destruction; it is presented as the final and most severe of the woman Jerusalem's crimes (23:36-39) and the reason for Yahweh's revenge (20:26; 24:8). In light of Ezekiel's prior accusations against Jerusalem, the reference in 36:18 to "blood poured out on the land" that is in turn "defiled through idolatry" evokes the image of the child sacrifice earlier attributed to the woman Jerusalem. Both the use of the term "*nddh*" and the accusation of idolatrous bloodshed link Yahweh's retrospective account of Jerusalem's past sins with her earlier personification as a woman.

Yahweh's summary in 36:17-21 of Israel's unclean past includes the only use of female sexuality as a symbol of defilement in chaps 36-39. Though the city is neither personified nor even mentioned by name, the behavior of the people was "like the pollution of a menstruant." The acts "like a menstruant" of which the people are accused are precisely those attributed to the woman Jerusalem. The metaphor of the city's pollution as sexual defilement has, however, after the city's fall, been translated into a simile. Ezekiel does not say that "she is [or was] unfaithful, unclean, or bloody," but that the (male) people have behaved "like" a menstruant. In Ezekiel 33-39, in the aftermath of the Babylonian invasion, the woman Jerusalem is neither condemned nor forgiven, but forgotten. The only remnant of Yahweh's former wife is the abiding memory of her uncleanness.

V. THE LADY VANISHES: THE TEMPLE CITY OF EZEKIEL 40-48

Ezekiel's vision in chaps 40-48 of the new temple city completes the cycle of the city's defilement, destruction, and restoration. The God who left in rage returns in triumph, and the city is renewed and recreated. Only Jerusalem, the chastened and forgiven wife, is absent from the scene. The new city is described as inanimate stone, and its private parts bear no reminders of their former, sexual signification. Yahweh's prophecy that, having been purified, Jerusalem would never open her mouth again (16:63) is fulfilled, albeit ironically. She does not open her mouth because, no longer portrayed as a woman, she cannot. The restored city is faithful, but only because the elimination of the city's female persona has made infidelity impossible.

A. *Purity without Danger: Ezekiel 40-48*

In 36:25 Yahweh promises that he will purify and then restore the house of Israel (cf. 16:63). This cleansing is accomplished in Ezekiel 39 where, having defeated Israel's last enemies, Yahweh hosts a banquet at which animals are invited to feast on human flesh and blood (39:17-20). The grisly gathering, which would ordinarily create defilement (Gen 9:4; Lev 17:10), is instead depicted as the final stage in the purification of the land prior to the restoration of Israel. Mary Douglas[48] notes that "pollutants are often used in renewal rites," first, to transform the negative power of the pollutant, and second, to emphasize the power of the one who, within the ritual system, can manipulate the power of the pollutant. In the blood-feast of Ezekiel 39 Yahweh, having re-established his military power in defeat of an apparently cosmic enemy, re-establishes his power over the life-force of blood. Yahweh uses human sacrifice (*zbh*; vv 17, 19) to purge the pollution caused by Jerusalem's sacrifice of her children. Once the pollution of the land has been remedied in chap 39, Yahweh takes steps to ensure against its future pollution. This prevention of pollution, specifically the pollution of Yahweh's new, holy dwelling, is the principle governing the structure and laws of the new temple depicted in chaps 40-48.

Ezekiel is brought in 40:2 to the land of Israel, where a "bronzelike" man (40:3; cf. 1:26-27; 8:2) takes him on a tour of the temple precincts, measuring its dimensions and pointing out its various features. This vision of the new temple city is presented as a balancing counterpart to Ezekiel's tour of the polluted temple in chaps 8-11. Whereas earlier Ezekiel had been shown, first the "abominations" that were "driving [Yahweh] from the sanctuary" (8:6), and then the actual departure of the divine chariot (11:23), in the new temple he sees fixtures and hears regulations that serve to "make a division between the holy and the common" (42:20). In the midst of this tour Ezekiel witnesses as Yahweh returns from the east and re-enters the new, pure temple (43:1-7), never again to leave.

The new temple is unlike the old precisely in its freedom from defilement. Both its architecture and its laws are designed to ensure a

---

[48] *Purity and Danger*, 163-64; and cf. Meigs, "Papuan Perspective," 309.

degree of holiness even greater than that prescribed for the former temple. The temple is set within a holy courtyard, enclosed by a ten foot thick wall. This in turn is surrounded by a holy district inhabited by priests (45:1-5) and Levites. Within the temple, stricter laws govern the purity of the priests than formerly (e.g., 44:22; cf. Lev 21:7), and for the first time all foreigners are excluded from the temple (44:9; cf. Josh 9:23; Num 15:14).

In light of Yahweh's earlier promise to Jerusalem (16:59-63) that, after punishing, he would cleanse, restore, and initiate a new covenant with her,[49] it would seem natural for Yahweh to describe his relationship with the new city as a new betrothal to his cleansed and penitent bride.[50] In Ezekiel's vision of the happy future, however, no such reconciliation takes place. In fact, the new temple city is never personified as a woman, nor is vocabulary associated with the woman Jerusalem of chaps 16 and 23 used to describe the city. The only use of such feminine imagery occurs in Yahweh's vehement denial that this city will be like the former one. In 43:7-9, swearing to remain in the new temple forever, Yahweh explains that he will be able to do so because "the house of Israel will never again defile my holy name . . . by their prostitution [znwt]. . . . Now they will put their prostitution far away." The use of the verb znh to describe what the house of Israel will not do is the only explicitly feminine imagery in the vision of Ezekiel 40-48.[51]

---

49 And cf. similar promises in the prophetic tradition in which Ezekiel shared (e.g., Hos 2:16-22 [Eng 14-20]; Isa 1:26).

50 The expectation of this new betrothal between Yahweh and the city is so strong that the author of Revelation, whose vision of the new city is directly modeled on that of Ezekiel 40-48, depicts the city as Yahweh's *bride*. After the defeat of the "whore" (who is *not* Jerusalem), John reports, "I saw the holy city, new Jerusalem, descending from heaven, from God, prepared as a bride for her husband" (2:12). John superimposes Ezekiel's image of Yahweh adorning Jerusalem as his bride onto the image of the restored city, thus supplying the symbolic reunion that Ezekiel lacks. The image of the restored city in 4 Ezra is similarly dependent on Ezekiel 40-48, and likewise presents the new city as a woman: "This woman whom you saw, whom you now behold as an established city, is Zion" (10:44).

51 The use of explicitly feminine imagery in Ezekiel 40-48 is thus equivalent to its use in chaps 33-39. In 36:17-21 feminine images are used to evoke the memory of Jerusalem's unsavory past, and in 43:7-9 they are used to deny that this past will be repeated. Because the city is never addressed directly, even the minimal level of personification required by the use of second person feminine verb forms is eliminated. The third person feminine pronoun is used only once, in 48:16, "These will be its [her] dimensions." Interestingly, English translations (e.g., RSV) that consistently render the feminine pronoun "her" throughout chaps 1-24 translate the 3fs possessive pronoun here as "it," reflecting accurately (if, perhaps, unconsciously)

This complete absence of the woman Jerusalem from the vision of the restored temple, while a departure from both earlier prophetic tradition and from Ezekiel's earlier prophecies, is consistent with Ezekiel's use of the marriage metaphor elsewhere. Ezekiel's Jerusalem is Jerusalem the prostitute, always and indelibly contaminated with blood, and insatiable in her adulterous lust. Ezekiel's depictions of Jerusalem the whore draw out the full implications of a symbolic system according to which woman's impurity is a source of male defilement, and her infidelity a source of male shame. In Ezekiel 1-39 the woman Jerusalem becomes virtually metonymous for defilement itself. Especially, she becomes a symbol of the defilement of the temple, defilement that threatens the very holiness of Yahweh. Having enlisted the reader to share in Yahweh's revulsion at the woman's bloody uncleanness (in 16:1-43; cf. 24:1-14), having shamed her, and excluded her from the bounds of the sanctified community, Ezekiel has effectively disqualified her from inclusion in the new creation. Given the history of Yahweh's wife's unrelenting perversity, it would have been no simple task to have reintroduced a female Jerusalem as a symbol of purity, and the guardian of both Yahweh's honor and of ritual law.

In chaps 16 and 23 (and less directly throughout chaps 1-24) Ezekiel presents the irremediable defilement of Yahweh's wife as the justification for Yahweh's abandonment and punishment of the people. The old Jerusalem's penchant, both for producing unclean blood and for allowing foreign men access to Yahweh's "private place," precludes the possibility of her remarriage to Yahweh. The incompatibility between the holy god and the personified city does not vanish with the cleansing of the city; the conflict is implicit within the marriage metaphor itself. If the city is Yahweh's wife, then both Yahweh's purity and his honor depend on the conduct and physical condition of that metaphorical "woman." If Jerusalem, however thoroughly cleansed, remains a woman, then Yahweh, as divine husband, remains in danger of defilement, whether through inadvertent contact with a *nddh*, or worse, through his wife's infidelity.[52]

Hosea, Isaiah, and Jeremiah overlooked or did not notice the marriage metaphor's implicit tendency to jeopardize Yahweh's purity and

---

both the implied personification of the city throughout chaps 1-39, and the emphatic lack of personification in chaps 40-48.

[52] The marriage laws of Leviticus 21, which Ezekiel makes even more strict, forbid priests from marrying (former?) prostitutes (v 7). Ezekiel is unlikely to depict Yahweh marrying a woman who would have been forbidden to an ordinary priest.

honor. The earlier prophets exploited the emotional force of the metaphor of a cuckolded god but did not focus on the problem of pollution inherent in the personification of Yahweh's dwelling place as a woman. This difference in focus may explain the earlier prophets' willingness to envision the restored city as a reconciled wife. Ezekiel, concerned above all with the purity of the temple, sees all too clearly the implications of Yahweh's broken marriage; the repugnance of the temple's pollution becomes even more offensive when Yahweh's presence in an unclean *house* is depicted as his intercourse with a menstruating or unfaithful woman. Once the dynamics of temple pollution have been fully explicated in terms of female sexual pollution, with its attendant danger of polluting the male, no personification of the temple as Yahweh's sexual partner could be tolerated.[53]

B. *The Return of the Repressed:*
The Feminine Identity of the New City

Having exposed the potential for defilement inherent in the marriage metaphor, Ezekiel necessarily refrains from personifying the new city as Yahweh's wife. Every trace of the city's former persona, including her name, has been purged from the restored city. Ezekiel's ability to dissolve entirely the marriage between city and god, however, is limited. Although the degree to which the personification of cities was a "dead" metaphor is impossible to determine, the fact that no city is ever portrayed or addressed as a *man* in the Hebrew Bible suggests that, though the city's female status could be ignored, it could not easily be contradicted.[54] Thus the new city/temple of Ezekiel 40-48, while never actually

---

[53] The coherent use of the marriage metaphor throughout Ezekiel supports the possibility that the book is substantially the work of a single author or editor (on which, see M. Greenberg, "The Design and Themes of Ezekiel's Program of Restoration," *Int* 38 [1984] 181-208). The integration of language suggesting the female persona of Jerusalem throughout chaps 1-24 furthers the impression of the conceptual unity of this section. The elimination of Jerusalem from the second half of the book, except in retrospective passages recalling its "whoredom" (43:7-9) and "menstruation" (36:18) is likewise consistent with the intolerability of the polluted woman of chaps 1-24. Finally, the absence of the city's female persona from the vision of restoration, while initially surprising, is in fact a logical solution to the problem of the pollution that drove Yahweh from his temple.

[54] Ezekiel's ability to portray the city of Tyre as, not a woman, but a ship (chap 26) suggests that the metaphor was not entirely "dead," or at least that other metaphors might be added to the dead metaphor of the city as a woman (so in English, the "face" of a clock might also be called a "full moon"). The depiction of Tyre as a ship harmonizes well with its portrayal as a woman, since ships are also traditionally, and

personified, nonetheless retains the role, and so some of the identity, of Jerusalem, the bride of Yahweh.[55]

Ezekiel presents the new temple as the opposite of the old, both in terms of its purity and of the many safeguards protecting that purity. The lack of feminine personification may be understood as one such safeguard against impurity. If the temple is no longer a woman, it is no longer in danger of being polluted either from within (by producing unclean blood) or from without (by breaking vows and "hosting" foreign men). The sacred building is more easily controlled than the sacred woman. The new temple, cured of its former waywardness by the absence of its former persona, is further protected by both physical and legal barriers. It is surrounded by a thick wall, beyond which foreign men are forbidden. Within the wall, Yahweh's representatives, the priests, order all activity. Blood, which so defiled the interior of the female "temple," is also present within the new temple, but now only its life-bearing power is operative, and that under the control of Yahweh's priests. Manipulated by sanctioned authorities, its polluting power is transformed into cleansing power, the force through which the defiled "other" may be reinscribed within the boundaries of Yahweh's domain.

Because the life-powers within are so carefully controlled, and the pollutants without so thoroughly excluded, the new temple is a suitable and acceptable dwelling for Yahweh. The new, ideal, and unpersonified city can now be trusted not to defile Yahweh's name (through sancta trespass). Therefore that divine name which the former Jerusalem so thoroughly defiled may safely be bestowed upon the new sanctuary

---

in Hebrew, grammatically, feminine. However, when Ezekiel applies specifically *masculine* imagery or pronouns to cities, the imagery is applied, not to the city itself, but to its king (so it is the king of Tyre, and not a personified, male "Tyre," that is addressed in Ezekiel 27; cf. the depiction of Pharaoh as a sea monster in Ezekiel 32), thus avoiding the use of masculine imagery for an entity understood to be metaphorically female.

[55] The reappearance of explicit personification in Revelation and 4 Ezra attests to the strength of the city's female persona. Modern commentators have similarly supplied "the missing woman" in their interpretations of Ezekiel 40-48. So, e.g., M. Parker ("Exploring Four Persistent Prophetic Images," *Bible Review* 6 [1990] 38-45) cites Ezekiel as typical of a pattern wherein "the bride turns adulteress or harlot and is humiliated by her lovers before she is finally restored as Yahweh's wife" (39). R. MacKenzie ("The City and Israelite Religion," *CBQ* 25 [1963] 60-70) reports the destruction of Jerusalem as "only a temporary interruption, a disciplinary interlude, in this divine romance; Sion after her chastisement will be for ever reunited with the Spouse who has pledged her his eternal faith" (68).

(48:35). Instead of "Jerusalem," the name of this city is "Yahweh Is There," a final reversal of the rejection of the old city.

Ezekiel depicts a temple city that is the opposite of the old, defiled, and rejected Jerusalem; in his very description of the new temple, he "makes a separation" (Lev 10:10; Ezek 42:20) between the clean temple to be and the unclean temple that was. Such radical opposition, however, has its limits. To the extent that the extreme and carefully guarded purity of the new temple city is a response to the unruliness and pollution of the old, the new city can be seen as a mirror image of the depraved woman Jerusalem. The new, inviolable city perforce plays the role of a well-behaved alter-ego to the old Jerusalem.

In addition to the comparison implied by the opposition between the new city and the old, the femininity of the new temple city is implicit in its very status as a capital city. The conceptual metaphor of the city as a woman would continue to exert an influence, whether or not Ezekiel intended to personify the city.[56] The attributes that originally gave rise to the personification of capitals as women would likewise characterize Yahweh's new dwelling: the city is an enclosed space, and the sacred home of the protector god. Moreover, in light of the biblical tradition of personifying capital cities, the city's feminine persona would be hard to eradicate entirely. The feminine persona, even when not presented, could be presumed.[57]

Ezekiel's new city, while separated insofar as possible from the old Jerusalem, exhibits the same "feminine" characteristics as its predecessor. Physically, it is an enclosed space, the sheltering "mother" of its inhabitants. The city contains within it a series of hidden enclosures, each of successively greater mystery and containing successively greater power. The innermost chamber is that place where the power of blood is controlled. That innermost chamber is also the jealously protected possession of the male god, whose honor depends on the inviolability of the inner sanctum. Such a space cannot avoid association with the feminine, given the parallel functions of the temple and the wife in the symbolic world of the Hebrew Bible. The temple is to its god as the woman, in her sexual capacity, is to her husband. The marriage metaphor merely expresses an existing system in which the mysterious and internal

---

[56] Neumann (*Great Mother*, 46, 283; and cf. Mumford, *City in History*, 12-16) argues that the "symbolism of cities as feminine is universal."

[57] Cf. the personification in Isaiah 1 and Nahum 3 in which the city's feminine persona is clear without being explicitly stated.

powers of both woman and temple must be carefully controlled by the male in authority over them.

Physically and symbolically, Ezekiel's new temple city retains an affinity with the defiled woman it replaces. The new temple, however, goes beyond the old in symbolic fulfillment of its subliminal sexuality: the new temple is fertile. The old Jerusalem had borne children to Yahweh but, "not remembering [her] own . . . birthblood" (16:22), promptly murdered them. The new temple, though inanimate, gives symbolic birth. After his tour of the temple fortifications, Ezekiel returns to the entrance of the temple. Here he sees a stream of water flowing from beneath the threshhold. The stream is fertile, supporting trees that perpetually bear fruit, and whose leaves have medicinal powers (v 12). All kinds of fish can live in the river, and they in turn support human life (vv 9-10). The stream is not only fertile, but also cleansing, turning salt water fresh (v 9). This life-giving stream, issuing from the "entrance" to the inner sanctum, is reminiscent of the flow of blood that earlier characterized the woman Jerusalem. This stream, however, like the blood contained within this temple, is both clean and cleansing,[58] the inverse of menstrual or other uterine blood. The flow from the interior of the new temple is a sort of symbolic amniotic fluid, a provider and sustainer of life.

Flowing water is a common image of female sexuality. The term "fountain" (*mqwr*) is commonly used in the Hebrew Bible to designate female sexual organs. In Lev 20:18 the woman's "fountain" flows with menstrual blood, and in Lev 12:7, with the blood of childbirth. Prov 5:15-18, however, describes a woman metonymically as a "fountain," and advises the prudent man to drink from his own and not another's, taking care lest his own "fountain" should go flowing out into the street. In this latter case the fountain remains a symbol of female sexual organs but apparently describes their flowing during intercourse rather than with blood. The female lover is also described as a fountain, first sealed and then flowing, in Cant 4:12-15.[59]

Images of a stream that flows from the city or temple are found elsewhere in the Hebrew Bible, as well as in the ancient Near East. Ps

---

[58] In the Mishnah, water from a flowing spring is considered the most purifying and therefore the most appropriate water for the cleansing of menstrual blood. Unlike rain water, it can purify objects for either sacred or secular use (*Miqw.* 1:8; J. Neusner, "From Scripture to Mishnah: The Origins of Tractate Niddah," *JJS* 29 [1978] 135-48).

[59] Cant 8:9-10 uses the image of a virgin as a "wall."

46:5 (Eng 4) speaks of the "river that rejoices" the city of God, and Joel 4:18 (Eng 3:18) predicts that a fountain will flow from the house of Yahweh. Zechariah (13:1; 14:8) likewise predicts that a fountain will flow from Jerusalem.[60] Two rivers are said to flow from the palace of El,[61] Baal is enthroned upon the "flood,"[62] and images of two rivers[63] flowing from a sacred place are common in Mesopotamian iconography.[64] The imagery of Ezekiel 40-48 is also reminiscent of Eden,[65] from which fertilizing rivers flow and in which the tree of life grows.[66] Ezekiel

----

[60] Cf. Ps 68:27, in which those who process into the sanctuary are called upon to bless Yahweh "from the fountain of Israel." So also in Ps 87:7 the celebrants on Zion say, "all my springs are within you."

[61] R. Clifford, *Cosmic Mountain*, 52 n28, 97.

[62] The sequence of events in Baal's battle on Mount Zaphon are strikingly similar to those of Ezekiel 38-47. Like Yahweh battling Gog (chap 38), Baal fights a cosmic battle on the mountain, after which he holds a feast (cf. Ezek 39:17-20). He then calls the goddess Anat to "put on the face of the goddess of fertility" and help him establish upon the mountain his new dwelling, out of which the rivers flow (see Clifford, *The Cosmic Mountain*, 66, 74, 77; and cf. the similar sequence of events after Gudea builds a temple [*The Harps That Once . . .*, 386-444]).

[63] The use of the dual, *nhlym*, in 47:9 is suggestive. Though it could be translated "two rivers," given the lack of any explicit reference to a second river in the passage, it is probably a plural of extension or of amplification, reflecting the abundance of water (GKC §§124b, e). Zechariah does depict two rivers (14:8), one flowing east and one west.

[64] See, e.g., the Assyrian cylinder seal described in Clifford (*Cosmic Mountain*, 95-96), in which two rivers flow from a heavenly source into two vases, and "a sacred tree blooms on a mountain, arising out of the same kind of vase that received the heavenly waters." The "flowing vase motif" is common in the depiction of goddesses, and in the iconography of their temples (see H. Frankfort, *The Art and Architecture of the Ancient Orient* [Harmondsworth: Penguin, 1954] esp. 58, 62-63; A. Moortgat, *The Art of Ancient Mesopotamia: The Classical Art of the Near East* [London: Phaidon, 1969] esp. his discussion of "water goddesses," 66, 70, 88-89, 94, 111-12, including an Old Babylonian water goddess whose headdress has "an altar or temple facade," 89).

[65] On the Eden symbolism of Ezekiel's vision, see M. Fishbane, *Text and Texture: Close Readings of Selected Biblical Texts* (New York: Schocken, 1979) 111-20; J. D. Levenson, *Theology of the Program of Restoration*, 25-43; G. J. Wenham, "Sanctuary Symbolism in the Garden of Eden Story," in *Ninth World Congress*, 19-25; Eliade, *Patterns*, 282.

[66] The "tree of life" is itself a feminine symbol (see Neumann, *Great Mother*, 48-52, 241-56; Eliade, *Patterns*, 280-86, 380-82; Frankfort, *Art and Architecture*, 17). M. N. Powers ("Menstruation and Reproduction: An Oglala Case," *Signs* 6 [1980] 54-65) cites the role of the fruit tree in Oglala rituals of both menarche and birth (58, 61). Within the OT, see Cant 7:7-8, in which the woman is portrayed as a fruit-bearing tree, and Prov 3:18, in which Torah (grammatically feminine) is called a tree of life.

presents the holy city as, like Eden, the center of the universe,[67] the source of life, and the point of contact between heaven and earth.

Ezekiel's new city performs a *symbolically* feminine role: a walled, protecting and protected space, from which defiling elements (specifically, foreign men) are excluded, but within which the mysterious power of life resides and from which fertile streams flow out to produce fruit-bearing trees. The pure, safe, and fertile city is a fitting consort for the male god. Unlike the personified woman Jerusalem, this city performs the functions of the "eternal feminine" without the attendant risks of pollution. The new city represents an assimilation of the powers associated with the female body into the ritual system as an object of priestly jurisdiction. Although, or perhaps because the female *body* has been excluded,[68] the temple's symbolically feminine role is no longer a symbol of otherness but of Yahweh's secure dominion.

VI. CONCLUSIONS

In chaps 1-24 Ezekiel, using the traditional image of the city as Yahweh's wife, describes in detail the sexual abominations of which the city, as a woman, is guilty. Following the logic of the marriage metaphor to its extremes, Ezekiel reveals the kind and degree of sexual defilement implied by the gross pollution of the temple. The visceral power of Ezekiel's resulting images reinforces a sense of horror at the uncleanness of Yahweh's holy place. Ultimately, the metaphor of the city as a woman becomes unusable, both because it has been associated with such intolerable levels of pollution and because the potential for that pollution is built into the metaphor itself. If the city is a woman, it is always possible for "the faithful city" to "become a whore" (Isa 1:21). The requisite purity of the new city does not allow for its explicit personification as a woman. Ezekiel accordingly does all he can to avoid depicting the new city as

---

The goddess Asherah is also represented by a tree or pole (e.g., 1 Kgs 15:12-13; cf. Olyan, *Asherah*, 5-9).

[67] On the mythology of the "omphalos," or center of the earth, see S. Terrien, "The Omphalos in Hebrew Mythology," *VT* 20 (1970) 315-38; Eliade, *Patterns*, 367-71, 374-79.

[68] The Qumran Temple Scroll provides an interesting parallel in this respect. Like Ezekiel 40-48, the Temple Scroll prescribes that the entire city about the temple must be holy. Y. Yadin argues (*The Temple Scroll* [3 vols.; Jerusalem: Israel Exploration Society, 1983] 1. 306-7) that in order to preserve the holiness of the city (and thus of the temple within it), women are forbidden from the city altogether, because of the danger posed by menstrual pollution.

Yahweh's wife. Nevertheless, the feminine cannot be entirely excluded from the vision. Both culturally and symbolically, the identification of the city as feminine proves impossible to eradicate fully.

Ezekiel foresaw that, faced with the people's continued and apparently incorrigible rebelliousness, Yahweh would literally have to reconstruct them, to make them able to choose obedience: "I will remove your stone heart from your body and give you a heart of flesh. I will put my spirit inside you and make you behave according to my statutes and keep my ordinances" (36:26-27; cf. 11:19; 18:31). God's people would be changed from stone into flesh. In light of her similar disobedience, Ezekiel foresaw that a similar transformation would be necessary to ensure the obedience of Yahweh's consort, Jerusalem. The woman Jerusalem, however, suffers the opposite fate from the people. Instead of being changed from stone to flesh, she is changed from flesh to stone— from a woman to a fortified wall. Given the pollution of the old Jerusalem and the connection drawn between that pollution and the sexuality of Jerusalem as woman, no explicitly female figure could represent the inviolable purity demanded for the new temple. If the catastrophe of Yahweh's abandonment were to be prevented from recurring, the new city must be less a consort and more a fortress. Ezekiel therefore envisions a city that will perform the symbolic functions of the former, female Jerusalem, but without the uncleanness of her sexuality.

VI

CONCLUSION: THE FUNCTION OF THE MARRIAGE METAPHOR IN THE BOOK OF EZEKIEL

This study has analyzed Ezekiel's metaphorical depiction of the city Jerusalem as Yahweh's wife. Ezekiel's personification of Jerusalem in chaps 16 and 23 is an appropriate vehicle to describe various aspects of the relationship between Yahweh and the city. First, the metaphor of marriage describes the proper relationship between the city and its god: gracious favor by the superior party and grateful fidelity by the inferior party. The metaphor of marital infidelity similarly describes Jerusalem's violation of that relationship. The marriage metaphor is also well suited for the retelling of Jerusalem's long history of infidelity; the device of biography allows Ezekiel to rehearse the various events of Jerusalem's past and to establish the city/woman's infidelity as a persistent character defect rather than as an isolated aberration. Finally, the use of the marriage metaphor, and specifically the metaphor of sexual infidelity, provides a convincing vehicle by which to depict (and justify) the intensity of Yahweh's outrage against the city. In fact, the use of the marriage metaphor may itself contribute to the reader's perception that Yahweh has been deeply humiliated and consequently must act to avenge his honor.

In addition to the explicit personification of Jerusalem in chaps 16 and 23, the city's feminine persona is implicit elsewhere in Ezekiel 1-24, in both the language and the imagery used to depict the city. Not only does Yahweh address the city using second person feminine singular forms, but also he describes Jerusalem's pollution in terms associated with female sexuality—"menstruant" (*nddh*; 7:19), "prostitute" (*znh*; 6:9), "perversion" (*zmmh*; 22:9; 24:13). The images chosen to represent the city—a pot with an unclean interior (24:6), a private place defiled by other men (7:22), an entity with "her blood in her" (24:7), and the sign-act of Ezekiel's wife's death as a representation of the city's fall (24:15-27)— are consistent with the association of Jerusalem with the feminine, and especially with feminine sexual impurity.[1]

In chaps 25-39, after the fall of Jerusalem, the city is no longer mentioned, but in 36:17 the people are remembered as having been "like a menstruant." In the final vision of chaps 40-48 the city is rebuilt but is not personified, either through the use of direct address, or through the use of metaphor. Although neither addressed nor designated as female, however, the city retains its role as home, as source of fertility, and as the exclusive possession of its lord. The restored city continues to be symbolically feminine, but this symbolism never is expressed by means of metaphor. The metaphor of the city as wife remains instead a metaphor exclusively of pollution and infidelity in the book of Ezekiel.

As has been discussed above, the marriage metaphor is well-suited to portray the relationship between Yahweh and Jerusalem. Because the metaphor had roots in Mesopotamia and had been widely used by earlier Hebrew Prophets, Ezekiel's readers would have been disposed to accept the proposition that the city was as a wife to Yahweh. Earlier prophetic depictions had also established the marriage metaphor as a means of depicting the relationship of subordination and obligation obtaining between Yahweh and the capital city. In addition, the metaphor captures well the twofold nature of Jerusalem's infidelity. Like sexual infidelity, in which trespass of a physical boundary simultaneously violates a legal obligation, so Jerusalem's cultic and political infidelities involved both the desecration of physical sancta and the violation of the legal and religious sancta of covenant obligation.

---

[1] Blood, especially shed blood (as in 22:3), would ordinarily, as an act of war, be associated with men. But as an image depicting a city, "bloodiness" is used in the Hebrew Bible only in personifications of cities as women (Nah 3:1; Jer 2:34; cf. Isa 4:4).

Two characteristics of the marriage metaphor make it especially apt for conveying Ezekiel's special concerns, namely, with the purity of the temple and with the honor of Yahweh, both of which must be protected if Yahweh is to dwell among the people of Israel. First, the metaphor of Jerusalem as a woman provides a powerful means for Ezekiel to explore his concern with the ritual pollution of the temple. If the city is a woman, then the temple is a symbolic vagina and womb, precisely those places most violated by the woman's sexual infidelity. Second, the symbolic defilement of Jerusalem's "womb" implies a shaming of her "husband." For this reason the marriage metaphor is an apt vehicle for describing the loss of honor to which Jerusalem's infidelity subjected Yahweh. The depiction of Yahweh expunging his own shame by punishing (including shaming) the unfaithful Jerusalem thus serves to reinterpret the destruction of the city as a *positive* event, one that reestablishes the honor and potency of Yahweh. This metaphoric refurbishment of Yahweh's honor not only would have allowed Ezekiel's readers to avoid the shame of acknowledging their god's humiliation and defeat, but also would have allowed male Judeans to expunge their own shame by transferring it to the personified woman, Jerusalem. As men in solidarity with a divine, punishing husband, male Judeans could, at least momentarily, have seen Jerusalem (and her shame) as "other," a woman justly shamed. The humiliation of personified Jerusalem would thus paradoxically serve to recapture a sense of power and control for the militarily humiliated male residents of the city.

A final aspect of Ezekiel's use of the marriage metaphor, one closely related to the metaphor's function as a means of expunging Yahweh's shame, is its use to establish symbolic control over the female. In Ezekiel, this quest for control is particularly expressed as the attempt by the male god and by Ezekiel, his representative, to control the woman through the power of the gaze. Ezekiel, who inspects the unpersonified temple as visionary in chaps 40-48, previously inspected the personified temple as voyeur. According to Laura Mulvey, voyeurism is a form of pornographic investigation in which the male's "pleasure lies in ascertaining guilt, . . . asserting control and subjecting the guilty person through punishment or forgiveness."[2] The voyeur "demystifies" the threateningly mysterious woman, first by investigating and exposing her secrets, and then by punishing and thus "saving" her.[3] The dynamics of voyeuristic

---

[2] "Visual Pleasure," 14. On the close relationship between pornography and investigation, see also A. Kuhn, *Power of the Image*, 20, 46.

[3] Mulvey, "Visual Pleasure," 13.

investigation are reproduced exactly in Yahweh's "revelation of the abominations" (16:2; 23:36) of the woman Jerusalem. Her story is traced in graphic sexual detail, her guilty uncleanness exposed, and her transgression punished. At the woman's punishment, Yahweh will be "sated . . . and calmed" (16:42), while the guilty woman will be humiliated, as much by her saving purgation (16:63) as by her punishment.

Ezekiel's role as divinely appointed voyeur is consistent, not only with his investigation of Jerusalem in chaps 16 and 23, but also with his two temple visions of chaps 8-11 and 40-48. Ezekiel's two visions of the temple, the polluted and the pure, encapsulate the plot of the entire book of Ezekiel. In the first vision, the prophet is led about the defiled temple and is asked by Yahweh to look at each feature of its defilement. He then witnesses as Yahweh's chariot abandons the rejected temple. In the second vision, Ezekiel is again given a tour of the temple in which he is continually told to "look" (40:4, 5, 17, 20, and so on), this time at the newly created temple and the features that safeguard its purity. Having thoroughly inspected this new edifice, Ezekiel then witnesses as Yahweh returns to the temple.

In light of Ezekiel's voyeuristic exposure of Jerusalem's sexual depravity in chaps 16 and 23, his two inspections of the temple can be understood as part of an overarching theme of control through focalization. In the old temple, Ezekiel peered through a peephole to discover the elders, themselves looking at their illicit pictures. In the new temple, the view is no longer shocking; investigation of the merely sanitary is without suspense. Ezekiel 40-48, the inspection of the demystified and objectified feminine, ceases to be voyeurism per se, taking on instead overtones of fetishism. According to Mulvey, the male faced with the feminine as threat may use a combination of two strategies to relieve his anxiety and establish control. He may demystify through voyeuristic investigation and punishment, or he may instead disavow the feminine "by the substitution of a fetish object or turning the represented figure itself into a fetish so that it becomes reassuring rather than dangerous. . . . This second avenue, fetishistic scopophilia, builds up the physical beauty of the object, transforming it into something satisfying in itself."[4]

Ezekiel's inspection of the new temple in chaps 40-48 represents precisely the substitution of a reassuring object in place of a threatening feminine subject. Originally, the woman Jerusalem was herself to be this

---

4 "Visual Pleasure," 13-14.

fetish. Cleansed of her defilement and decked with the symbols of Yahweh's authority, she "became his" (16:8), "perfect in beauty" (16:14) and inscribed within the realm of the god's control. Pornographic perfection, however, includes submission, and the woman Jerusalem failed in her role as fetish by her disobedience. The woman Jerusalem could therefore give satisfaction only by her punishment; true perfection must instead be sought in a symbolic object. That object is the restored city/temple, inanimate but "satisfying in itself," because in all its parts it reflects only the ideals and intentions of Yahweh. The new city's identity consists solely in its ownership by Yahweh: "Henceforth the name of the city is, 'Yahweh Is There'" (48:35).

The metaphor of the city as Yahweh's wife fulfills, among various roles, the role of mediating between prophet as visionary and prophet as voyeur. The woman Jerusalem functions as a metaphor of the chaos and castration that threaten Yahweh in light of both the desecration of his temple, and ultimately, its destruction. Yahweh's struggle for control emerges over the course of Ezekiel as a struggle between male and female, depicted in chaps 16 and 23 through a form of pornography, a whore's biography with the woman's sexual subordination as its goal. After the destruction of Yahweh's unfaithful wife, Ezekiel envisions a more perfect partner, a substitute in stone for Yahweh's ancient consort, "reassuring rather than dangerous," whose beauty will eternally reflect upon its maker.

BIBLIOGRAPHY

Ackerman, James S. "Satire and Symbolism in the Song of Jonah," *Traditions in Transformation: Turning Points in Biblical Faith* (ed. Baruch Halpern and Jon Levenson; Winona Lake, IN: Eisenbrauns, 1981) 213-46.

Adler, Elaine J. "The Background for the Metaphor of Covenant as Marriage in the Hebrew Bible" (diss., Berkeley, 1989).

Ahuis, Ferdinand. "Das Märchen im Alten Testament," *ZTK* 86 (1989) 455-76.

Andersen, Francis I., and David Noel Freedman. *Hosea* (AB 24; Garden City: Doubleday, 1980).

Andre, G. "ṭāmēʾ," *TDOT* V (1986) 331-42.

Bal, Mieke, ed. *Anti-Covenant: Counter-Reading Women's Lives in the Hebrew Bible* (JSOTS 81; Sheffield: Almond Press, 1989).

————. *Murder and Difference: Gender, Genre, and Scholarship on Sisera's Death* (Bloomington: Indiana University Press, 1988).

————. *Narratology: An Introduction to the Theory of Narrative* (Toronto: University of Toronto Press, 1985).

Ballantine, William. *Ezekiel: A Literary Study of His Prophecy* (New York: Fleming H. Revel, 1892).

Bartlett, John R. *Edom and the Edomites* (JSOTS 77; Sheffield: Journal for the Study of the Old Testament, 1989).

Batto, Bernard Frank. *Studies on Women at Mari* (Baltimore: Johns Hopkins Press, 1974).

Beardsley, Monroe C. "The Metaphorical Twist," *Philosophical Perspectives on Metaphor* (ed. Mark Johnson; Minneapolis: University of Minnesota Press, 1981) 105-22.

Begg, Christopher T. "The Non-mention of Ezekiel in the Book of Jeremiah," *ETL* 65 (1989) 94-95.

―――. "*berit* in Ezekiel," *Proceedings of the Ninth World Congress of Jewish Studies* (Jerusalem: World Union of Jewish Studies, 1986) 77-83.

Biddle, Mark. "The Figure of Lady Jerusalem: Identification, Deification, and Personification of Cities in the ANE," *The Biblical Canon in Comparative Perspective* (Scripture in Context 4; ed. W. W. Hallo, et al.; Lewiston, NY: Edwin Mellen Press, 1991) 173-194.

Bird, Phyllis. "To Play the Harlot: An Inquiry into an Old Testament Metaphor," *Gender and Difference in Ancient Israel* (ed. Peggy Day; Minneapolis: Fortress Press, 1989) 75-94.

Black, Max. *Models and Metaphors: Studies in Language and Philosophy* (Ithaca, NY: Cornell University Press, 1962).

―――. "Metaphor," *Proceedings of the Aristotelian Society,* NS 55 (1954-55) 273-94; reprinted in *Philosophical Perspectives on Metaphor* (ed. Mark Johnson; Minneapolis: University of Minnesota Press, 1981) 63-82.

Blenkinsopp, Joseph. *Ezekiel* (Louisville: John Knox Press, 1990).

Block, Daniel I. "Ezekiel's Boiling Cauldron: A Form-critical Solution to Ezekiel xxiv 1-14," *VT* 41 (1991) 12-37.

Boadt, Lawrence. "The A:B:B:A Chiasm of Identical Roots in Ezekiel," *VT* 25 (1975) 693-99.

―――. "Rhetorical Strategies in Ezekiel's Oracles of Judgment," *Ezekiel and His Book: Textual and Literary Criticism and Their Interrelation* (ed. J. Lust; BETL 74; Leuven: University Press, 1986) 182-200.

Booth, Wayne. "Metaphor as Rhetoric: The Problem of Evaluation," *On Metaphor* (ed. S. Sacks; Chicago: University of Chicago Press, 1978) 47-70.

Bourguet, Daniel. *Des Métaphores de Jérémie* (EBib 9; Paris: Gabalda, 1987).

Braaten, Laurie J. "Parent-Child Imagery in Hosea" (diss., Boston University, 1987).

Brandes, Stanley. "Like Wounded Stags: Male Sexual Ideology in an Andalusian Town," *Sexual Meanings: The Cultural Construction of Gender and Sexuality* (ed. S. B. Ortner and H. Whitehead; Cambridge: Cambridge University Press, 1981) 216-39.

Breasted, James H. *Ancient Records of Egypt: Historical Documents from the Earliest Times to the Persian Conquest* (5 vols.; New York: Russell and Russell, 1962).

Bright, John. *Jeremiah* (AB 21; Garden City: Doubleday, 1965).

Brinkley, Timothy. "On the Truth and Probity of Metaphor," *Philosophical Perspectives on Metaphor* (ed. Mark Johnson; Minneapolis: University of Minnesota Press, 1981) 136-53.

Brinkman, J. A. *A Political History of Post-Kassite Babylonia 1158-722 B.C.* (AnOr 43; Rome: Pontificium Institutum Biblicum, 1968).

Broome, Edwin C. "Ezekiel's Abnormal Personality," *JBL* 65 (1946) 277-92.

Brownlee, William H. "Ezekiel's Copper Cauldron and Blood on the Rock," *For Me to Live: Essays in Honor of James Leon Kelso* (ed. R. A. Coughenour; Cleveland: Dillon/Liederbach, 1972) 21-43.

Bucher, Christina. "The Origin and Meaning of '*znh*' Terminology in the Book of Hosea" (diss., Claremont, 1988).

Calvin, John. *Commentaries on the Prophet Ezekiel* (2 vols.; Edinburgh: The Calvin Translation Society, 1849-50).

Camp, Claudia V. *Wisdom and the Feminine in the Book of Proverbs* (Bible and Literature 11; Decatur: Almond Press, 1985).

Carroll, Robert P. *Jeremiah: A Commentary* (OTL; Philadelphia: Westminster Press, 1986).

Cassem, Ned H. "Ezekiel's Psychotic Personality: Reservations on the Use of the Couch for Biblical Personalities," *The Word in the World* (ed. Richard Clifford; Cambridge, MA: Weston College Press, 1973) 59-63.

Cazelles, Henri. "Fille de Sion et Théologie mariale dans la Bible," *Mariologie et Oecuménisme* (vol. 3; Paris: Lethielleux, 1964) 51-71.

Charlesworth, James H., ed. *The Old Testament Pseudepigrapha* (vol. 1; Garden City: Doubleday Press, 1983).

Clark, David J. "Sex-related Imagery in the Prophets," *BT* 33 (1982) 409-13.

Clifford, Richard J. *The Cosmic Mountain in Canaan and the Old Testament* (HSM 4; Cambridge, MA: Harvard University Press, 1972).

Cogan, Morton. *Imperialism and Religion: Assyria, Judah, and Israel in the Eighth and Seventh Centuries B.C.E.* (SBLMS 19; Missoula, MT: Scholars Press, 1974).

Cohen, Chaim. "The Widowed City," *JANESCU* 5 (1973) 75-81.

————. *Biblical Hapax Legomena in the Light of Akkadian and Ugaritic* (SBLDS 37; Missoula: Scholars Press, 1978).

Cooke, G. A. *The Book of Ezekiel* (International Critical Commentary 21; 2 vols.; New York: Scribners, 1937).

Danby, Herbert, ed. *The Mishnah* (Oxford: Oxford University Press, 1933).

Davidson, A. B. *The Book of the Prophet Ezekiel* (The Cambridge Bible for Schools and Colleges; Cambridge: Cambridge University Press, 1892).

Davidson, Donald. "What Metaphors Mean," *On Metaphor* (ed. Sheldon Sacks; Chicago: University of Chicago Press, 1978) 29-46.

Davis, Ellen. *Swallowing the Scroll: Textuality and the Dynamics of Discourse in Ezekiel's Prophecy* (JSOTS 78; Sheffield: Almond Press, 1989).

Day, John. *Molech: A God of Human Sacrifice in the Old Testament* (Cambridge: Cambridge University Press, 1989).

van Dijk-Hemmes, F. "The Imagination of Power and the Power of Imagination, An Intertextual Analysis of the Two Biblical Love Songs: The Song of Songs and Hosea 2," *JSOT* 44 (1989) 75-88.

Dolan, Jill. "The Dynamics of Desire: Sexuality and Gender in Pornography and Performance," *Theatre Journal* 39 (1987) 156-74.

Douglas, Mary. *Purity and Danger: An Analysis of the Concepts of Pollution and Taboo* (London: Routledge & Kegan Paul, 1966).

———. *Implicit Meanings: Essays in Anthropology* (London: Routledge & Kegan Paul, 1975).

———. *Natural Symbols: Explorations in Cosmology* (London: Barrie and Jenkins, 1973).

Driver, G. R. "Linguistic and Textual Problems: Ezekiel," *Bib* 19 (1938) 60-69, 175-87.

———. "Ezekiel: Linguistic and Textual Problems," *Bib* 35 (1954) 145-59, 299-312.

Durlesser, James. "The Rhetoric of Allegory in the Book of Ezekiel" (diss., University of Pittsburgh, 1988).

Dworkin, Andrea. *Intercourse* (New York: The Free Press, 1987).

Edelman, Diana. "Biblical Molek Reassessed," *JAOS* 107 (1987) 727-31.

Eichrodt, Walther. *Ezekiel: A Commentary* (OTL; Philadelphia: Westminster Press, 1970).

Eissfeldt, Otto. "Hesekiel Kap. 16 als Geschichtsquelle," *JPOS* 16 (1939), 286-92 (*Kleine Schriften II*; Tübingen: J. C. B. Mohr, 1963. 101-06).

Eliade, Mircea. *Patterns in Comparative Religion* (Cleveland: World, 1963).

Epstein, I., ed. *Hebrew-English Edition of the Babylonian Talmud* (New York: Soncino Press, 1974).

Erlandsson, S. "*zānāh*," *TDOT* IV (1980) 99-104.

Falkenstein, M. "La Cité-Temple sumérienne," *Journal of World History* 1 (1954) 784-814.

Fensham, F. C. "The Marriage Metaphor in Hosea for the Covenant Relationship between the Lord and his People (Hos. 1:2-9)," *JNSL* 12 (1984) 71-78.

Fishbane, Michael. *Text and Texture: Close Readings of Selected Biblical Texts* (New York: Schocken Books, 1979).

———. *Biblical Interpretation in Ancient Israel* (Oxford: Oxford University Press, 1985).

Fisher, Eugene. "Cultic Prostitution in the Ancient Near East?," *BTB* 6 (1976) 225-36.

Fitzgerald, Aloysius. "The Mythological Background for the Presentation of Jerusalem as Queen and False Worship as Adultery in the OT," *CBQ* 34 (1972) 403-16.

———. "*btwlt* and *bt* as Titles for Capital Cities," *CBQ* 37 (1975) 167-83.

Fohrer, Georg. *Die Symbolischen Handlungen der Propheten* (Zurich: Zwingli, 1953).

———, and Kurt Galling. *Ezechiel* (HAT 13; Tübingen: J. C. B. Mohr [Paul Siebeck], 1955).

Fox, Michael V. "Jeremiah 2:2 and the 'Desert Ideal'," *CBQ* 35 (1973) 441-50.

———. "The Rhetoric of Ezekiel's Vision of the Valley of the Bones," *HUCA* 51 (1981) 1-15.

Frankena, R. "The Vassal Treaties of Esarhaddon and the Dating of Deuteronomy," *OTS* 14 (1965) 122-54.

Frankfort, Henri. *Art and Architecture of the Ancient Orient* (Harmondsworth: Penguin, 1954).

Freedy, K. S., and D. B. Redford. "The Dates in Ezekiel in Relation to Biblical, Babylonian, and Egyptian Sources," *JAOS* 90 (1970) 462-85.

Friedman, M. A. "Israel's Response in Hosea 2:17b: 'You Are My Husband'," *JBL* 99 (1980) 199-204.

Frye, Northrop. "Allegory," *Princeton Encyclopedia of Poetry and Poetics* (ed. Alex Preminger; Princeton: Princeton University Press, 1974) 12-15.

Frymer-Kensky, Tikvah. "Pollution, Purification, and Purgation in Biblical Israel," *The Word of the Lord Shall Go Forth: Essays in Honor of David Noel Freedman in Celebration of His Sixtieth Birthday* (ed. Carol L. Meyers and J. M. O'Connor; Winona Lake, IN: Eisenbrauns, 1982) 399-414.

Gaenssle, Carl. *The Hebrew Particle ʾšr* (Chicago: University of Chicago Press, 1915).

Ginsberg, H. L. "Studies in Hosea 1-3," *Yehezkel Kaufmann Jubilee Volume* (ed. M. Haran; Jerusalem: Magnes Press, 1960) 50-69.

Ginzberg, Louis. *The Legends of the Jews* (7 vols.; Philadelphia: Jewish Publication Society, 1968).

Glassner, Jean-Jacques. "Women, Hospitality and the Honor of the Family," *Women's Earliest Records from Ancient Egypt and Western Asia* (ed. Barbara Lesko; Brown Judaic Studies 166; Atlanta: Scholars Press, 1989) 71-90.

Goldsmith, Nancy F., and E. Gould. "Sumerian Bats, Lion-headed Eagles, and Iconographic Evidence for the Overthrow of a Female-priest Hegemony," *BA* 53 (1990) 142-56.

Good, E. M. "Ezekiel's Ship: Some Extended Metaphors in the Old Testament," *Semitics* 1 (1970) 79-103.

Greenberg, Moshe. *Ezekiel 1-20* (AB 22; Garden City: Doubleday, 1983).

———. "The Design and Themes of Ezekiel's Program of Restoration," *Int* 38 (1984) 181-208.

Greenfield, Jonas. "Lexicographical Notes I," *HUCA* 29 (1958) 203-28.

Greengus, Samuel. "A Textbook Case of Adultery in Ancient Mesopotamia," *HUCA* 40 (1969) 33-43.

———. "The Old Babylonian Marriage Contracts," *JAOS* 89 (1969) 505-32.

Greenspahn, Frederick. *Hapax Legomena in Biblical Hebrew: A Study of the Phenomenon and Its Treatment Since Antiquity with Special Reference to Verbal Forms* (SBLDS 74; Chico: Scholars Press, 1984).

Griffith, F. L., ed. *Catalogue of the Demotic Papyri in the John Rylands Library* (3 vols.; Manchester: The University Press, 1909).

Gubar, Susan. "Representing Pornography: Feminism, Criticism, and Depictions of Female Violation," *Critical Inquiry* 13 (1987) 712-41.

Hals, Ronald M. *Ezekiel* (FOTL 19; Grand Rapids: Eerdmans, 1988).

Hammond, Mason. *The City in the Ancient World* (Cambridge, MA: Harvard University Press, 1972).

Haran, Menachem. *Temples and Temple-Service in Ancient Israel: An Inquiry into the Character of Cult Phenomena and the Historical Setting of the Priestly School* (Oxford: Clarendon Press, 1978).

Harris, Rivkah. "The naditu-Woman," *Studies Presented to A. Leo Oppenheim* (Chicago: The Oriental Institute, 1964) 106-35.

Hauck, F., and S. Schulz. "*porne*," *TDNT* VI (1968) 579-95.

Hayes, John H. "The Usage of Oracles Against Foreign Nations in Ancient Israel," *JBL* 87 (1968) 81-92.

————, and Stuart Irvine. *Isaiah, the Eighth-Century Prophet: His Times and His Preaching* (Nashville: Abingdon Press, 1987).

————, and Paul K. Hooker. *A New Chronology for the Kings of Israel and Judah* (Atlanta: John Knox Press, 1988).

Hays, H. R. *The Dangerous Sex: The Myth of Feminine Evil* (New York: G. P. Putnam's Sons, 1964).

Heider, George C. *The Cult of Molek: A Reassessment* (JSOTS 43; Sheffield: Journal for the Study of the Old Testament, 1986).

Hengstenberg, E. W. *Die Weissagungen des Propheten Ezechiel* (Berlin: Gustav Schlawitz, 1867).

Henle, Paul. "Metaphor," *Philosophical Perspectives on Metaphor* (ed. Mark Johnson; Minneapolis: University of Minnesota Press, 1981) 83-104.

Herodotus. *The Histories* (Middlesex: Penguin Press, 1954).

Herrmann, J. *Ezechiel* (KAT 11; Leipzig/Erlangen: A. Deichert, 1924).

Hillers, Delbert R. *Treaty-Curses and the Old Testament Prophets* (BibOr 16; Rome: Pontifical Biblical Institute, 1964).

————. *Lamentations* (AB 7a; Garden City: Doubleday, 1972).

Hitzig, Ferdinand. *Der Prophet Ezechiel erklärt* (Leipzig: Weidmann'sche Buchhandlung, 1847).

Holladay, William L. "On Every High Hill and Under Every Green Tree," *VT* 11 (1961) 170-76.

————. *Jeremiah 1, 2* (Hermeneia; Philadelphia: Fortress Press, 1986, 1989).

Hölscher, Gustav. *Hesekiel: Der Dichter und das Buch—eine literarkritische Untersuchung* (BZAW 39; Giessen: Töpelmann, 1924).

Honig, Edwin. *Dark Conceit: The Making of Allegory* (Evanston: Northwestern University, 1959).

Hooks, Stephen M. "Sacred Prostitution in Israel and the Ancient Near East" (diss., Hebrew Union College, 1985).

Horney, Karen. *Feminine Psychology* (New York: Norton, 1967).

Hurowitz, V. "Isaiah's Impure Lips and Their Purification in Light of Akkadian Sources," *HUCA* 60 (1989) 39-89.

Hurvitz, Avi. *A Linguistic Study of the Relationship between the Priestly Source and the Book of Ezekiel: A New Approach to an Old Problem* (Cahiers de la Revue Biblique 20; Paris: Gabalda, 1982).

———. "The Usage of šš and *bwts* in the Bible and its Implication for the Date of P," *HTR* 60 (1967) 117-21.

Irwin, William. *The Problem of Ezekiel: An Inductive Study* (Chicago: University of Chicago Press, 1943).

Jacobsen, Thorkild. *The Treasures of Darkness: A History of Mesopotamian Religion* (New Haven: Yale University Press, 1976).

———. *The Harps That Once . . . : Sumerian Poetry in Translation* (New Haven: Yale University Press, 1987).

Janzen, J. Gerald. "Rivers in the Desert of Abraham and Sarah and Zion (Isaiah 51: 1-3)," *HAR* 10 (1986) 139-55.

Jay, Nancy. "Throughout Your Generations Forever: A Sociology of Blood Sacrifice" (diss., Brandeis University, 1981).

Joyce, Paul. *Divine Initiative and Human Response in Ezekiel* (JSOTS 51; Sheffield: Journal for the Study of the Old Testament, 1989).

Kadman, L. *The Coins of Aelia Capitolina* (Jerusalem: Israel Numismatic Society, 1956).

Kaiser, B. Bakke. "Poet as 'Female Impersonator': The Imagery of Daughter Zion as Speaker in Biblical Poems of Suffering," *Journal of Religion* 67 (1987) 164-82.

Kalluveetil, Paul. *Declaration and Covenant* (AnBib 88; Rome: Biblical Institute Press, 1982).

Kedar-Kopfstein, B. "*dām*," *TDOT* III (1978) 234-50.

Keel, Othmar. *The Symbolism of the Biblical World: Ancient Near Eastern Iconography and the Book of Psalms* (New York: Seabury Press, 1978).

Keil, Karl F. *Biblical Commentary on the Prophecies of Ezekiel* (2 vols.; Grand Rapids: Eerdmans Publishing Company, 1950).

Kelso, J. L. "Ezekiel's Parable of the Corroded Copper Cauldron," *JBL* 64 (1945) 391-93.

Kennedy, James. "Hebrew *pithon peh* in the Book of Ezekiel," *VT* 41 (1991) 233-35.

Koch, Klaus. "Der Spruch, 'Sein Blut bleibe auf seinem Haupt'," *VT* 12 (1962) 396-416.

Koester, Craig R. "The Tabernacle in the New Testament and Intertestamental Jewish Literature" (diss., Union Theological Seminary, 1987).

Kramrisch, Stella. *The Hindu Temple* (Delhi: Motilal Banarsdass, 1976).

Kristeva, Julia. *Powers of Horror: An Essay on Abjection* (New York: Oxford University Press, 1982).

Kruger, P. A. "Israel, the Harlot (Hos. 2:4-9)," *JNSL* 11 (1984) 107-16.

Krüger, Thomas. *Geschichtskonzepte im Ezechielbuch* (BZAW 180; Berlin: de Gruyter, 1988).

Kuhn, Annette. *The Power of the Image: Essays on Representation and Sexuality* (London: Routledge & Kegan Paul, 1985).

Kutsch, Ernst O. *Die chronologischen Daten des Ezechielbuches* (ObO 62; Freiburg: Universitätsverlag, 1985).

Lakoff, George, and Mark Johnson. "Conceptual Metaphor in Everyday Language," *Philosophical Perspectives on Metaphor* (ed. Mark Johnson; Minneapolis: University of Minnesota Press, 1981) 286-329.

Lang, Bernhard. *Ezechiel: Der Prophet und das Buch* (Erträge der Forschung 153; Darmstadt: Wissenschaftliche Buchgesellschaft, 1981).

de Laurentis, Teresa. *Alice Doesn't: Feminism, Semiotics, Cinema* (Bloomington: Indiana University Press, 1984).

Levenson, Jon. *Theology of the Program of Restoration of Ezekiel 40-48* (HSM 10; Missoula, MT: Scholars Press, 1976).

Levey, Samson H. *The Targum of Ezekiel* (The Aramaic Bible 13; Wilmington, DE: Michael Glazier, 1987).

Levine, Baruch. *In the Presence of the Lord* (SJLA 5; Leiden: Brill, 1974).

Lewy, Julius. "The Old West Semitic Sun God Hammu," *HUCA* 18 (1944) 436-44.

Lindblom, Johannes. *Prophecy in Ancient Israel* (Philadelphia: Muhlenberg Press, 1962).

MacKenzie, R. "The City and Israelite Religion," *CBQ* 25 (1963) 600-70.

MacLaurin, E. C. B. *The Figure of Religious Adultery in the Old Testament* (Leeds: Leeds University Press, 1964).

Malul, Meir. *Studies in Mesopotamian Legal Symbolism* (AOAT; Neukirchen-Vluyn: Butzen & Bercker Kevelaer, 1988).

———. "Adoption of Foundlings in the Bible and Mesopotamian Documents: A Study of Some Legal Metaphors in Ezekiel 16.1-7," *JSOT* 46 (1990) 97-126.

Mays, James L. *Hosea: A Commentary* (OTL; Philadelphia: Westminster Press, 1969).

McCarthy, Dennis J. "The Symbolism of Blood and Sacrifice," *JBL* 88 (1969) 166-76.

———. *Old Testament Covenant: A Survey of Current Opinions* (Oxford/Richmond: Basil Blackwell/John Knox Press, 1972).

———. "Further Notes on the Symbolism of Blood and Sacrifice," *JBL* 92 (1973) 205-10.

McKeating, Henry. "Sanctions Against Adultery in Ancient Israelite Society, with Some Reflections on Methodology in the Study of Old Testament Ethics," *JSOT* 11 (1979) 57-72.

———. "A Response to Dr. Phillips," *JSOT* 20 (1981) 25-26.

Meigs, Anna S. "A Papuan Perspective on Pollution," *Man* 13 (1978) 304-18.

Milgrom, Jacob. "A Prolegomenon to Leviticus 17:11," *JBL* 90 (1971) 149-56.

———. *Cult and Conscience: The Asham and the Priestly Doctrine of Repentence* (SJLA 18; Leiden: Brill, 1976).

———. "Israel's Sanctuary: The Priestly 'Picture of Dorian Gray'," *RB* 33 (1976) 390-99.

———. *Studies in Cultic and Levitical Terminology* (SJLA 36; Leiden: Brill, 1983).

———. "The Priestly Impurity System," *Ninth World Congress of Jewish Studies* (Jerusalem: World Union of Jewish Studies, 1986) 121-25.

———, and D. P. Wright. "*niddāh,*" *Theologisches Wörterbuch zum alten Testament* (vol. V; ed. G. Johannes Botterweck and Helmer Ringgren; Stuttgart: Verlag W. Kohlhammer, 1972) 250-53.

Miller, J. Maxwell, and John H. Hayes. *A History of Ancient Israel and Judah* (Philadelphia: Westminster Press, 1986).

Monloubou, L. "La Signification du Cult selon Ezekiel," *Ezekiel and His Book: Textual and Literary Criticism and Their Interrelation* (BETL 74; ed. J. Lust; Leuven: University of Leuven Press, 1986) 322-29.

Moortgat, Anton. *The Art of Ancient Mesopotamia: The Classical Art of the Near East* (London: Phaidon, 1969).

Moran, William. "The Ancient Near Eastern Background of the Love of God in Deuteronomy," *CBQ* 25 (1963) 77-87.

Moulton, Richard. *Ezekiel* (The Modern Reader's Bible; New York: Macmillan, 1897).

Mulvey, Laura. "Visual Pleasure and Narrative Cinema," *Screen* 16 (1975) 6-18.

Mumford, Lewis. *The City in History: Its Origins, Its Transformations, and Its Prospects* (New York: Harcourt, Brace and World, 1961).

Muraoka, T. *Emphatic Words and Structures in Biblical Hebrew* (Jerusalem: Magnes Press, 1985).

Neumann, Erich. *The Great Mother: An Analysis of the Archetype* (Bollingen Series 47; New York: Pantheon Books, 1955).

Neusner, Jacob. "From Scripture to Mishnah: The Origins of Tractate Niddah," *JJS* 29 (1978) 135-48.

———. *A History of the Mishnaic Law of Women* (SJLA 33/1; Leiden: Brill, 1980).

Newsom, Carol A. "A Maker of Metaphors: Ezekiel's Oracles Against Tyre," *Int* 38 (1984) 151-64.

Nicholson, Ernest. *God and His People: Covenant and Theology in the Old Testament* (Oxford: Clarendon Press, 1986).

Oden, Robert A., Jr. *The Bible without Theology: The Theological Tradition and Alternatives to It* (San Francisco: Harper and Row, 1987).

Olyan, Saul. *Asherah and the Cult of Yahweh in Israel* (SBLMS 34; Atlanta: Scholars Press, 1988).

Origen. *Homélies sur Ezechiel* (Sources Chrétiennes 352; ed. Marcel Borret; Paris: Cerf, 1989).

Parker, Margaret. "Exploring Four Persistent Prophetic Images," *Bible Review* 6 (1990) 38-45.

Parunak, H. van Dyke. "Structural Studies in Ezekiel," (diss., Harvard University, 1978).

Paul, Shalom. "Adoption Formulae: A Study of Cuneiform and Biblical Legal Clauses," *MAARAV* 2 (1980) 173-85.

Peristiany, J. G. *Honour and Shame: The Values of Mediterannean Society* (London: Weidenfeld and Nicholson, 1965).

Petersen, David, ed. *Prophecy in Israel: Search for an Identity* (Issues in Religion and Theology 10; Philadelphia: Fortress Press, 1987).

Phillips, Anthony. "Another Look at Adultery," *JSOT* 20 (1981) 3-25.

———. "A Response to Dr. McKeating," *JSOT* 22 (1982) 142-43.

Pitt-Rivers, Julian. "Honor," in *International Encyclopedia of the Social Sciences* (ed. David Sills; New York: Crowell Collier and Macmillan, 1968) 6. 503-11.

———. *The Fate of Shechem and the Politics of Sex* (Cambridge: Cambridge University Press, 1976).

Powers, Morna. N. "Menstruation and Reproduction: An Oglala Case," *Signs* 6 (1980) 54-65.

Propp, William H. *Water in the Wilderness: A Biblical Motif and Its Mythological Background* (HSM 40; Atlanta: Scholars Press, 1987).

Rabinowitz, J. J. "The 'Great Sin' in Ancient Egyptian Marriage Contracts," *JNES* 18 (1959) 73.

Reider, Joseph. "Contributions to the Scriptural Text," *HUCA* 24 (1952/3) 85-106.

Reventlow, Henning Graf. "'Sein Blüt komme über sein Haupt'," *VT* 10 (1960) 311-27.

Richards, I. A. *The Philosophy of Rhetoric* (Oxford: Oxford University Press, 1936); reprinted in part in *Philosophical Perspectives on Metaphor* (ed. Mark Johnson; Minneapolis: University of Minnesota Press, 1981) 48-62.

Ricoeur, Paul. *The Rule of Metaphor* (Toronto: University of Toronto Press, 1977).

———. "The Metaphorical Process as Cognition, Imagination, and Feeling," *On Metaphor* (ed. S. Sacks; Chicago: University of Chicago Press, 1978) 141-57.

Robinson, Gnana. *The Origin and Development of the Old Testament Sabbath* (Beiträge zur biblischen Exegese und Theologie 21; Frankfurt: Peter Lang, 1988).

Rooker, Mark F. *Biblical Hebrew in Transition: The Language of the Book of Ezekiel* (JSOTS 90; Sheffield: Almond Press, 1990).

Rosenberg, Joel. *King and Kin: Political Allegory in the Hebrew Bible* (Bloomington: Indiana University Press, 1986).

Rowley, H. H. *Men of God: Studies in Old Testament History and Prophecy* (London: Thomas Nelson and Sons, 1963).

Saggs, H. W. F. "The Nimrud Letters, 1952—Part VI," *Iraq* 25 (1963) 70-80.

Sanday, Peggy R. *Female Power and Male Dominance: On the Origins of Sexual Inequality* (Cambridge: Cambridge University Press, 1981).

Sarna, Nahum. "The Abortive Insurrection in Zedekiah's Day (Jer 27-29)," *EI* 14 (1978) 89-96.

Scalise, Pamela D. J. "From Prophet's Word to Prophetic Book: A Study of Walther Zimmerli's Theory of 'Nach-interpretation'," (diss., Yale University, 1982).

Schley, Donald G. "The *šālīšîm*: Officers or Special Three-Man Squads?," *VT* 40 (1990) 321-26.

Schmitt, John J. "The Gender of Ancient Israel," *JSOT* 26 (1983) 115-25.

———. "The Wife of God in Hosea 2," *BR* 34 (1989) 5-18.

———. "The Virgin of Israel: Referent and Use of the Phrase in Amos and Jeremiah," *CBQ* 53 (1991) 365-87.

van Selms, A. *Marriage and Family Life in Ugaritic Literature* (Pretoria Oriental Series 1; London: Luzac, 1954).

Selvidge, Marla J. "Mark 5:25-34 and Leviticus 15:19-20," *JBL* 103 (1984) 619-23.

Setel, T. Drorah. "Prophets and Pornography: Female Sexual Imagery in Hosea," *Feminist Interpretation of the Bible* (ed. Letty M. Russell; Philadelphia: Westminster Press, 1985) 86-95.

Silverman, Kaja. "Masochism and Subjectivity," *Framework* 12 (1980) 2-9.

———. *The Subject of Semiotics* (Oxford: Oxford University Press, 1983).

Smend, Rudolf. *Der Prophet Ezechiel für die zweite Auflage erklärt* (Kurzgefasstes exegetisches Handbuch zum alten Testament 8; 2te Auflage; Leipzig: S. Hirzel, 1880).

Smith, Morton. "A Note on Burning Babies," *JAOS* 95 (1975) 477-79.

Smith, W. Robertson. "Moloch," *Encyclopaedia Britannica* (9th ed.; New York: Henry Allen, 1889) 16. 695-96.

Snodgrass, Klyne. *The Parable of the Wicked Tenants: An Inquiry into Parable Interpretation* (Wissenschaftliche Untersuchen zum Neuen Testament 27; J. C. B. Mohr [Paul Siebeck], 1983).

Soskice, Janet M. *Metaphors and Religious Language* (Oxford: Clarendon Press, 1985).

Steck, O. H. "Zion als Gelände und Gestalt. Uberlegungen zur Wahrnemung Jerusalems als Stadt und Frau im Alten Testament," *ZTK* 86 (1989) 261-81.

Steingrimsson, S. "*zimmāh*," *TDOT* IV (1980) 89-90.

Stone, Michael E. *Fourth Ezra: A Commentary on the Book of Fourth Ezra* (Hermeneia; Minneapolis: Fortress Press, 1990).

Stummer, F. "*ʾāmulla* (Ez xvi 30 A)," *VT* 4 (1956) 34-40.

Talmon, Shemaryahu. "The 'Desert Motif' in the Bible and in Qumran Literature," *Biblical Motifs* (ed. A. Altman; Cambridge, MA: Harvard University Press, 1966) 31-63.

———, and Michael Fishbane. "The Structuring of Biblical Books: Studies in the Book of Ezekiel," *ASTI* 10 (1976) 129-53.

TANAKH: A New Translation of the Holy Scriptures According to the Traditional Hebrew Text (Philadelphia: Jewish Publication Society, 1985).

Terrien, Samuel. "The Omphalos in Hebrew Mythology," *VT* 20 (1970) 315-38.

Te Stroete, G. A. "Ezekiel 24:15-27: The Meaning of a Symbolic Act," *BTFT* 38 (1977) 163-75.

Thompson, J. A. "Israel's 'Lovers'," *VT* 27 (1977) 475-81.

van der Toorn, Karel. "Female Prostitution in Payment of Vows in Ancient Israel," *JBL* 108 (1989) 193-205.

Tsevat, Matitiahu. "The Neo-Assyrian and Neo-Babylonian Vassal Oaths and the Prophet Ezekiel," *JBL* 78 (1959) 199-204.

Tucker, Gene M. "Covenant Forms and Contract Forms," *VT* 15 (1965) 487-503.

Visser, Margaret. "Vengeance and Pollution in Classical Athens," *Journal of the History of Ideas* 45 (1984) 193-206.

Wakeman, Mary. "Sacred Marriage," *JSOT* 22 (1982) 21-31.

Weems, Renita. "Gomer: Victim of Violence or Victim of Metaphor?," *Semeia* 47 (1989) 299-303.

Wegner, Judith R. *Chattel or Person?: The Status of Women in the Mishnah* (New York: Oxford University, 1988).

Weinfeld, Moshe. "*běrîth*," *TDOT* I (1974) 253-79.

———. "Zion and Jerusalem as Religious and Political Capital: Ideology and Utopia," *The Poet and the Historian: Essays in Literary and Historical Biblical Criticism* (ed. R. E. Friedman; HSS 26; Chico, CA: Scholars Press, 1983).

Wenham, G. J. "Sanctuary Symbolism in the Garden of Eden Story," *Proceedings of the Ninth World Congress of Jewish Studies* (Jerusalem: World Union of Jewish Studies, 1986) 19-25.

Westbrook, Raymond. "The Prohibition on Restoration of Marriage in Deuteronomy 24:1-4," *Studies in Bible* (ed. S. Japhet; Scripta Hierosolymitana 31; Jerusalem: Magnes Press, 1976) 387-405.

———. *Old Babylonian Marriage Law* (AOr 23; Horn, Austria: Ferdinand Berger & Sohne, 1988).

———. "Adultery in Ancient Near Eastern Law," *RB* 97 (1990) 542-80.

Westenholz, J. G. "Tamar, Qedesa, Qadistu, and Sacred Prostitution in Mesopotamia," *HTR* 82 (1989) 245-65.

Wevers, John. *Ezekiel* (New Century Bible Commentary; Grand Rapids: Eerdmans, 1969).

Widengren, Geo. "King and Covenant," *JSS* 2 (1957) 1-32.

Wiken, Uni. "Shame and Honour: A Contestable Pair," *Man* 19 (1984) 635-47.

Williams, Ronald. *Hebrew Syntax: An Outline* (2nd ed.; Toronto: University of Toronto Press, 1976).

Wilson, Robert R. "An Interpretation of Ezekiel's Dumbness," *VT* 22 (1972) 91-104.

———. *Prophecy and Society in Ancient Israel* (Philadelphia: Fortress Press, 1980).

Wiseman, D. J. *Chronicles of Chaldean Kings (626-556 B.C.) in the British Museum* (London: The British Museum, 1956).

Wolff, Hans W. *Hosea* (Hermeneia; Philadelphia: Fortress Press, 1975).

Wright, D. P. *The Disposal of Impurity: Elimination Rites in the Bible and in Hittite and Mesopotamian Literature* (SBLDS 101; Atlanta: Scholars Press, 1987).

Yadin, Yigael. *The Temple Scroll* (3 vols.; Jerusalem: Israel Exploration Society, 1983).

Young, F. W. and A. A. Bacdayan. "Menstrual Taboos and Social Rigidity," *Ethnology* 4 (1965) 225-40.

Zimmerli, Walther. *Ezekiel 1, 2* (Hermeneia; Philadelphia: Fortress Press, 1979, 1983).

Author Index

Printed in the United States
66689LVS00002B/16-21

9 781555 407568